Polio, the A-Bomb and Me

A Memoir by Paula C. Viale

A pound of flesh, a pound of wishful thinking and a pound of hazy images you can't quite make out. Voila! You have a memoir.

This book is dedicated to my husband Rusty
and to the memory of Dr. Jonas Salk.

CONTENTS

ACKNOWLEDGEMENTS

It takes a village to write and publish a book. I would like to thank and acknowledge the following individuals for their support and encouragement: My editor, Alice Peck; proofreaders Terri Niccum, Rusty Jorgensen and Gale Lawrence; graphic designer, Lee Lehrman; and to all the members of my memoirs writing class of 2014-2016.

My husband Rusty Jorgensen shared this journey with me, providing love, maintenance and an infinite amount of patience that has kept my spirits up when they were flagging. For a little girl who never believed in miracles, I found one and he is the love of my life.

PROLOGUE

It was every parent's worst nightmare—sending your energetic six-year-old son off to school only to have him returned home by the school nurse due to a high fever and chills. Or watching as a sudden bout of diarrhea and nausea forced your teenaged daughter to hang up her ballet shoes and miss an important recital. First the pounding headache and muscle cramps might be attributed to normal growing pains and treated with aspirin.

The invisible menace passed through some children unnoticed, causing no symptoms or impairment at all, but your child might be the one tucked into bed complaining of a stiff neck only to wake up paralyzed the next morning.

This disease also struck down adults in the prime of life. It diminished the godly stature of the Roman Emperor Claudius, jeopardized the political ambitions of F.D.R., one of America's best-loved presidents, and cast its shadow across the childhoods of musician Itzhak Perlman, artist Frieda Kahlo, actress Mia Farrow, photographer Dorothea Lange, track star Wilma Rudolph, and singer-songwriter Joni Mitchell. During the worst outbreak in 1952, 57,628 cases were reported, killing 3,145 Americans, 1,874 of whom were children under the age of five.

The highly contagious virus entered the body through hand-to-mouth contact or could spread via contaminated food or water. It settled briefly in the intestine before invading the central nervous system where it killed the horn cells designed to activate motor neurons within the spinal cord, brain stem, or motor complex. It could lead to temporary or permanent paralysis. In children, only one in every thousand cases resulted in muscles destroyed, limbs misshapen, and lives derailed.

I was one of those children destined to play host to this disease. I was the one in a thousand whose life changed forever. This is the story of my struggle to outwit and overcome the effects of polio.

1

MY SHAKY START

If you listened carefully you could hear the rafters of our tiny log cabin groaning under the weight of lingering grief that spread throughout its rooms on the day I was born in the autumn of 1948. The heady optimism following the Allied victory in World War II had been replaced by two threats that loomed large in the minds of most Americans: the horrifying, unimaginable destructive power unleashed by the atom bomb and the menace of the polio epidemic sweeping across the country.

My father turned up the car radio and halfway listened to the morning news. President Harry Truman, who had introduced us to nuclear war, was touring California along with his family. The most powerful man in the world opened his campaign speech with a stab at humor. "I wonder if you would like to see my wife and daughter? Here is the First Lady—she is the boss. And I will introduce *her* boss to you—Margaret."

Most likely, neither the A-bomb nor polio occupied the presidential family's thoughts as they soaked up the golden rays in sunny Los Angeles. None of them had the slightest idea that my birth, soon to be complicated by the polio virus, was occurring in Eureka, a gritty little logging town hugging the North Coast of California.

Jack changed the dial to an all music station and stepped on the gas. A two-hour journey from Sequoia to Eureka lay ahead of him as he coaxed his old black and white Ford north. He smiled to himself, thinking of his wife Lill and their new baby daughter waiting to be picked up at the hospital. Maybe things would improve with that new life; maybe it would lessen the sting from Preston's premature death. He pushed aside memories of the baby boy who had died the year before, barely a day old. My father rolled down the car window, letting a blast of fresh air clear his head and help him focus on the road winding through the redwoods.

He concentrated on the local weather report until the intrusive, recurring memories faded and for a while he forgot that day when he and Lill drove home from the hospital, arms empty and spirits crushed. Their two-year-old son David had stood waiting for them on the front steps of their cabin holding tightly to his Grandmother Momo's hand. Jack helped his wife out of the car, brushing by David and Momo without a word as he steered her towards their bedroom.

Before shutting the door, Jack had caught a glimpse of David's puzzled look. "No baby?"

Bessie, known to her grandchildren as Momo, picked David up and cradled his head on her shoulder. "Not this time, little one."

Jack regretted slipping by David without a hug or words of explanation. Death had no reality for a two-year-old anyway and Jack's main concern right then centered on how cold and detached his wife had been acting.

Preston's death unhinged Lill for months, draining her of the energy that David and my father required to keep their small family functioning. Fortunately, both my parents came from large, extended families; brothers and sisters, aunts and uncles, and most importantly grandmothers who stepped in to fill the gaps left by my mother's instability. Everyone agreed no mention should be made of Preston's death unless Lill brought up the subject. She never did.

In the days that followed, my father turned to his mother—our Momo—whose steadfast faith in a loving God helped strengthen his own flagging belief. "I know your hurt," Momo reminded him.

Still, he wrestled with debilitating guilt for Preston's death. "I should have paid the extra money for a private nurse like the doctors recommended," he'd told her.

"Jackie, you're not to blame yourself. You have to leave it in God's hands."

The faith that infused his mother's life now seemed pitiful to him.

Jack pulled the little Ford to the side of the road and got out to stretch his legs. He stood overlooking the Eel River near Myers Flat. My father was a handsome man, of average height and though he had very little Italian blood in him, it expressed itself in his dark complexion and thick black hair. He was born on July 5, 1918, so he assumed the fireworks set off on the Fourth of July were in preparation for his birthday.

A cool breeze forced him to zip up his khaki jacket and return to the car. Tuning in the CBS station, he eased onto the two-lane highway. Through the radio's static, he heard about the overproduction of potatoes that year, forcing market prices down to an all-time low. Maybe life would get better. After all, today's news had reported the glut of potatoes instead of the number of casualties suffered on some foreign battlefield.

Death had been hounding my father for a long time. He was the third of nine children. According to my grandmother Momo, her Jackie was the dreamer in the family, "but he still did well in school," the one-time teacher bragged. Dreams and intellect hardly mattered with The Depression in full swing. They gave way to long hours of eking out a living just to survive. Poverty took its toll.

Momo teased that Jackie had an angel on one shoulder and a chip on the other. "You're blessed to have clean clothes to wear," she scolded him when he balked at dressing in his brother's hand-me-down shirts and pants.

He took it personally when he learned that his father had lost a good-paying job because prejudice against Germans after World War I had forced the Müller Cement Factory to close down.

He asked his mother why God had allowed their family to lose everything.

"God works in mysterious ways," she explained. "Look at the beautiful land we own now. We have to make the best of things."

My grandfather did make the best of things. He purchased some cheap, logged-over land near Myers Flat, California where he moved his growing family in a covered wagon borrowed from a neighbor. Here he scraped out a living selling second-growth timber and loading homegrown produce onto the Northwestern Pacific train to be sold as far south as San Rafael.

Jack began to question God's mysterious ways. He hid his sense of shame and inferiority beneath a cloak of contrived arrogance. He boasted about his high I.Q. and outstanding grades. He wrote love poems to his grammar school sweethearts and lost himself in the worlds of Thornton Burgess and Robert Louis Stevenson.

Jack and his brothers Raymond and Robert fancied themselves the Three Musketeers. They spent their childhood in tiny Sequoia, trapping and taming a host of baby raccoons, orphaned foxes, and a large box turtle named Snippet. After school and performing the list of chores that had to be completed before dinner, they finished their homework and spent what remained of the evening training their wildlife menagerie.

Soon after he turned thirteen, Jack caught the bus to South Fork High School—miles away from Sequoia and light years away from the habits and customs of that backwater town. My father's image of himself as a hayseed loser tormented him; low self-esteem prevented him from exploring the few decent options left open to a man of his capabilities. Eventually he enrolled in an apprenticeship as a press operator in Eureka until World War II and the draft caught up with him.

During his two-and-one-half years in the army, my father was stationed in the Pribilofs, a four-island archipelago marooned in the Bering Sea, three hundred miles from Alaska's mainland. There he guarded the arctic shores against Japanese kamikaze pilots, learned to eat whale blubber offered to him by his Eskimo hosts, and nearly froze to death in the subzero temperatures. He endured the glacial isolation, thanks to the close friendships he developed with a few men in his unit. Their camaraderie and appreciation of his intelligence and wit helped build his confidence and he often stated those years were some of the best in his life.

Jack, Raymond, and Robert had dreamt of becoming veterinarians after the war, perhaps sharing an office. So many plans for the Three Musketeers…plans that turned to ashes and blew away on the winds of the South Pacific. Of the three romantics who marched off to World War II, only my father returned. Survivor's guilt haunted him for the rest of his life. Where were God's hands then?

Jack realized the gas tank arrow pointed to empty. A mile later he pulled his Ford into a Flying A station in Scotia and asked for a fill-up. He handed over $2.40 in exact change and pulled back onto the road. Would his wife be happy to see him when he arrived to take her and their baby home from General Hospital? *Please God, let her be.*

My mother was one of thirteen children. She was raised by her two older sisters as a family pet of sorts. Bertha and Bessie had reached their early teens when they assumed responsibility for Lill, her twin brother Bill, and Donny, the last of the litter. My aunts' timely intervention came as a welcomed relief for Grandma Ida. Although her sturdy Swedish roots sustained her, the passel of thirteen children had aged her beyond her years and she happily abandoned her maternal role to the next generation.

Despite the Great Depression, my mother lived a comfortable existence made possible by the generosity of her sisters. Both Bess and Bert worked at the Humboldt Creamery and devoted a sizable amount of their salaries to the purchase of pretty dresses and playthings for their blue-eyed towheaded sibling. They seized the opportunity to compensate for their own early deprivation. They delighted in coddling their little sister, decorating her small, but cheerful bedroom at the back of their house and showering her with toys, inexpensive jewelry, and the latest fashion dolls for every birthday and Christmas. The dark days of the twenties left Lill unscathed.

Timid and shy, my mother had natural beauty on her side and while she did poorly in school, her looks made her popular with both girls and boys. Her nine brothers called her "Fraidy Cat," sometimes chased her with their boisterous horses, and teased and frightened her with their drinking and carousing, but they too indulged their baby sister.

Unlike her adventurous twin Bill and her baby brother Donny, Lill circumvented the riskier pleasures of childhood. She squeezed her eyes shut tight whenever Bill grabbed onto the frayed rope hanging from the willow tree and flew out over the deep gulch behind their house. She sidestepped the thrill of starting small grass fires using her brother's magnifying glass and while her siblings jumped on and flattened the neatly piled hay stacks in her father's field, Lill imagined the thrashings that might await them at the end of the day.

Lill had no set chores assigned to her, but she obeyed any rules her sisters set down and never questioned their validity. Darkness frightened her so she often slept at the foot of the bed Bert shared with Bess. It was to them and not her mother and father that she turned for comfort and safety. Her parents, worn out by thirteen children to feed and clothe, had little energy left to share with her and she surely felt the absence.

Lill had a passion for paper dolls and eagerly awaited the arrival of her sisters' monthly magazines featuring Betsy McCall and Polly Dingle. As she grew older, she bought sets of popular movie star cutouts and spent hours creating beautifully designed and stylish outfits to add to their wardrobes. Lill displayed considerable artistic talents, but no one took them seriously, so neither did she.

Lill remained a bit of a mystery to her sisters. They never guessed that their well-intended interventions would later lead to much of my mother's inability to cope with adulthood. She rarely cried and when she did, she couldn't say why. She simply shrugged if some one asked her what she wanted to do when she grew up—not that many people asked. She walked home from her first day of school to report that her teacher had divided her garden of children into roses and thorns and though Miss Candy had mentioned no names, my mother knew she was and always would be one of the thorns. When Bess laughed and said "Maybe so," Lill wove those thorns into the fabric of her self-image.

Bess and Bert squashed any signs of rebellion my mother exhibited. Female nerves, however, were acceptable to them. Jumpy nerves, after all, ran in the Wahlund family and a secret list of ancestral suicides proved it.

My mother put little effort into high school, leaving academics to the scholars while she enjoyed the companionship of fellow teenagers. As a freshman, she became best friends with Auntie Margaret, Jack's youngest sister. Margaret made my mother laugh with the practical jokes she played on her elders and the comical faces she made at the dinner table when no one was looking. Lill spent hours at Margaret's home, escaping the eagle eyes of Bertha and Bessie. The fourteen years that separated them from their little sister gave them parental status and a heavy influence over my mother. As role models they displayed few attributes of other flappers in the roaring twenties. The only bit of rebellion they expressed was when they shortened their old-fashioned names to Bert and Bess once they married.

Lill graduated with a C average and a paucity of practical skills. Like most women of the thirties and forties, few opportunities outside of marriage and childrearing awaited her. She gave little thought to her future, but Bess and Bert made it clear when it was time for Lill to earn some money, at least enough to pay for her wardrobe and trips to the movies.

"There's nothing I know how to do." Lill sighed. "It makes me nervous to learn something new. Everything's over my head. I guess I'm just stupid." She displayed growing signs of helplessness that her sisters unwittingly fostered.

Rather than helping to build Lill's self-confidence by teaching her how to tackle new challenges, Bert and Bess found it easier to rescue their sister from life's day-to-day problems. When Lill faced the daunting task of job-hunting, Bess and Bert rushed in, finding her employment as an egg-candler at Humboldt Poultry Producers. Lill relied upon their helpful guidance, but theirs was a recipe for disaster because it failed to teach their little sister the basic skills of surviving as an independent and competent adult.

The Poultry Producers building stood just a stone's throw away from where Bess and Bert wrapped butter at the local creamery. Their physical proximity reinforced Lill's dependency on them, providing her with the security she sought. Constantly available to help her balance on her own two feet, they unfortunately robbed her of the opportunity she needed to stand on her two feet alone.

Lill did take pride in her work, learning how to hold fresh eggs up to a light to make sure no developing fetus lurked inside. She shuddered the first time she discovered the shadow of a purple veined blob and hastily threw it in the reject bin. That a living fetus could have hatched into a fluffy yellow chick never occurred to her. Lill's lack of curiosity stifled any movement towards exploring the world and the people around her.

Almost everything outside her daily routine disturbed my mother. Fast cars, upscale social events and any sort of turmoil upset her. While her twin brother Bill prepared to enter the military, Lill remained content with the routine of her work and spent most of her lunch break devouring movie magazines and chatting about Guy—her high school boyfriend—with the other young female employees.

When my handsome Italian father Jack began courting my beautiful Swedish mother, he was completing his apprenticeship as a press operator at the *Humboldt Standard* newspaper. After work he often joined my mother and his sister Margaret at family dinners. His good looks charmed her and she delighted in his compliments. Jack soon replaced Guy in my mother's diary entries.

My parents exchanged letters while my father served time in the army and married when he returned home from Alaska on furlough. Against my aunts' strong objections (Lill should stay closer to home so they could keep an eye on her) the newlyweds moved to Seattle where my father was stationed while waiting to be discharged.

That's when my mother's sheltered life came to an abrupt halt. She had only a vague idea of what went on between a man and woman in a marriage. My father was clumsy when he introduced his wife to lovemaking. The act of sex shocked and repulsed her and left my father feeling rejected and ashamed. My mother submitted enough times to get pregnant, but the marriage limped along without much intimacy. In no way was she motivated to acquaint herself with the facts about pregnancy and childbirth. She took a wait-and-see attitude while she learned the ins and outs of being a housewife and pined away for her happy life back in Eureka.

With twelve brothers and sisters, my mother had never learned how to be alone. Without her sisters' approval or help to lessen her nervous worries, anxiety began to build inside her. What would happen when the baby came? How would she manage to take care of it? Babies had never much interested her. She wasn't even sure she wanted one.

My father worked part-time selling tickets at the Seattle Racetrack. His other job involved sorting through surplus military goods for resale at the US Army Surplus store. He and his buddies did a little pilfering to supplement their low wages. "After all," Jack joked to his co-workers, "we are the 'US' in army surplus. This stuff is meant for *us*." He took particular pride in the special army sleeping bags that came with an extra layer of down to keep out the frigid air of the Pribilofs.

My father often returned from work to find my mother downhearted and depressed, so he convinced her to join him at the surplus store. The work helped her push aside her anxiety and homesickness. Always leery of breaking the law, Lill finally threw caution to the wind and stole two silk parachutes and with the coaching of a friendly neighbor fashioned them into a complete layette for the baby to come. A short-lived rush of self-confidence buoyed her sagging spirits

This spurt of maternal activity pleased Jack no end. He took pride in his wife's beauty and creativity. He considered himself a lucky man and this gratitude began to wear down his resistance to Lill's desire to return to Eureka once his discharge papers came through. Jack believed that, unlike Eureka, Seattle offered him a wider array of employment opportunities. He also enjoyed the friendship of his old Army buddies who, along with their wives, expanded the young couple's social connections beyond the limitations of family ties and filial obligations.

My homesick mother peremptorily dismissed his arguments for staying. Once she gave birth to my brother David in the fall of 1945, the regimen of dirty diapers, warming baby bottles, and endless nights of colicky cries kept her nerves on edge a good part of each day. She missed the companionship of her family and the web of connections offered by a small hometown. Jack finally caved in. Shortly after David's delivery at Seattle's Swedish Hospital, my father packed up his bag of dreams and moved back to Eureka with my mother and John David Junior.

My father, strapped for money, ended up buying eighty-eight acres of logged-over land on Pigeon Point Hill from his father-in-law, my Grandpa John. He did this reluctantly because the parcel lay outside of the city limits, which prevented him from qualifying for a GI loan. He found this bitter pill hard to swallow. It would be one of many.

Jack harbored the suspicion that God's plan for his life differed somewhat from his own expectations, but putting his best foot forward, he settled his starter family into a three-room cabin on the property and began what would become a lifelong project of expanding the tiny log house. At about the same time my mother slowly realized the trap she had fallen into with her marriage to my father and the highly intimidating task of raising a child without a clue about how to do so.

David was a fussy baby who suffered from painful bouts of colic. His wailings robbed the young couple of a good night's rest and left them exhausted. Sad to say, their combined levels of anxiety and lack of basic nurturing skills made them poor parenting material. Both took my brother's disruptive behavior personally.

"I never really wanted children," Lill told her sister Bess soon after David's birth. "I don't know what to do with babies." Baffled, she looked down at my brother squirming and fussing in her reluctant arms. "I don't know what he wants when he cries." She handed the infant to Bess and collapsed into a kitchen chair. "Motherhood has made me a nervous wreck, but what else can I do with my life?" Bert never had any children and Bess had stopped at one so they had little personal experience to pass on to Lill.

My mother continued to flounder. She spent long hours alone in the log cabin atop Pigeon Point, frustrated and overwhelmed by the ordinary demands of an infant she failed to soothe or satisfy. She shared morning coffee with a clutch of neighborhood mothers who, like her, were making do living in tents, tarpaper shacks, and trailers while they waited for their dream houses to come true. She was no different than most housewives of the forties and early fifties who lacked any occupational opportunities outside of marriage and childrearing. Now married with a child to raise, Lill could hardly return to her work at Humboldt Poultry Producers.

Bert broke with family tradition when she wed and moved away to Berkeley. My mother loved visiting Bert and her husband George. They invited her often, but she lacked the desire to leave the safe environs of Eureka for more than a few weeks. My mother enjoyed playing with Bess' child Reid, but she happily escaped from any responsibilities for him at the end of the day.

"I make a better aunt than a mother," she once cried to Bess. This worried Bess as my mother was becoming increasingly prone to sudden emotional outbursts. It prompted her to ask, "You haven't had another one of your spells have you, Sis?"

The question irritated Lill. "Only when I'm pressured," she muttered, eager to shut down any conversation regarding her *spells*. However, what are young married life and motherhood if *not* a series of pressures?

Somehow my parents survived David's difficult infancy. Nevertheless, Lill began to experience more worrisome anxiety spells. They came out of nowhere and made her feel like she was suffocating or having a heart seizure. She didn't admit that they also left her feeling detached and disoriented. She finally confessed to Jack that she feared she might be going crazy. At twenty-three, her life began to come apart and both she and my father knew it.

Lill's second pregnancy failed to improve her mental health or general outlook on life. She was flattened by post-partum depression following the death of Preston. A cloud of frantic despair descended over her and cast its shadow over Jack's life as well. He suspected that the steadfast God of his childhood had transformed into a God of random acts, most of them cruel or petty.

As time passed, Lill's nervous spells and fears of going berserk multiplied. She had little experience with personal loss and no understanding of how to express it. How could she know that the painful emotions flooding through her were signs of grief and not madness?

Jack ultimately turned to his mother for advice. "What do I do to shake Lill out of this? I need something a little stronger than prayer."

She ignored his sarcasm. "Lill needs to see a doctor."

My father took little convincing. He left work early the next afternoon to drive my mother to their family doctor's office. Dr. Ely knew of the young family's history; he'd delivered Preston, and in fact, signed the baby's death certificate.

"I feel like the top of my head is coming off," Lill repeated to the balding ex-Army, no-nonsense physician. "I don't know what's happening to me?"

My father stood to one side, agitated and eyeing the floor. "It's just her nerves," he stammered, mindful that his own were ragged as well.

The well-upholstered Dr. Ely nodded in agreement, folding and unfolding his double chins. He patted my mother's trembling arm. "The good news is, Lill, I can give you something to help." With inscrutable penmanship, he wrote out a refillable prescription for phenobarbital and handed it to my father.

"My women patients swear by it," he consoled my mother. "And so do their husbands," he added with a wink meant to reassure my father. The well-intentioned physician never mentioned the highly addictive nature of this wonder drug or that its hypnotic side effects could render the user incapable of fairly important emotions like love and compassion.

Dr. Ely also recommended my parents get pregnant again and as soon as possible. "You need to get started on another baby right away," he advised, little realizing it was the last thing they needed. "It's the only way to put Preston's death behind you."

Jack slowed the car as he entered the city limits of Eureka. He turned into the General Hospital's parking lot and switched off the engine, wiping his sweaty palms on his jeans. His wildly conflicting emotions churned, making his next step, any step, difficult. On one hand, he could hardly wait to see his wife and their two-day-old daughter; on the other, this new addition to an already stressful situation left him with a strong compulsion to drive away as fast as he could.

2

QUARANTINED

My mother gazed down at her dark-haired, nine-pound, twenty-two-inch baby girl, just three days old, asleep in her arms. The drive home from the General Hospital to Pigeon Point Hill took barely half an hour. A few minutes earlier, she had told my father she looked forward to getting back to their little cabin. This came as music to his ears and the pressure that weighed him down during the long drive from Sequoia lifted.

The radio played the latest hit, "The Woody Woodpecker Song," while my mother hummed along. A news bulletin broke in to report that President Truman had ordered an airlift of food and supplies to Berlin rather than using military force to end Stalin's blockade of the city. WWIII was avoided once again while I slumbered in my mother's lap.

My father had the day off, it being Sunday, and he and my mother stopped by Momo's where my three-year-old brother had spent the past few days. Momo helped David into the back seat of our black and white Ford. "He's been a good little boy," she told my parents. "Don't let him get lost in the shuffle." Momo reached through the front window, patting Daddy on the back. "You have a beautiful little girl there, Jackie. Now you have one of each." She winked at David.

"What's her name, Mommy?" David asked excitedly, jumping up to peer over my mother's shoulder.

"Hush, you'll wake her," Mommy whispered. "Her name is Paula Christine. Now sit still and be quiet."

David sighed and rolled down the window. "So long, Momo," he called out as she stood in full bloom waving goodbye in her red, pink, orange, and yellow dahlia patch. Her hair, which had turned white prematurely, floated around her head like a puffy cloud. David thought she looked beautiful. He leaned back against the seat, picking at an old scab on his knee. He already missed Momo and wished that he could live with her and Pop for always.

Our cabin stood ready and waiting. My father, careful of the sleeping cargo she carried, helped my mother out of the car, and then turned to retrieve David from the back seat. He watched his son prance his way up the steps. Aware of his new status as a big brother, David held the cabin door open to allow my mother and me to pass through. "Good boy," my father praised, bringing up the rear.

In the past few months, my mother had spruced up the log house, sewn curtains for the kitchen and throw pillows for the Chesterfield sofa. She and my father painted all four rooms of our cabin a soft yellow that made everything look cozy.

Overjoyed by David's homecoming, our collie Lady jumped around delightedly, nearly knocking him over with her wagging tail. My mother bent down to introduce me to Chico, the Boston terrier she had owned since high school. "How's my little man?" she asked her standoffish pet. "Did you miss me?" She made kissing noises in the air.

David tugged on my mother's coat sleeve, anxious to share in her affection "Can sister sleep with me, Mommy?"

Mommy laid me down in David's old wicker bassinette. She smiled at him, something she rarely did. "For now, Paula's going to sleep in this," she explained. "In our bedroom."

David stood on tiptoes to observe me. He carefully drew the covers off for a better look.

"Oh, Mama, she has the cutest little paws," he squealed, a reflection perhaps of his early maternal bonding with our collie. "Can I pet her?"

Within a month, a new routine reshaped my mother's days. She gradually made peace with her roles as wife and mother. At four weeks old, I had both a lusty cry and happy-go-lucky nature. David, at first taken with me, now accepted the newest member of the family with a carefree nonchalance.

"She's an easy baby," Mommy told Grandma Ida, feeling more confident as my chief caregiver. She still grew restless and lonely up on the hill, so most every day Daddy dropped her, David, and me off at Grandma's on his way to work. All nine of Mommy's brothers stopped by regularly, first to have a helping of Grandma's fried potatoes and then to take a gander at me, the latest member of the tribe. Babies and children in general continued to baffle my mother. She constantly worried about my brother and me. She confused that worry with parental love, probably because she herself grew up without it.

The four-week honeymoon that followed my uneventful birth, gave everyone some time to adapt to the present and look forward to the future.

The calm collected before the storm, then almost overnight, home life took a turn for the worst. Without rhyme or reason, at six weeks old I morphed from an easygoing infant, pleased with herself and the world, into a screaming baby banshee. After hours of nonstop wailing, I'd switch to a lethargic and non-responsive infant, refusing to take my bottle.

"Why is she crying so much?" David asked, watching Mommy change my diaper. "She hurts my ears!" He clomped around the changing table in his new red leather cowboy boots, determined to stomp out my squalls.

"Babies do that sometimes," Mommy sighed, a familiar anxiety beginning to squeeze her chest, making it difficult to breathe. She picked me up in another futile attempt to soothe me. "You go outside and play with your truck," she ordered. My brother eagerly complied, dragging Lady along. For the next hour, he rode her around the yard, shooting at robbers with his water pistol.

My mother staked herself at the back door, pouncing on my father when he returned from work that afternoon. "I'm at the end of my rope," she warned in the low monotonous voice that caught his attention. "Something's wrong with her, Jack."

Daddy tried to ignore the panic in his wife's account of her harried day attending to me. "She's fine," he said, silently praying that I was. Or did this mark the beginning of another round of chaos God had in store for him? Was he being punished for his wavering belief?

Leaving David with Momo and Pop, my distraught parents took me to see Dr. Ely.

Cases of polio had been cropping up in Eureka throughout the summer of 1948, but Dr. Ely initially ruled that diagnosis out. "We just don't see polio in infants."

"All she does is sleep," Lill reported to Dr. Ely. He grabbed up his prescription pad and wrote out another order for phenobarbital. He handed the paper to my father and then leaned over the examination table, placing his stethoscope on my tiny chest.

"Could be sleeping sickness," the doctor muttered, mostly to himself.

Daddy pushed Dr. Ely aside, picked me up from the examining table and tried to rouse me. "Look how limp she is."

"She definitely needs to be hospitalized and put under observation," Dr. Ely told him. "You get her over to General Hospital and I'll call ahead and tell the staff there to expect you."

The pediatrician who admitted me to the hospital initially concurred with the diagnosis of sleeping sickness, the everyday name for encephalitis. "I don't like the look of her," he shrugged. My mother and father reluctantly left me isolated in the critical-care ward of the nursery where a cadre of white-masked strangers poked and prodded me, running tests and proposing various theories about my deteriorating condition. Just to rule it out, a spinal tap screening for the polio virus was performed shortly before my release.

On Sunday morning, Dr. Ely phoned to break the bad news. "I'm afraid it's polio," he informed my parents. "She's been transferred from General to the quarantined unit at County Hospital."

"When can we see her—I mean actually hold her in our arms?" Daddy demanded.

"If she survives, she'll be in isolation until County Health officials deem her free of the polio virus. There's a staff of two doctors and two registered nurses trained and willing to work with polio victims. It's a risky business since your baby is still likely to be contagious."

"So how long will that take?" my father persisted.

"Hard to tell…three weeks, maybe a month. We haven't seen a case of polio in a child as young as Paula, so we have no way to determine her chances. At this point, she can breathe with the help of an oxygen tent. It will take months, even years to fully understand the extent of her disabilities. We do know that at this time all four limbs appear to be paralyzed and her neck and swallowing muscles are affected. She may live, but your daughter will never sit up or walk on her own."

Stunned by the alarming diagnosis and equally pessimistic prognosis, my father covered the phone's receiver and conveyed the information to my mother. A parent's worst nightmare unfolded in the tiny kitchen of the log cabin.

"Oh, God, no…oh, God, no…" my mother repeated. My father stood by, too dazed to comfort her.

"Are you still there, Jack?" Dr. Ely asked from the other end of the telephone line.

"Yes, I'm here. What do we need to do next?"

"Wait," the doctor answered. "You and Lill need to come see me next week. By then, we may know more about her condition and prospects for recovery. I don't recommend that you see Paula right now. You know, best not to get too attached. And I have some concerns about Lill's abilities to cope," the doctor continued. "Some parents are opting to institutionalize their children in light of the burden caring for such a severely handicapped child entails."

My father slammed down the phone, angry at the doctor's matter-of-fact tone, but equally upset because my mother was barely up to handling a normal child like David, let alone a severely disabled one like me.

The clock ticked off hours, then days of waiting. I remained in isolation for two weeks, paralyzed, although I could now breathe on my own. California had 326 cases of polio diagnosed in mid-September 1948. Swimming pools and movie houses shut down whenever new outbreaks cropped up. Parents panicked, many refusing to let their children play with any child who contracted the disease, even long after the contagion was over. Eureka was no exception. Scores of my parents' friends and family refused to visit our home, fearful that they might expose their own children to the virus. They did so with good reason.

Polio was highly contagious. Incubating in the gut, the virus invaded the spinal cord and sometimes the brain. Once established, polio killed off delicate horn cells, small units that conduct signals from motor neurons to muscles. With horn cells destroyed, the muscles they had been attached to ceased to function. Sometimes surviving horn cells branched out, eventually reconnecting to damaged motor neurons; this branching often resulted in partial or complete recovery of damaged muscles and the individual regained full functioning.

Polio rarely killed or crippled those who became infected. Muscular paralysis only affected one in every 1,000 cases. Treatment often involved keeping the muscles "at rest" while they recovered. If they recovered.

Each day after work, my father stood outside the glassed-off contagious ward, attempting to monitor my progress. The doctors argued over my survival chances, doing little to ease my parents' concern. Presented with predictions like "difficulty swallowing, will never sit up or walk, better to be placed in a long-term care facility" there was little room for faith or hope. Jack urged Lill to follow Dr. Ely's orders and not visit me until the odds looked more promising.

This separation from my parents and the world around me left an indelible mark. Hospital staff restricted their hands-on touch to feeding, bathing, and diapering my wasted body. My spirit miraculously survived the stark isolation surrounding me. Call it resiliency. Still, I didn't escape unscathed. The seeds of loneliness and anxiety took hold within me; they took root throughout most of my childhood and adolescence.

1948 proved to be a bad year for polio, but a good one for me. In spite of the odds, I prevailed over the tiny malevolent virus that left my body in such a mangled state.

3

MERE ANARCHY

On my first birthday, September 23, 1949, President Truman's voice came over the radio to announce that Russia had exploded her first atomic bomb. Along with the arms race, I was launched into a world of unbridled fear and turmoil, none of which I recall. Those who might have known the facts are long gone, so I have only a few impressions of that period of my life. I was in and out of the County Hospital in Eureka and later spent a few days being assessed at Stanford Medical Center near San Francisco.

I'm told I returned home after doctors declared there was nothing they could do for me until my condition stabilized. This left my mother to care for an active three-year-old boy and an infant who sometimes gasped for air and at other times choked on it. Both my mother and father shared the guilt and self-blame of any parent with a less than healthy child. It seemed once again that God was randomly punishing them. But for what?

My need for constant supervision placed an especially heavy burden on my mother. She tried her best to cope with the demands of a nearly paralyzed child, but the grim reality of my diagnosis and the bleak picture doctors painted for my future *and therefore hers,* finally broke her already vulnerable spirit.

In the forties, doctors hospitalized such broken spirits. Mommy, convinced that she was going mad, agreed to be admitted to the General Hospital for a few days. Dr. Ely put her on complete bed rest and prescribed high doses of tranquilizers. Undoubtedly medicated into a drug-induced fog, my mother recalled very few details of her hospitalization or what was happening with me at the time.

Crucial questions regarding what transpired during my early infancy remain unanswered. How long was Mommy hospitalized? Where did my brother stay in her absence? Who took care of me? Was I hospitalized during some of that period? Days and weeks are missing.

Accounts of my life resumed when Mommy returned home to her routine on Pigeon Point Hill—but just barely. My father continued at the newspaper where he put in six days a week, spelling my mother only on Sundays. Daddy had a better set of nerves than Mommy did, but my precarious condition left him as emotionally overwrought as she was. He sacrificed hours of overtime so he could catch the Greyhound bus down to San Francisco to visit me in various hospitals. Desperate to prevent another emotional collapse, whenever he was at home he tried to bolster Mommy's sagging spirit.

He attempted to search for help and took on a Native American girl to foster, hoping she might assume some of my care. Alice evidently loved to carry me around on her hip while singing to me. She taught me to warble a muddled version of "Good Night, Irene," but Daddy sent her back to the Hupa Indian reservation when my mother discovered some of her jewelry had disappeared. Later, while sweeping under David's bed for dust bunnies, she found her missing jewelry hanging from the bedsprings.

It still fell largely to my mother to uphold the daily regimen of the hot baths and vigorous massages doctors recommended to help restore some use to my traumatized muscles. This course of therapy was inspired by the work of the Australian nurse, Sister Kenny. Though highly controversial as a treatment, Mommy had seen the movie of this nurse's life and I think Rosalind Russell, who played Sister Kenny in the movie, convinced her it was worth a try. The smell of baby oil and my mother's off-handed touch remain a vivid memory for me. I soaked up these rare moments of intimate connection.

She left the painful foot and neck stretching exercises to my father when he came home from work. She stole out of the cabin then, eager to block out my baby cries of pain. Though she received encouragement and praise for her dedication to me from extended family members, she most highly valued the respite from my care offered by my Grandma Ida.

My four-year-old brother David surely felt abandoned by two parents who spent much of their time fixated on me. That his needs were ignored is clear from a picture of him at four. He smiles into the camera revealing that most of his baby teeth have rotted out, probably due to neglect. He spent increasingly longer periods with Momo, shadowing and clinging to her. Thankfully, the love both Momo and Grandma Ida lavished upon David rescued him from an otherwise intolerable situation.

I was too young to register my parents' guilt and resentment over being saddled with a nearly paralyzed child. That realization came later. The first feat I achieved in my own personally constructed myth was my unexpected victory over a life-threatening disease. As soon as I mastered baby talk, I started babbling to anyone around me that I was the youngest baby to catch polio and live to tell about it. Although a somewhat off-putting claim to fame for a child, I took pride in my survival skills and savored my first taste of self-esteem.

I remember waking up to rays of sunshine filtering through the venetian blinds of my parents' bedroom, leaving yellow stripes across my baby blanket. Like any other day, Mommy propped me up in a corner of my crib with a bottle and a pacifier to soothe me while she left to tackle her daily chores. The ringing telephone interrupted our normal routine and Mommy ran to answer it.

My cribbed-in world was becoming too small to meet my simplest needs. I wanted to be on the living room linoleum, licking the pretty pink roses that covered it. I wanted to roll on my back, kick my right leg in the air, and wave it in excitement. This brought our collie Lady to my side where, true to her breed, she herded me in circles with her nose, barking and wagging her tail.

Bored and lonely, I stared at the book and stuffed elephant on the other side of the bed, both beyond my reach. Scooting closer to them, I lost my balance and plopped over on my stomach, landing on my face.

Facedown in my crib, I struggled to lift my head so I could breathe better and see between the bars. Mommy had returned with Auntie Bess behind her.

"See, Bess, she won't stay put," Mommy explained. "I don't know what to do with her."

Auntie Bess sat me back up while I kicked my good leg to show my enthusiasm. "She wants to be moving around," Auntie Bess lectured.

Mommy resented suggestions coming from a woman raising a perfectly normal, healthy six-year-old son. She held up one of my lifeless arms and let it drop back down on the bed. She glared at her older sister, pain in her eyes. "Well, she can't move around, can she, Bess?"

Auntie Bess shrugged. "Like it or not, Paula's heading for the terrible twos, so you best put her on the floor and let her explore her world."

I gurgled with delight when Auntie Bess lifted me from the crib and laid me down on the living room floor. By rolling and shoving myself along with my good leg, I reached the picture window, catching a glimpse of the fluffy white clouds.

"See," Auntie Bess remarked. "She's learning how to get from here to there in her own way."

Mommy picked me up in her arms so I could look out the window. I nestled close to her, unaware of the way her body stiffened against my weight. Colors streamed in from the outside world and I soaked up the blue, blue sky.

Daily life shifted a little after that. Upon awakening, Mommy sat me on the living room floor, propping me up in a corner with my tiny, easy-to-handle toys. Once I was bored with that, I'd slide down onto my back and slither towards the kitchen, pushing myself along with my good leg. While my personal world grew larger every day, Mommy's shrank in size, leaving little time for a life of her own.

One of my earliest memories is of a meeting of *The Club,* a huge monthly gathering of my mother's many female relatives. On a blanket spread out on the grass, Mommy sat me up for the umpteenth time that day. To her surprise and delight, I remained upright when she let go!

"Quick, Mom! Get your camera," Mommy shouted excitedly. Grandma Ida ran inside to fetch her trusty Brownie and took a snapshot of me smiling, pleased as punch. My accomplishment met with raves from aunts, great-aunts, and cousins in attendance. My extended family provided me with my first live audience. A star was born.

My second performance of note featured me walking solo at two, tempted to do so by the prospect of holding my newly-born cousin, Debbie, if I took some fledging steps. My father stood me up in Grandma Ida's kitchen. When he saw that I was balanced, he took his hands away. "Off you go."

I studied the black and white tile floor, carefully placing my right high topped shoe on a white square. I dragged my weaker leg forward, placing this shoe on a black square. I was off and running—well, staggering, but I made it to the other side of the kitchen.

I swaggered my way into the living room and parked my behind on Grandma Ida's couch. Still a bit shaky, I nonetheless demanded my prize. Auntie Dot arranged pillows around me and propped up my arms. Debbie was mine to hold. Gently I cooed over her the way I'd seen Auntie Dot do. I hugged my baby cousin in my arms as best I could, enchanted by her curly blonde hair and rosebud mouth. She looked like an angel, with no polio hands or feet.

"Where did she come from?" I asked her mother, my Auntie Dot.

Uncle Bill, Mommy's twin brother, looked over at his wife. "Well, Dot?"

Auntie Dot grinned at me. "Why, she came to us by airmail. They dropped her wearing a baby parachute and your Uncle Bill caught her in his arms." As we grew older, Auntie Dot became our go-to source if we ever had questions about bodily functions or sex. At the time though, I embraced the airmail delivery system as a wonderful explanation for the process of childbirth. Eventually I discovered Auntie Dot's was not the only version out there.

After my visits to Baby Debbie, I pumped Mommy for details of my own birth. "Mommy, did I get dropped from a plane and Daddy catched me in his arms? Can I see the chute?" I begged.

Mommy grinned over at Daddy. "I guess she's old enough to hear how she came into our family."

Daddy nodded. "It's time."

"When Daddy lived on the Pribolof Islands near Alaska," Mommy began, "he hiked into the woods every morning. One day he heard a baby crying, and then he stumbled upon you, abandoned by someone in a big mud puddle of melting snow. He washed you off and brought you home to me."

"I'm an Eskimo like the people where Daddy lived?" Daddy had told my brother and me exciting stories about being in the army, visiting igloos and eating blubber with the natives. So *that* was my original family. Maybe this explained the source of my sadness—I missed them.

Daddy squirmed in his chair. "Actually you're Aleutian," he clarified, stopping a moment to bring my birth story to a happy conclusion. "We fell in love with you right away and decided to keep you and raise you as our own little girl."

Mommy retrieved my baby book from her bedroom. She opened to a picture of me, dressed in a bright red snow suit, my black hair poking out in all directions from under the hood.

I certainly looked like a baby Eskimo. "Did I have polio yet? Is that why they left me behind in a mud puddle?"

Without answering, Mommy cut up the hamburger she had cooked for our evening meal. "Finish your dinner or we'll miss the Ed Sullivan Show."

I leaned over my plate and picked up a bite of meat.

"Mommy, she's not using her spoon," my brother prattled.

Mommy grabbed up the special spoon with the curved handle that lay idle at the side of my plate. She wrapped my three usable fingers around it. I struggled to scoop up some potatoes and direct them towards my mouth. I hit my eye with the first bite, but my aim improved on the next try.

One weekend we drove across Humboldt County to Trinidad's rugged coastline. I loved to watch the waves crash over and around giant rocks and listened with new interest to the barking seals offshore calling me home to Alaska.

While there, we visited Mommy's favorite garden nursery where I enjoyed poking through the dull brown iris and daffodil bulbs. Mommy reminded me that they would bloom bright yellows and purples in the spring. She bought me one of each. She patiently shared her love for and knowledge of gardening with me, providing another source of connection between us. At the same time, I longed to be with Daddy and David chasing waves on the beach below the cliffs. I liked to see Daddy playing with David instead of hitting him.

The garden lady had a magical gift shop at the back of her house, a mixture of tacky plastic replicas of starfish and sea horses along with the real things that cost more. I had no desire for the bags of poor lifeless starfish, sea dollars, and dried out baby crabs but I persuaded Daddy to buy me a cheap Indian doll mother with a papoose strapped to her back. Much to my disappointment and the garden lady's regret, she had no such items from Alaska, but Daddy convinced me that Native Americans and Eskimos came from the same family line and that was good enough for me.

The mother-daughter figurine became a favorite talisman of mine. I wanted Mommy to carry me like that. As soon as I grew up, I would sail to the Aleutian Islands to find my real mother. I never spoke to Mommy about my plans.

Trips to Trinidad and drives in the country, visiting with relatives, attending the annual rodeo and the Barnum and Bailey circus, or spending a Saturday night at the Midway Drive-In all marked the good but infrequent times we did things together as a family. These occasions helped balance the relatively somber periods of life where my mother lapsed into one of her escalating *nervous spells* and my father descended into the noisy bowels of the *Humboldt Standard Newspaper*.

In retrospect, I understand why my father escaped to the newspaper, working overtime to earn more money, especially during the holidays when our parents piled presents three feet high around the tree. Incidentally, overtime also provided Daddy with a valid reason to spend less time with my mother. He forgot that he abandoned my brother and me to the care of an edgy stay-at-home mother whose behavior could often be perplexing, full of threats and warnings. On her bad days, Mommy's disappearance into a haze of drug-induced lethargy took its toll on our young psyches.

Between the ages of two and three, Mommy considered me old enough to be left alone to entertain myself. While David could play outside with the neighbor kids, I spent solitary hours poring over my brother's and my baby books, albums designed to highlight developmental milestones in black and white images. I lingered over the first photos of me before polio had wasted the muscles in both my arms and left leg.

Try as I did, I naturally failed to recollect my first six-weeks of life; the time when I still had usable limbs that could clap, wave, and kick in an orderly sequence. I lost myself in the eyes of a fully functioning dark-haired five-week-old baby in a buggy, smiling back at me before the virus did its damage.

A few pages later, a picture of me posing behind the white picket fence surrounding my grandmother's back garden particularly resonated with me. I stood erect, my head turned sideways to the camera, looking off into the distant hills with determination. The snapshot captured the first signs of what Grandma Ida admired in me and referred to as "gumption."

"When you fall down and almost break your head open, you can cry just a little, but then you get right back up and on with the rest of your day," she told me repeatedly. "Show your gumption." She believed I had quite a lot of this gumption and it would take me a long way in life if I applied myself.

Gumption, however, provided no substitute for a lack of maternal love and attachment. I have few early memories of being held or interacting with my mother beyond her dressing me, feeding me in my high chair and sitting me up in my crib. It was my father who took me in his arms to comfort me. He walked me around the house, bent over and holding me up under the arms, while I moved my scrawny baby legs as best I could. Soon I yearned to meander with him through the second growth redwood forest on our land. "Walk me, Daddy, walk me," I begged the minute he returned from work each afternoon or early on a Sunday morning.

"Let's go get the eggs," I pleaded constantly. Daddy picked me up and I rode high on his shoulders out to the chicken coop where he took my weakened hand and forced it under a setting hen. Together we studied the egg I retrieved. "Oh, Daddy, it's still warm." I put the egg up against my cheek, then his. Nature became my second mother and I delighted in any interaction with her.

With support from a tiny leg brace, my balance and walking continued to improve. The little steel device held in place by wide leather straps was stabilizing although it kept my leg stiff and pinched my skin. I willingly accepted the encumbrance that allowed Daddy and me to sneak off on our little adventures. These outings fired up my attempts to push the boundaries of safety, as I dared to try new things like digging for treasured baby potatoes, or plucking and scooping out the still-steaming entrails of a newly butchered chicken. Daddy always cut off the feet so we could pull the tendons and make the old hen tap dance. Some mornings he stuffed me into my stiff yellow raincoat and red galoshes and together we splashed through the deep mud puddles left from the previous night's storm. Best of all, he would wake me up early and pack me out to our tiny barn. I was the first to set eyes on a newborn colt or goat, still slick and wet. Once I experienced the thrill of putting my hand on top of Daddy's and feeling the powerful vibrations from his chainsaw as it chewed up logs for our woodstove. I swore not to tell Mommy of our more dangerous escapades because she, being overprotective when it came to risk-taking, would get upset.

Daddy sat me astride our pony, Soxy, holding me firmly by my waist as we trotted around the pasture. When I grew steadier in the saddle, Daddy put the reins in my hands and let me ride Soxy a few feet ahead of him. To be on horseback all by myself exhilarated me. Over time, my self-confidence blossomed because Daddy honored my drive for independence, letting me take the many small risks necessary to a child's normal development.

Since my father had to work six days a week, my only dose of his undivided attention came on Sundays. I couldn't wait until daylight savings arrived and left us with longer times to tromp down to the Ten Acres, a few miles away.

Late one Sunday afternoon, Daddy sat on a fallen redwood log holding me between his knees so I could survey the gullies of ferns and stretches of black berry brambles. I imagined I stood all by myself and delighted in the sensation.

I scanned the deep undergrowth a few feet away. A rustle in the briars caught my attention. A small red fox nosed its way out of a nest of brambles and stared me straight in the eyes.

"Daddy, look."

"I see it," he whispered. We remained stone still, sharing the moment the way we shared a strawberry milkshake at the Fresh Freeze.

"Your Uncle Robert and I had a pet raccoon when we were boys."

"Was that when you wanted to be a veterinarian once you grew up?"

"It was." Daddy got a faraway look as his eyes misted up a little.

The fox bolted across the narrow trail and vanished into a nearby hole under a log. His black nose and eyes stayed with me like the smile of the Cheshire cat.

"What can I be when I grow up?"

"You know...I've been thinking about that lately. Maybe you and I could own a pet store together."

The idea enchanted me. "We could sell dogs and cats and those giant aquariums with the neon and angelfish in them," I proposed, flying off on his dream.

Daddy studied the place where the fox had disappeared under the log. "We could call it *Paula's Pet Parade*."

There, far away from the house and Mommy and the evening chores waiting to be performed, Daddy and I hatched a dream. "Could I make a living out of the store?" Long before I'd started school, Daddy thought up ways that I could earn a living and not have to depend on anyone else when I grew up.

"You could."

"It'd be hard to sell the animals, especially to total strangers."

Daddy laughed. "I could help with that. I'd make sure our animals went to people who would take good care of them."

Darkness settled over us by the time we'd planned out my future livelihood. We headed home, me riding high on his shoulders. I fell asleep that night dreaming of the little red fox and envisioning a sign above a store announcing Paula's Pet Parade was open for business.

To keep myself in the spotlight, I became a notorious ham, ferreting out the recognition, praise and affection of others when and wherever I could. I belted out many of the popular hits of the day like "How Much Is That Doggie in the Window?" or "I'm a Little White Duck," and everybody's favorite, "Good Night, Irene."

My brother and I entertained and leaned on one another when no well-adjusted adults were available to nurture and console us; set adrift in the same leaking boat, we realized early on that we couldn't afford the luxury of sibling rivalry. I depended on David to comfort and reassure me, especially when Mommy threatened to run away from home. "I'm leaving and I'm never coming back," she announced one rainy autumn afternoon. David and I sat playing Chinese checkers on the kitchen floor, squabbling over whose turn it was.

"Don't go, Mommy," I pleaded, desperate to stop her. "We won't fight anymore." I hadn't yet learned to distinguish between her empty threats and the ones she was likely to carry out.

"Don't cry," David soothed me after Mommy disappeared through the back door. "I want to show you something." Lifting me under the arms, he dragged me over to the window above the kitchen sink. It took some lifting, pushing, and flailing, but eventually he maneuvered me onto the counter.

He scrambled up next to me. "Look." He helped me lean over to peer outside.

Mommy was crouched there, a light rain falling on her. She didn't realize we could see her. We watched until she left her hiding place and came back into the house. From that point on, I never took Mommy's threats to abandon us very seriously. I remained nonchalant when she ran out the back door, slamming it behind her. My brother and I would look at each other and smile.

Bon voyage, Mama!

4

THE BIG DREAM

Until I was three years old or so, I depended on Mommy or Daddy to stand me up whenever I wanted to walk. Without their help, I had to scoot around the house on my butt or walk on my knees. My arms lacked the strength to support my upper body, so crawling was out of the question.

To my great delight, I discovered I could sit on top of my brother's flatbed toy truck and propel myself with my good foot. This mode of transportation wore me out fast though and David resented my commandeering his vehicle for my own purposes.

"Leave my stuff alone," he ordered one day as I careened around the living room. "You're not supposed to ride on it, stupid. I don't mess with your dolls."

He had a point, but it continually irked me that I had to count on someone else, often my harried mother, to help me.

Fortunately, the antics of Mommy's Boston terrier taught me an important lesson. I was making inroads into Chico's loyalty to Mommy; increasingly he was taking my side. I was still jealous of the dog because Mommy called him her *good little man* while she referred to me as *Little Moaning Mary*.

Watching Chico jump on and off our Chesterfield sparked my imagination. With Chico sniffing at my feet, I scooted over to the sofa and tried to climb up on it. It was too high. In frustration, I grabbed one of the cushions in my teeth and pulled it onto the floor. Having removed the cushion, I was at the perfect level to lean over and push myself onto the Chesterfield. Next, I sat myself up, placed both feet on the floor, tipped forward, and like magic, I stood up! All by myself. The thirty-minute workout exhilarated and empowered me—no more waiting for somebody to help me. This sense of independence fired my determination to find more ways of gaining physical and psychological freedom.

Careful not to trip, I tottered into the kitchen to show Mommy my newest achievement. Her response dampened my spirits.

"You see, you could have been doing that all along if you'd only tried harder. I won't be around to help you forever, you know."

That would be a pleasurable turn of events. I still entertained hopes of finding my Eskimo mother.

"But I do try." I smiled at Chico who padded over and nosed my arm up around his neck. "We hate Mommy, don't we?" I whispered to him, feeling smug when he nodded his head in agreement.

When my father came home that afternoon, I excitedly scooted into the living room and repeated my climb up onto the Chesterfield. All thirty-six inches of me swayed back and forth on my feet.

"Daddy's so proud of you." His smile made me stand even straighter. "You did it!"

That, in a nutshell, was the difference between my mother and father.

The daily hysteria of my mother and the sporadic rages of my father fueled the nightmares haunting my sleep throughout early childhood. The common theme involved one of my parents shape-shifting into a variety of wild animals—a roaring lion, a growling grizzly bear, or a towering King Kong. I'd dream I heard a terrifying scratching at my bedroom door and when I opened it, I'd find my mother or father, their smiles changing into snarls as their faces transformed into monster masks.

Oddly, my father played both a starring role in my nightmares as well as being the hero who rescued me when I cried out from night terrors. As soon as I heard his reassuring footsteps thumping toward my bedroom, I knew he would lie beside me until I fell back to sleep. The monster vanished. It was just my father snuggling with me, no longer a threat, but a comfort.

My inner world began to compensate for my everyday life where I remained stranded. By using my active imagination I filled the empty hours with fairy friends and fantasy excursion into the world of local wildlife where I rescued injured rabbits and motherless fawns like Bambi. I coaxed birds to perch on my finger and sing to me and slept with the little red fox curled at my feet. The dreams that came during the night fascinated me and often spilled over into my waking hours. Where did they come from and what did they mean?

I was quite young when I had what psychologists refer to as a "big" dream—the kind so vivid they're recalled for a long time. The memory of it remains fresh to this day. In the dream, I am standing in a large field behind Grandma Ida's house, watching our pony Soxy give birth. Living on a farm, I had witnessed live births so this helped inform the dream. A beautiful blue colt emerges from the birth sac, wet and wobbly in the sunshine. I immediately know that this blue baby horse belongs to me, and contently watch Soxy lick her newborn clean. My attention is drawn to a dark figure staggering towards me, wielding an axe. A sense of foreboding sweeps over me as he rushes forward, chops the head off my baby blue horse, and tells me it is too wounded to live in the world. The man is my father.

Despite my immediate grief and terror, this dream left me filled with awe and a sense of mystery. Once awake, I knew this magical blue horse must be kept secret, so I vowed to protect it with my silence. From then on though, a growing part of me believed I had powers, as yet unexplored and that polio had left untouched. This dream added to that experience of myself; it struck me as something grownup and significant.

Years later, a Jungian professor interpreted my dream as one where my father attempted to kill off my unique, but damaged spirit for "my own good." In Jungian terms, the dream played out my father's unconscious disavowal of me. Certainly, it reflected his conflicted feelings; he both loved and feared for me. What strikes me now is that early on, I had picked up on the shame, guilt, and responsibility my father felt over my broken body. His brothers' deaths, the death of Preston, and finally a daughter who contracted polio left Daddy feeling increasingly alienated from God. To make matters worse, he feared this alienation might be responsible for my polio.

"You see, honey, God may have given you polio because I turned my back on Him."

My four-year-old mind grappled with the disturbing notion that God may have given me polio to punish Daddy for his lapse of faith. This incensed me.

"I hate God for giving me polio."

"Don't hate God. God loves you."

"Then why did God give me polio instead of you?"

The question stumped my father. He shook his head sadly. "I only wished he had."

I endeavored to make sense of Daddy's God and my place in His creation. I was aided in my struggles by *The Little Golden Book of Bible Stories*, one of a series of inexpensive children's books Mommy bought David and me at the grocery store. As if by magic, the book opened at a page displaying a reassuring illustration of Jesus surrounded by a crowd of children. I immediately identified with a little boy leaning against Jesus, a small crutch underneath one arm. I figured he had polio too and yet, from the loving look in Jesus eyes, I could see that this child was special to Jesus. The notion comforted me. I doubted if He'd given me polio to punish Daddy or me. Along with my father, Jesus provided me with the perfect parent to internalize and keep present; the Son of God was just plain old Daddy to me. By giving me polio, God showed me I was strong enough to be chosen for a life as a crippled kid. It gave my suffering some meaning.

That Little Golden Book offered something even more valuable. There on the frontispiece was Jesus as a toddler, his little arms spread open in a show of love. Unable to restrain myself, I tore out the page and waved it at Mommy. "Look," I exclaimed, "he's a perfect paper doll."

One of the only things my mother enjoyed playing with me was paper dolls like the ones we purchased at Jones' Five-and-Dime. She had collected them as a child and I came to share her enthusiasm for these ephemeral families; they offered a vital bond between us, which I savored. Unlike my rubber dollies, paper dolls were light to handle and easy to dress. Even with weak hands and arms, I could manipulate my paper friends and lose myself in their paperweight world.

"You shouldn't be tearing up your books," Mommy scolded. She examined baby Jesus and then, smiled down at me. "We'll have to paste him to some stiffer paper," she mused as she somewhat reluctantly cut the figure out with her sewing scissors.

Next, she dug in the kitchen garbage can until she found a baseball trading card my brother had thrown away. "This will do nicely," she declared, pasting Jesus to the cardboard and cutting him out for the second time. She handed me the Jesus paper doll.

"Thank you, thank you, Mommy."

"Shall I draw some clothes for him?"

I was beside myself. Mommy was in a good mood and I wanted to make the most of it. "Yes, please!"

Mommy found some paper and a box of crayons and we sat down together at the kitchen table. If only it could always be like this.

"Since Jesus is wearing a dress, I'm going to pretend he's a girl and call him Jesse Jesus," I explained to Mommy. "That way I can dress him in skirts and sweaters."

I watched contentedly as Mommy traced around Jesus, making him a collection of skirts, sweaters, and party dresses fit for a princess. She remained relaxed and attentive. The moment felt enchanting. Just Mommy and me...

Trapped in an unresponsive body, I also learned to compensate for my lack of mobility by focusing my energy on close observation and practiced recall. This sharpened my memory of the events happening around me. I vividly recollect days spent in the "standing table" my father built for me. It enabled me to be outdoors in an upright position—rain or fog—while the tray attached to it provided space to color or play with my paper dolls. It allowed for some psychological distance between Mommy and me. She could safely leave me unattended except for our collie Lady and I could enjoy a bit of independence.

Out in our large yard, I memorized the sweet smell of honeysuckle and stored away the orange, red, and yellow colors of nasturtiums. I passed hours sitting in my sandbox watching my mother hanging out the laundry, a bunch of clothespins in her mouth, all the time imagining what it would feel like to raise my arms high above my head. I entertained myself by making up stories and poems and later found numerous occasions to recite them, delighting those around me and stoking my literary ego.

Everyone's favorite poem went:

I am Paula,

On my own.

But big enough to write this poem.

Of course I had to recite my poem since reading and writing were not yet a part of my world.

Anything that I could accomplish alone yet in relative safety pleased my mother. Besides my solitary stints in the standing table and sandbox, Mommy often left me in the sunroom off our porch, sitting on the floor amid boxes of dolls from around the world. These ancient treasures had been passed down to me courtesy of Great Aunt Bertha who inherited them from a rich Catholic lady she worked for as a maid. I yearned to visit places where people wore furry Eskimo jackets, hula skirts, or silky kimonos, where they performed Irish jigs and kicked their legs up high in the French can-can; I dreamed of countries where they lived in grass huts or igloos like Daddy had seen in Alaska. My lifelong wanderlust was born and nurtured by the dusty relics of bygone times.

I lost myself for hours soaking in the bathtub. I filled empty bottles with water and pretended to pour it into tiny cups held by the dwarves and fairies I conjured up. Occasionally, I would fall over when no one was around. Not a problem—I simply held my breath and used my good leg to splash the water around until my harried mother arrived and sat me back up. Never once did I entertain the notion that I might have drowned waiting to be rescued. I only knew that I could hold my breath longer than any of my friends could—another feather in my cap.

Social and educational mainstreaming of handicapped children wasn't a concept back in the early fifties. Those bygone times held few of the threats that limit today's kids to organized sports, music lessons, and play dates. Luckily for me, I was integrated into the neighborhood gang by way of my brother's wagon. I was just a little over three when David loaded me into his Red Flyer and pulled me along with a group of neighborhood kids ranging from two years all the way up to eleven. The oldest doubled as babysitters for the younger children.

Sharon Barnhart, my age and of a like mind, often joined me in the wagon and in a pinch we could squeeze in a dog or two. I yearned to look just like Sharon with her golden hair and cute chubby figure like a cherub.

Her brothers, Barney, Keith, and Mikey comprised the rest of the Barnhart brood with Richard and Gary Harris joining Judy and Ricky Lermo to make us a party of eleven—more if visiting cousins or schoolmates showed up. Everyone took turns pulling me in the wagon. In the summers and on most Saturdays, we gathered right after breakfast; we played, fought, and made-up with only a short break for lunch. Then we were off again until five or six p.m. when hunger pangs called us home for dinner.

Parental rules bordered on negligence: no going up to the Ten Acres where tramps often slept in a cabin abandoned years before; no spitting at or hitting each other; and no picking berries unless we asked permission from the owner of the property where they grew. None of us followed these guidelines with any regularity.

One experience we shared and never forgot were the earthquakes that shook Eureka from time to time. One Christmas vacation, Sharon and I sat on my family's living room floor next to the woodstove. We were playing the "visiting game," pretending Sharon had stopped over to say hi and drink tea from my blue willow teacups. Without warning, a frightening rumble shook the house, growing louder by the second. The logs of our cabin moaned and groaned like a monster. The woodstove jumped a few inches closer to Sharon and me, prompting us to move farther from the fire.

My mother ran in from the kitchen, shrieking all the way. She snatched me up, while poor Sharon could only cling to Mommy's skirt. Meanwhile the front door flew open and shut and before Mommy could reach it, the Christmas tree tipped over smashing several ornaments to bits.

"My God, where are the boys?" Mommy cried, temporarily forgetting they were playing horseshoes in a neighboring field.

She didn't have to wait long for an answer. We heard frantic knockings on the door and when Mommy opened it, my brother and the Barnhart boys collapsed onto our braided rug.

"Mommy, the trees are laying down on the ground," David reported, his brown eyes wide with both terror and wonderment.

"And the ground got all wavy," Barney sputtered.

"I got knocked clean over," Keith chimed in.

Following a few small aftershocks, Mommy shepherded us over to the Barnhart's to check things out. Bernie Barnhart counted all her roly-poly children and when she finished, we spent the afternoon sitting outside so we wouldn't get hit by shards of glass or flying bricks from the small aftershocks that followed.

When the newspaper account came out the next day, we oohed and aahed over pictures of giant cracks in city sidewalks, houses slipped off their foundations, and two serious car collisions. Still, nothing topped the near-death experiences of our neighborhood gang—by the time Christmas vacation ended, we'd spun out an elaborate tale of our earth-shattering day. The saga featured giant redwoods trees flattened to the ground, barely missing my brother. Keith claimed a sinkhole opened up, almost swallowing him alive. By now Barney's story had newly added drama—he remembered he had just missed being killed by a falling chimney. Naturally, Sharon and I added our bit about the stove jumping over two feet and nearly burning us to death.

If no one was around to pull me in the wagon, I rode in my outgrown "tailor tot," an early version of today's stroller. Once seated, I rested my bad leg on the luggage shelf between the wheels and stretched my good leg far enough out so my shoe could reach the pavement, enabling me to propel myself forward. Where there were sidewalks, I cruised at breakneck speeds, especially when I sailed down a ramp.

I loved visiting my cousin Robbie in Hollywood where pavement covered everything and made pushing myself along easy. Born a month apart, he and I had an intensely combative relationship. On the positive side, he enjoyed the thrill of forbidden adventures as much as I did so we often declared a truce long enough to carry out prohibited and therefore exciting escapades.

Early one morning, I talked Robbie into hopping on his tricycle and joining me on a trip downtown. We whizzed along for two or three blocks, finally stopping to look back when we heard our names bellowed out in the crisp morning air. Mommy and Auntie Marg, both still in bathrobes and wearing slippers, charged down the sidewalk, breathless when they finally reached us.

Robbie and I escaped any punishment, probably because our mothers didn't want to reveal their disciplinary methods to each other. My punishment came later that day, when the four of us boarded a bus to a doctor's office in Los Angeles. A Hollywood doctor had designed a specialized treatment to help hasten recovery from polio and Mommy and Daddy had decided to try him. Or have *me* try him, that is.

For over an hour the doctor stuck little needles into my muscles and shot bolts of electricity through them to see which ones jumped and which never moved at all. The newly developed torture completely ruined a day that had started so well. And nothing came of it except another disappointment for my parents.

When Mommy and I returned to Eureka, Daddy surprised me by putting the finishing touches on the new tricycle he and Mommy presented me for my birthday. My father designed an adaptation to my tricycle—a ring that went around my waist and attached to the seat, providing stability as I swayed side to side. My "bad" leg was tied to the left pedal while my "good" leg hung free to do the lopsided pedaling. My scrawny right arm more or less flapped around as I steered with my stronger left hand. Soon I left my tailor tot in the dust, delighted with my newfound three-wheeled freedom.

My father's imaginative modifications to everyday objects played an important role in promoting my ever-growing desire and at times desperate push for independence. Now I could go anywhere accessible by tricycle or my brother's Radio Flyer wagon. On a foggy Saturday morning, the gang of us pedaled up to play house in the forbidden log cabin on the Ten Acres. All five of us peered inside. To our amazement, we spied a tramp curled up on a dirty old mattress in the corner.

Sharon, Keith, my brother, and I tiptoed around the tramp.

"Is he dead?" Sharon whispered.

"Nah, I can see his chest going up and down," David replied.

When the old man twitched a little in his sleep, we got spooked and pedaled for our lives, stealing backward glances to make sure he wasn't following us.

"He could have a knife and butcher us," Keith speculated. The thought sent us flying to the Barnhart's home in a panic.

The boys' mother, Bernie Barnhart, met us at the door, eyeing her two sons warily and giving David, Sharon, and me a close inspection.

"Where were you kids and what were you up to?" she asked.

We stood by silently, waiting for someone to take charge of our explanation. "We were building a fort," my brother began. The brambles he had caught in his summer crew cut added some much needed authenticity to his story.

"And don't worry, we stayed right on our own property," Barney assured his mother. "We didn't see a single no trespassing sign." Barney's stomach growled noisily. "We worked up an appetite, though."

Bernie folded her arms suspiciously. "Uh, huh...well, why don't I make you some lunch? Then I'd love to see your little project."

We stood there dumbfounded. None of us had anticipated a visit by Bernie to examine our mythical fort.

David finally answered, "We're not quite done, Bernie. You'll have to visit us later after we finish the roof." Our trio nodded in agreement. My brother had saved the day, at least for a little while. For the next half hour, we crowded around the kitchen table, devouring our peanut butter and jam sandwiches, hoping Sharon wouldn't break down under the stress of her overly active conscience and spill the beans for all of us.

Our little lie cost us a lot of blood, sweat, and tears. We spent the rest of the afternoon frantically building a fort. To make room for rabbit hutches and chicken houses, several large redwood trees had been removed from the fields around our neighborhood by using dynamite to blow away their cores. We located a large hollowed out stump on the Lermo property down the hill and set to work. The boys laid a few rotted two-by-fours across the hollowed out stump, making a roof. Sharon and I picked ferns to fill in the spaces between the boards and dug up some moss and baby's tears growing nearby. In no time, we'd planted a plush carpet inside the stump. Everyone lay down cheek to jowl and gazed up through the board-and-fern roof as we feasted on red and black currents, salmon berries, thimble and huckleberries. The juices of summer ran down our chins.

Sunlight filtered through the greenery, flooding the fort with a fairy tale glow. My world was enchanting at times and this enchantment offered me a vital escape from the dreary existence of everyday life. Surrounded by giant sequoias, I felt small and insignificant, but mesmerized by their majesty.

"Yoo-hoo," Mrs. Barnhart called from outside our magical stump. "Can I come in and take a peek?"

"Sure," we urged her on.

"Well, would you look at this," Mrs. Barnhart exclaimed, smiling as she examined the project we had completed in an afternoon of frenzied activity. "You really were building a fort! I have to admit I thought you might be up to no good, but it's obvious you put a day's labor into this." She carefully stepped over our moss carpet so as not to crush it. "You did such a nice job. Looky here what I baked for your dessert," she said in her soft Southern accent. "Blackberry pie and it's still warm."

Mrs. Barnhart left the whole pastry with us, handing out forks so we could eat it right out of the dish. We fell asleep before we'd digested the feast, totally exhausted. Several days passed before we regained our nerve and returned to the Ten Acres.

5

GREAT EXPECTATIONS

Throughout our childhoods, Mommy and Daddy continued to panic over the mundane family challenges that arose on a regular basis because neither of them had a clue about child development or what qualified as normal behavior. Like so many young parents, ours imagined David and I spent our time thinking up terrible things to do or say just to irritate them.

Mommy frequently reminded me that my disability weighed heavier on her than me. Not only did she have to feed and dress me; she had the added chores of lifting me onto the duck-shaped potty seat that saved me from falling down the toilet, as well as struggling every morning to jam my polio leg into a full-length brace of unforgiving steel.

After months of my mother's daily massages and my father's less soothing stretches of my tightly-coiled muscles, I gradually gained some strength in my limbs, enough to be able to move my left arm and right leg. The support of a brace on my weakened left leg made standing and walking possible. In spite of her consistent dedication to the doctor's prescribed exercise routine for me, my mother failed to interact with me in other ways. She lacked the instinctual impulses to hold or play with either my brother or me. That lack had serious ramifications for both of us.

My brother dealt with situations no young child should have to face on his own. Lacking the ability to brainstorm his way through difficult circumstances, my father relied on David to come up with creative solutions that would resolve the tensions and reduce the chaos of our family life.

One afternoon, as my father drove David home from Momo's, he pulled our green Studebaker truck to the side of the road, killed the engine, and turned to my brother.

"How in the hell can I work six days a week, then help out with Paula and all the doctors' appointments she has? Of course, I also need to make sure your mother doesn't take her tranquilizers with a glass of wine and end up dead. You tell me, how I can do all that? Tell me."

Five-year-old David was at a loss. "I don't know, Daddy, I'm just a kid." He squeezed up small against the door of the truck.

My father turned beet-red and slapped my brother across the face. "Don't be a smart aleck with me!" He interpreted David's confused silence as stubborn defiance, unaware of the obvious fact that his young son lacked any perspective on the serious matters troubling our family. Neither of my parents sought advice from the adults in their world. In their mutual ignorance of a child's need for nurturing and patient support, Mommy and Daddy turned to us for those very things. They expected our gratitude for the normal sacrifices parents make for their children.

Since our parents grew up during the Depression, my brother and I were constantly reminded to be thankful for having clean clothes, good food, and warm beds to sleep in. It never crossed my parents' minds that at three and six, we lacked the proper perspective to appreciate these finer things in life. Meanwhile, my parents failed to see that they needed to look to each other for the love and mutual support lacking in their fragile marriage.

Throughout the years, David's normal behavior and needs continued to enrage my father and upset my mother. Growing up, I learned to sit quietly while Mommy and Daddy shared all the terrible things that could happen in the scary outside world. Potential catastrophes included nuclear war, Mommy having a nervous breakdown, and Daddy losing his job. By the time I could talk, both parents confessed to me about how unhappy they were with each other, putting me in the middle of their many disputes. Occasionally, I too received a slap or spanking for "being smart," but nothing like the irrational whippings my brother's childish antics inspired. Fear ruled our household.

The terrifying chaos I saw in the world did nothing to dampen my desire to be an active part of it. The challenge of caring for my growing demands to be mobile intensified, draining my mother of her physical and emotional stamina. My increased ramblings around the cabin and outside in the yard resulted in constant falls and injuries that kept her ever on high alert.

I wanted out! The days dragged on in loneliness and monotony. One activity I could enjoy by myself was playing music on the black and white record player I received for my third birthday. Some of the records featured children's stories and songs that entertained me for hours, but the melancholy of the "you broke my heart" western music left me feeling sad. To me, it reflected my own sense of being rejected by my mother. I saw Mommy as my lost love-object whose desertion was expressed in the lyrics of Gene Autry, Woody Guthrie, and Hank Williams. I took comfort in the fact that there were lots of broken-hearted people in the world to keep me company and share my pain.

After my brother started school, Daddy continued to drop my mother and me off at my Grandma Ida's house three or four days a week. Boredom never arose with Grandma there. "Want to help Grandma bake?" she'd ask me if I started to get on Mommy's nerves.

"Can I make tarts?" Bingo—the next thing I knew, Grandma had swept me off Mommy's lap, spread out newspapers on the kitchen floor, sat me in the middle and tossed me a wad of dough to shape into lopsided hearts. With nobody watching, I pressed the dough flat by stepping on each ball with my shoe. Grandma understood that my hands were too weak to use and she always complimented me for finding novel ways to carry out my baking projects. I merrily stamped out my jelly tarts, always a bit gritty from the leftover dirt that clung to the soles of my brown high-tops.

While Mommy rested, Grandma bustled around the kitchen, making a variety of tasty pies: berry, pumpkin, apple, cherry, plum, and mincemeat from the remains of the deer my uncles shot on one of their many hunting trips. Grandma left the tough pieces of fat and sinew drying on a clothes rack in front of the woodstove. The resulting jerky topped my list of favorite foods for years to come.

Sometimes Grandma rescued me from the tedium of my days by allowing me to go through her sewing basket. Crammed inside were packets of embroidery thread in every color and squares of material she had cut up and saved for her quilts. If she had a little extra time, she sat on the couch with me, telling stories about the swatches she'd fish out of the basket. We had all donated worn-out clothing to her quilt-making projects and I loved identifying pieces of my old nightgowns and David's raggedy play clothes stitched together with Daddy's work shirt and Uncle Charlie's bandanas. Grandma patched together the bits and pieces of her children's and grandchildren's lives. Her quilts became a collection of family histories and she made one for each of her offspring.

My cousin Debbie, who grew to be cute as a bug's ear, lived across the field from Grandma, so she and her mother, Auntie Dot, visited on a regular basis. If Debbie and I played nicely and didn't fight, Grandma allowed us to enter her tiny bedroom and rummage through her valuables. First we picked out our favorite hats, always the ones with veils we could pull down over our faces. Donning her necklaces and earrings, we wriggled into grandma's silk nightgowns and slips pretending we were dancehall girls like on the *Gunsmoke* television show.

Debbie and I loved to straddle the arms of Grandma's overstuffed rocking chair, imagining we were riding a matched pair of palomino horses. Every once in a while, we rocked the chair so hard it tipped over, spilling us onto the floor.

"What are you girls doing in there?" Grandma called from the kitchen. If the noises sounded life threatening, she came to check on us. With any luck, before Grandma appeared, we could right the chair and squeeze into the seat, rocking quietly like the genteel ladies of Dodge, although the blowsy women who hung around the bars in that city fascinated us even more. "We're saloon girls," Debby explained to Grandma. "We're riding this stagecoach as far as Dodge City." Then, before I could get a word in, Debbie would announce, "My boyfriend is Matt Dillon."

I glared at Debbie. "She always gets Matt Dillon," I complained. "I have to have Chester for my boyfriend every time. It's no fair."

Debbie smiled one of her coy little smiles. "That's because Chester has a limp, just like you, Paula. Maybe he had polio too," she liked to point out.

My disability had several disadvantages—like me having to put up with Chester or even an Indian if white men were in short supply. Little by little, I began identifying with these down-and-out characters, imagining we had hardships in common. I remember asking for a black baby doll one Christmas, sensing that she and I were both outsiders, and therefore kindred spirits. I went so far as to amputate one of my favorite doll's arms so she could be more like me. The need for role models and figures with whom I could identify went unaddressed in the 1950s.

I suppose this gravitation toward outsiders like myself, explains my attraction to Unk.

6

GOOD OLD UNCLE CHARLIE

My Great Uncle Charlie was the best-loved drunk in town; most days you could see him staggering bandy-legged along Ryan Slough Road, his beet-red face as shiny as his balding head. He made a daily round-trip into Eureka, either buying or bumming as many drinks as possible before returning to his little cabin across the hill from Grandma Ida's house.

Soon after my Grandpa John died and vacated the red captain's chair next to the woodstove, Unk laid claim to it, sitting there for a spell each morning before setting out on his daily quest for odd jobs and fortified wine. Most afternoons he returned home in time for dinner at Grandma's. If he was more than three sheets to the wind, he stumbled back to his cabin without eating. Nobody knows how many times he collapsed at Tony Beckencourt's where he'd sleep off the worst of his hangovers in the empty stall next to Tony's horse, Belinda.

Tony and Uncle Charlie had grown up together. Even though both men experienced difficult lives, Tony's seemed the worse by far. Lightning struck him while he milked the cows and flung him across the barn. This made him kind of jumpy.

Moreover, Tony's wife Janie, had pitched herself headfirst down the family well, becoming one in a long list of suicides plaguing our family and friends. My mother told me how one of my great uncles grew so despondent over his son's alcoholism that he roped dynamite sticks around his body and blew himself up. It took days to find all the pieces.

Unk fascinated me with his bleary eyes and toothless grin and I believe he took a genuine interest in me. More than once he slipped a raw potato into my dress pocket—a sure cure for polio, he'd promise me.

"Oh for pity's sake, Charlie, leave the child be," Grandma Ida snapped, slapping his hand and putting the potato back in the pile she cut up every morning to fry in her big cast iron skillet. Unk would wink at me and smile his empty grin.

I preferred Uncle Charlie's potato cures to some adults' well-intentioned recommendations to a new doctor for a new treatment, not because their suggestions bothered me that much, but because I hated to let down my parents when the cures proved to be useless.

My failure to respond to polio cures in the guise of special healers, herbs, and even nasty tasting vitamin regimens disappointed my parents and left me feeling guilty and unworthy of earthly or heaven-sent love. Up until I became a cynical teenager, I spent many a Sunday afternoon with my hand plastered to the television screen on top of Reverend Oral Robert's outstretched palm in an attempt to pick up a miracle via the TV antenna.

Grandma Ida and Uncle Charlie came from a family with three sets of twins. Grandma's twin was Great Aunt Alta, while Great Aunt Bess twinned with Great Aunt Bertha. Uncle Charlie shared his birthday with Great Aunt Ann, a hilarious prank of nature because Great Aunt Ann married a rich antique dealer and acted very hoity-toity. She would have croaked if people in town knew Unk was her brother, not to mention her twin.

According to Mommy, when Unk reached nine or ten, older boys thought it a big joke to get him drunk and watch him wobble around. By the time he hit his teens, Unk's blood had reached ninety proof.

After Unk burnt his cabin down during one of his binges, some of my uncles drove him "down below" and left him to dry out in a clinic for drunks. Eurekans designated anything beyond San Francisco's city limits as "down below." For a long time, I thought the state fell off into the ocean at that point, and I pictured Unk locked up in a prison tottering on the edge of oblivion.

While Unk dried out somewhere in Napa, his nine nephews joined forces to build him a brand new cabin, this time without a fireplace. My Uncle John visited the army surplus store where he bought Unk three pairs of long johns, a heavy-duty raincoat, boots, and lots of socks. "Don't want the old bugger to freeze this winter," he told Grandma Ida.

Grandma had lost all patience with her brother. "He can have these old horse blankets from the shed for bedding," she snapped, loading them onto Uncle John's outstretched arms. I had spent the day with her making sugar cookies and I was surprised to hear anger in her voice. "I have washed my hands of that man," she confided to me, though I knew she really hadn't.

Uncle Charlie returned from the clinic a month later, dressed in a too-tight double-breasted suit and a wrinkled blue work shirt. He had Brill-

Creamed his wisps of white hair flat to his head and he wore a snazzy fedora with a feather in the brim. He looked and acted like a new man.

As Mommy and I sat at the table with him for lunch one day, I watched him cutting corn off the cob so he could gum it more easily. "Lost my choppers at that stink hole down below," he informed us. He winked at me.

Sober like that, he told woeful stories of his boyhood back in the olden days. "Pop put me to work at eight years old," he recounted for the umpteenth time. "The old duffer had me doing the work of a grown man." I could tell he was proud of the fact, but Grandma yawned right in the middle of his stories without even covering her mouth.

"So what? Ma had me scrubbing clothes and sweeping the floor as soon as I could walk. So, don't go complaining to me," Grandma snapped. I felt sad for both of them and their rotten childhoods.

Unk stayed sober until the Fourth of July when he fell off the wagon while lighting firecrackers with a bunch of his cronies. After a few rounds of "Yankee Doodle" and even more swigs of fortified wine, he headed straight home to his nice new cabin. He'd reformed enough to go hungry rather than sit at Grandma's dinner table in a drunken state.

I identified with the down and outs like Unk, even feeling a little superior to them. Like me, Unk attracted a lot of unwanted attention. I only wished there was a place I could go to dry out from my polio virus, but the closest thing to a place like that was the Sunshine School for Girls, and they couldn't cure you, just keep you out of the way. More than once Mommy threatened to send me there after leaving David at the County's Child Welfare Department.

According to Mommy, lots of parents sent their crippled or thankless offspring to these far away institutions. "You should be grateful that you have parents who keep you at home," she told me one morning as she helped me on with my leg brace. "You should thank your lucky stars that I keep you clean and presentable."

"Well I don't," I mumbled under my breath. I daydreamed about boarding at the Sunshine School for Girls, which had been built as part of Franklin Roosevelt's New Deal. Maybe saner guardians could adopt me.

7

WEEKENDS

Up until the time I started school, life at home with Mommy consisted of long stretches of loneliness and boredom, broken up by visits to Grandma Ida's, play dates with my cousin Debbie, or occasional trips to the Eureka Zoo and Sherwood's Forest Nursery. Saturdays and Sundays were different matters altogether. I loved weekends because my brother had no school and Daddy got off early on Saturday afternoons as well as all of Sundays. Mommy fled the scene, opting to go shopping with my Auntie Bess. She returned hours later with a trinket or two she'd purchased for us from Jones's Five and Dime.

At eight o'clock every Saturday morning, I begged David to let me climb in bed with him to listen to *Uncle John and Sparky Story Time* on the radio. With great ceremony, my brother drew an imaginary line down the center of the bed, demanding that I scoot over and wedge myself into the crack against the wall. I would eventually inch my way across the line and badger my brother until his patience ran out. "Move over. I don't want to catch your cooties." If I didn't comply, he'd pinch my arm until I rolled back into the crack where I belonged.

The two of us lay there under the covers, listening to Uncle John on a little white radio that had once belonged to my mother. I loved the pink marbling that covered the radio. I learned later that this design had been achieved when my brother left a wad of bubblegum on the radio's top and it melted down the sides and front. David told me Mommy had been furious, but he figured that by ruining her radio, he had come to inherit it.

If the Barnhart boys and Richard Harris were unavailable for companionship, David allowed me to play Cowboys and Indians with him. Sometimes I persuaded my brother to set up his Western town. Made of tin sheets that fastened together with tabs, it included a jail, a blacksmith shop, and best of all, a saloon with swinging doors. Cowboys and Indians populated the town along with horses to ride and wagons to pull. I always claimed the Western woman figure and her two children.

"Here." He thrust a handful of plastic Indians at me. "You gotta be the bad guys or you can't play."

I was happy to oblige, having nothing against Native Americans, although I preferred Lincoln Log cabins to the phony-looking plastic teepees that my guys lived in.

"Can I build a log cabin for them, please, David?" I pleaded one rainy Saturday morning. We had just finished a breakfast of pancakes and Mommy was in such a good mood that she poured the batter into shapes of rabbits and dogs instead of moons and suns.

At times generous, David shrugged and passed me the canister of redwood logs.

"I'm going to make a two-storey cabin," I declared, ever optimistic about my attempts at construction. I carefully lined up and linked together the wooden logs. Lost in my attempts to build a second story, I didn't see David grab a fistful of marbles. "Bombs away," he shrieked, pelting my cabin to smithereens.

I knew not to cry. Such babyish behavior would end our play almost immediately. I begrudgingly accepted the fact that bombing raids on log cabins occurred on a daily basis back in the olden times of the West.

David and I staged numerous shootouts at the O.K. Corral. Most of our plots came directly from radio and television programs like *Gunsmoke* and the *Roy Rogers Show*, featuring Trigger his golden palomino, and Bullet his faithful German shepherd. One morning to add a bit of realism to our play, my brother whipped out his pocket knife, waving it wildly and trying to look sinister.

"What are you doing?" I cried, watching him pick up a cowboy and with great skill and effort slice off his leg.

"Don't look at me that way. It had to be amputated. He got shot in the leg and they couldn't get the bullet out. He would have died from blood poisoning," he argued convincingly, his voice deadly serious.

It made sense to me. After all, hadn't our mother been hospitalized for blood poisoning in her arm? "Dr. Ely told Daddy she almost lost it," David solemnly reminded me.

From then on, we continued to ratchet up the realism in our play, my brother amputating the arms and legs of slow-on-the-draw, nearsighted cowpokes. He recycled his wounded warriors by replacing missing limbs with modeling clay so we could shoot them off all over again. Mommy intervened when we spilled a bottle of her red nail polish on the floor in our attempt to add blood and guts to the cowboys' wide array of injuries.

Flagrant sexism infiltrated toy stores in the 1950s. It took the 1960s to bridge the great divide between the boys' and girls' departments. The same Christmas that David received his tin Western town, I unwrapped a crummy tin dollhouse with most of the furniture painted on the walls except for a table and chairs, a sofa, two beds, and a plastic molded stove. I must admit the bathroom furniture delighted me; along with a freestanding tub and sink came a toilet with a seat that flipped up and down.

Better yet, that Christmas Santa brought me a set of comic book figures. Dick Tracy, Gravel Gertie, Blondie and Dagwood, and Little Orphan Annie with her Daddy Warbucks soon occupied the rooms of my dollhouse. I prized these characters, preferring them to the bland-looking mom, pop, and kids that originally came with the set.

More than anything though, I lusted for the toy service station featured in the *Sears and Roebuck* catalog. The station came equipped with three gas pumps with tiny hoses attached, and a lift you could put a car on while you jacked it up for easy access. Later, after I started school, Mrs. Beck, my physical therapist, set one up in her exercise room and when we completed my practice falls and muscle stretches, she let me drive a toy car up the ramp to the station's rooftop where there was lots of free parking. I never fulfilled my dream to be a gas station owner, although my mother recalls me asking for the set several years in a row.

"Why didn't you and Daddy give it to me as a birthday or Christmas present?" I confronted her years later.

She smiled sadly. "You were a girl and girls didn't play with service stations back then." Case closed.

Sundays at home provided another relief from the humdrum weekdays. Except for summer Bible School at my friend Sharon's church, my father took on the responsibility of David's and my religious education. Every Sabbath morning we'd sit in a circle around the woodstove in our living room while Daddy took out the enormous family bible and read to us. We learned about Noah and his ark, Daniel in the lions' den, and Cain slaying Abel in a fit of sibling rivalry. I pored over the colorfully illustrated pages jammed in the middle of the book, especially attracted to the ones where idolaters hurled babies against rocks and heathens roughed up women. The vivid depiction of the flood haunted me when, during our winter rains, the Van Duzen and Eel River swelled up and threatened to overflow their banks.

Mommy never participated in our religious homeschooling. She sat in the corner of the room in our big black rocking chair, rolling her eyes whenever Daddy teared-up over some particularly touching verse. The best part of these morning sessions occurred when Daddy asked us if we had any questions.

"Do you think God made the aliens that fly around in their UFOs?" I inquired after a rash of UFO sightings had been reported on the radio.

"Well," he began, "if there really are aliens, I expect that God made them." He continued along this line of logic, proposing that God could have peopled other planets as well. To Daddy, life unfolded in one great mystery after another. "Consider all the stars in the sky and rainbows, the Northern Lights of Alaska…and don't forget He made all of this beauty from empty space. There was no beginning, God was always here."

He never revealed his doubts about God's purpose in allowing wars to break out and get two of his brothers killed or why God let me get polio and nearly die.

I interrupted Daddy to get him back on track. "But what about the aliens? Did he make them out of clay and blow them up with the breath of life? Are they God's children, too?"

He mulled over my question. "You know that Jonah sat in the belly of a whale and Moses parted the Red Sea," he theorized, "so I don't think we should rule out the possibility that God had a hand in making aliens."

"Daddy, would you go up in an UFO if one landed in our pasture?"

Instead of answering, Daddy liked to turn the tables on us. "Would *you* take a ride, Paula?"

I'd been entertaining this possibility for months. "I'd be scared, but I think I would go and talk to them because they might have found a cure for polio."

David scoffed at my bravado. "You're crazy," he laughed. "The aliens could suck the blood and brains right out of you and give you back something worse than polio."

"God wouldn't make evil aliens," I protested.

"Well, he made Hitler," David pointed out.

I moved a little closer to my father. "Do you think God made Hitler, Daddy?"

My father glanced over at my mother. "Well, Lill, do *you* think God made Hitler?"

Mommy heaved a big sigh and stood up. "I know damn well God never made breakfast," she huffed, brushing past our cozy circle on her way to the kitchen. With Mommy's pancakes stacking up on the griddle, Daddy closed out our discussion by reading one of the Psalms.

Mommy swore every day of the week and Sundays were no exception. She learned an impressive number of powerful cuss words growing up with nine brothers. Unlike Auntie Bert and Auntie Bess who rarely used more than a damn or a shit, Mommy peppered her speech with swear words every chance she got.

Frequently my brother and I woke up to a barrage of "God damn it to hell" and "Jesus Christ Almighty" blasting from the kitchen as she banged pots and pans around, making us brunch on the holiest of days. Her sheer originality impressed me, though I died of embarrassment if she started a tirade in front of my friends or relatives.

Mommy came up with hilarious responses to people who offended her. One day as she and I poured over the paper doll rack at Jones', deciding whether to buy the curvaceous Doris Day or Natalie Wood, an uppity acquaintance bumped into us without so much as an "Excuse me" or "I'm sorry."

Mommy looked down at me and whispered, "That lady thinks she's shit on a stick," followed by the comment "and I bet she thinks her shit don't stink." I spent the next few minutes imagining the woman parading around town with shit on a stick. Did it fall off after a while or dry up and blow away? Mommy concluded her character assault of the la-di-da lady by flinging one last insult, albeit under her breath. "Old fart handles like her should be thrown out of the human race."

I looked up at my mother and saw she was smiling. "What's a fart handle, Mommy?"

"Tell you what. When we get home, I'll draw one for you." We laughed, each knowing that Mommy had no intention of doing so.

My parents' role reversals confused me. It struck me as peculiar that my mother swore like a sailor and never shed a tear, while my father cried like a baby over a sad movie and rarely used a cuss word even when he stubbed his sore toe or accidently hit his finger with a hammer. My father spent most of my childhood remodeling our cabin, so he encountered all sorts of opportunities to use foul language.

Along with the pleasure of pancakes for Sunday brunch, David and I looked forward to the hour on the radio where a consistently jovial man read the Sunday comics out loud, commenting on the way Lil' Abner had pulled another trick on Daisy Mae or why Dagwood got on Blondie's nerves. In the drab monotonous desert of my younger years, weekends provided a welcomed and appreciated oasis. If asked then to share my idea of heaven, I would have claimed paradise started with pancakes on the griddle and the comics read aloud over the airwaves on a Sunday morning. Life didn't get much better.

8

BOMBS AWAY

Although our household provided few opportunities to promote our intellectual development, both my mother and father made sure we had a good supply of children's books, not to mention comics, at our disposal. Even more exciting were our subscriptions to children's magazines, because with the exception of an occasional letter or birthday card from our Auntie Bert in Berkeley, magazines were the only mail we received. *Wee Wisdom*, a publication of the Unity Church, featured decent stories of moral courage and spiritual fortitude without sinking to maudlin sermonettes, but best of all, every issue offered a paper doll page to add to my growing collection of cutouts. David eagerly awaited his monthly issue of *Boy's Life* while I counted on my copy of *Jack and Jill* to supplement our reading material.

Then there were the catalogs…*Sears and Roebuck* and *Montgomery Ward* came just before the school year started and again at Christmas. We fell into a delirium of greedy paging through these Christmas "wish books."

Two pieces of mail especially intrigued David and me. One was the titillating *Fredericks of Hollywood* catalog that came at random times throughout the year. No one knows how our household got on Frederick's mailing list, but my brother and I appreciated a sneak peek into the forbidden realm of pornographic underwear for women. The sheer baby doll nighties introduced us to a world of pointy breasts, bras that had holes for nipples to poke through, and crotchless panties. Mommy rushed to confiscate the catalogue before my brother and I could get our sweaty little hands on it, but sometimes we got to it first.

The other type of mail arriving with increasing frequency were the pamphlets, often published by insurance companies, informing us of ways to survive if an atom bomb happened to land in our neighborhood. As a child of the fifties, I knew our world hovered on the edge of destruction. The Cold War and Communism threatened to wipe out our entire generation. Accounts of the escalating arms race dominated the news, and these government publications shoved into our mailbox offered helpful hints on how to keep your life on an even keel following a nuclear holocaust.

Our reading comprehension skills weren't quite up to the task, so one Saturday afternoon, I persuaded Cora Mae, our teenaged babysitter, to read us the most recent pamphlet sent to us by *Mutual of Omaha*. Hot summer days were rare in Eureka, so Cora Mae flopped on her stomach in our backyard, tanning herself as she nonchalantly shared the life-saving information with us.

My recruits, Sharon and Gary, sat next to me in rapt attention as Cora Mae studied the brochure entitled *How to Survive a Nuclear Bomb*. It was dense reading material and many of the words were unfamiliar to us, but we got the general idea.

"It says here," Cora Mae began, "that if you notice an intense light in the distance you *should not* look in that direction!" We all agreed that this was going to be next to impossible to do and would take a lot of practice. How could we *not* look?

"If no shelter is nearby," Cora Mae continued, "you should drop to the ground face down."

The three of us rolled over on our stomachs, pressing our faces into the sweet-smelling grass. That step proved easy enough.

"In all cases you must shield yourself from the flash of brilliance. If indoors, drop to the floor with your back towards the window or crawl behind or beneath a protective piece of furniture."

"Let's go into the house," I ordered. "We need to practice with furniture."

Nobody moved. "It's too hot," Gary whined.

"Okay, let's pretend we're in the house. We can shelter in place behind the lawn chairs," I suggested.

"Can't we just pretend to shelter in place?" Sharon sat up, flapping her arms to cool off. Sweat glued her bangs to her forehead.

"Fine," I sputtered, "you just better hope they drop a *pretend* bomb."

"Do you want to hear this or not?" Cora Mae broke in. "I have other things to do with my time." At sixteen, Cora Mae had developed utter contempt for anybody under the age of twelve. She cleared her throat. "Curl up in such a way as to shield your face, neck, hands, and arms," she droned on. We rolled into fetal positions.

Cora Mae paused for a moment, scanning the next paragraph.

Sharon, Gary, and I looked up. "Don't stop reading!"

"Okay, but it really isn't for children's ears." Cora Mae smirked at us. "Unless you happen to be close to the immediate area of the bomb, your greatest danger would be from flash burns which could seriously damage exposed areas of the skin. Remain in this curled up position for at least ten seconds."

We did just that, too unnerved to move on to the next bit of information.

"I'm skipping some of this cause it's over your heads. It just goes on to explain that thermal radiation...or the burning brightness...can be dangerous as far away as two miles, but if you instantly shelter yourself from those rays, you may avoid serious burns.

Oh, here's the good part," our sarcastic babysitter read on, "it says at least protect yourself with your own body. Let your back take the brunt of the rays. Lightly colored clothing can usually prevent rays from reaching your body."

"We can wear the nurses' uniforms we got for Christmas!" I told Sharon excitedly "and Gary can wear one of his dad's dress shirts."

Cora Mae really seemed to be enjoying herself as she finished reading about the doomsday scenario. "Listen up," she cautioned, "you should be alert to the blast wave which spreads outward for as much as a minute or more after the explosion. If you happen to be on the street when the wave hits, press close to a building so that you are sheltered from breaking glass or falling debris."

"What's debris?" I asked so I'd know what to look out for.

Cora Mae stood up and brushed herself off. "It's stuff like roof shingles and bricks. Oh yeah and flying body parts," she added with an evil smirk. "Here's your mom, Paula. I'm outta here."

Mommy paid Cora Mae and invited Gary and Sharon to stay and eat lunch with me. Learning about nuclear bombs had killed our appetites though, and Sharon wanted to go home and check on her mother to make sure she hadn't vaporized.

I became obsessed with the notion of staying alive following a nuclear war, and since it was clear that our parents were too irresponsible to build a fallout shelter, I convinced some of the neighborhood gang to participate in air raid drills to insure our way of life continued after an atomic explosion. Naturally, I assumed the role of drillmaster.

Constructing an underground bunker was no job for sissies. Shaken by the knowledge of the dangers of atom bombs, Sharon and Gary volunteered to do the digging. With my weakened arms, I had to be the straw boss, ordering Sharon to bring the biggest spoons she could get from her house and sending Gary off to retrieve his Grandpa Moore's shovel.

The job went smoothly at first. While Sharon and Gary ran off to gather the necessary tools, I managed to dig a six-inch deep hole in the lawn using the heel of my shoe. I kneed my way over to the hose and pulled it back, clamping my teeth around it. Turned on full blast, the water deepened the hole beyond my wildest expectations. By the time Sharon and Gary returned, the ground was soft enough for Gary to complete a three-foot hole by the end of the afternoon, using just a garden spade. The spoons proved to be useless.

Exhausted by their digging efforts, Sharon and Gary collapsed on the ground next to me and together, we let our imaginations finish the job for us. While we rested in our muddied clothes, I described how I could use a slide to get down into our underground bunker. I reminded Sharon and Gary that they would have to pull me back out when the world was once again safe for democracy.

By the time Daddy arrived home from work, we had completely stocked and decorated our shelter while lying on our backs and watching the clouds sail overhead. Daddy yelled at us for digging up the lawn, but he proved very understanding when he listened to our explanation. That weekend, Daddy filled up the hole and built me a clubhouse attached to the backyard fence. It had real glass windows and a door complete with a working handle. Best of all, Gary, Sharon, and I could all squeeze inside and take shelter if the atom bomb struck close to home.

9

ALL ABOARD

Every few months throughout the first four years of my childhood, Mommy and I boarded a train from Eureka to San Rafael where Auntie Bert picked us up and drove us to her home in Berkeley. The next day she accompanied us to the Shriners Hospital for Crippled Children in San Francisco for my three-or six-month check-up. My stomach ached just thinking about Shriners.

These trips proved to be a mixed bag for me. On the one hand, I loved riding the train and buying a doughnut when the food cart came by, always steered by the same black porter who took a shine to me. My mother usually gave me the dime, and sometimes the porter sneaked me a second donut for free if I flashed him a cute smile.

I also loved my aunt's house on 2225 Ward Street. Once there, the chaos and tension of life back home evaporated. Auntie Bert and Uncle George doted on me and I never understood why the same behavior that riled my mother and stirred up her nerves back home brought smiles and even laughter from my aunt and uncle. Why couldn't I be good like this back in Eureka? It never occurred to me that I acted the same way. The difference was my aunt and uncle saw me as a spunky, sometimes sassy little girl while Mommy found that same behavior irritating.

The downside of train travel included a visit to Shriners on 19th Avenue. Built to care for low-income children, the massive red brick building looked inviting from the outside with its beautiful gardens, fairy statues, fountains, and reflecting ponds.

The beauty vanished when Mommy, Auntie Bert, and I walked through the heavy glass doors and took our seats in the dimly lit waiting room. Fifteen or twenty kids—wearing braces, casts, and slings—shared the space with me.

"I hope they get to her pretty soon," Mommy whispered to Auntie Bert. "Last time, the doctors showed up nearly three hours late."

I dreaded hearing my name called and walking down a long hall of examination rooms. Built out of bricks of wavy glass, they screened you from any prying eyes. Mommy lifted me onto a cold steel table and following the nurse's orders, stripped me down to my underpants. About an hour later, Dr. Ramsey and Dr. Shultz barged in with a posse of young interns waving around x-rays and fat folders bursting with notes and charts.

"And how are you today, Mrs. Viale?"

"Fine," Mommy began, but they usually ignored her, focusing on me, their little specimen of a polio victim, all the while conferring with each other in low mumbles. I feared these figures of terror, dressed in stiff white coats, carelessly pulling at my arms and stretching my legs while my mother sat quietly in the corner on the aluminum chair.

An encounter with Shriners was the last thing on my mind when I woke up to a soppy Eureka morning a few months before my fifth birthday. I heard hushed voices drifting in from the kitchen. The paws of my Felix-the-Cat wall clock pointed to twelve and seven and Daddy hadn't left for work yet. Something was up.

I slid out of bed and shuffled into the kitchen. "Why is Daddy still here?" Time stopped as I watched my parents eye one another, each nodding for the other one to go first.

Daddy pulled out a chair and had me sit down. "We're planning a trip," he said casually. "Daddy's going to drive you and Mommy down to Auntie Bert and Uncle George's."

"Like a vacation?" I immediately pictured a visit to Fairyland in Oakland or an excursion into San Francisco's Chinatown. "Is David coming too, Daddy?"

"Afraid not. He'll be staying with Momo and Pop. This time I'm going with you and Mommy to the Shriners clinic. In fact, we're going to get up very early tomorrow and drive all the way to Berkeley."

I tried to say something, but a cold stone of fear blocked my words. I sucked in a deep breath. "Won't you get fired if you don't go to work, Daddy?"

"No, honey, Mr. McCane is giving me some time off."

"Oh." I felt dizzy and even though I wanted to know what came next, I ignored my curiosity, which I knew could kill cats. I took no chances.

"Can I have Rice Krispies for breakfast, Mommy?"

Her face brightened. "You can have anything you want!"

That's when I realized I had no appetite for either breakfast or an account of what awaited in the very near future. The account came anyway.

Daddy and Mommy explained that my rich Great Uncle Ralph had arranged for me to get very special treatment at the world-renowned hospital. "He's a Shriner himself and has some pull with the organization," Daddy stood up and poured himself a second cup of coffee.

I scooted off my chair and hurried back to my bedroom. "I don't feel so good," I called over my shoulder. "I'm going back to bed. Wake me up tomorrow when it's time to go."

Bright and early the next morning I curled up in the back seat of our blue Ford, playing with a shiny red cash register Daddy had given me for being a brave little girl. I didn't feel very brave. I checked the pocket of the red dotted Swiss dress Mommy bought me for our journey. Jesse Jesus gave a comforting crackle. I waited for my parents to fill me in on Shriners plans for the rest of my life, but we wordlessly poked our way down Old Redwood Highway, pulling off to the side of the road whenever a rude logging truck driver blasted his horn at us. I looked out the window as we drove through Garberville, Miranda, and Laytonville. Somewhere around Ukiah, I couldn't stand it anymore.

"What's going to happen to me?" I blurted out, making Mommy jump.

"Nothing bad," she said, avoiding my eyes. "It's just that this time you're going to stay for a while."

Dead silence.

"All by myself?" My heart sunk lower with every mile.

"You won't be alone," my mother insisted. "There'll be lots of girls just your age to play with and when you come home, you'll be stronger."

"What are they going to do to me?"

"Fix you up so you can walk better and maybe use your arm."

"My bad arm?" My voice quivered.

"Your *right* arm," Mommy corrected me, turning around in her seat to pat my useless hand. How I wished that she would take me in *her* arms and comfort me the way my father did.

"And your cash register will be full when you come home," Daddy explained. "I'll put a nickel in it every day you're gone."

"You mean I can't I take my cash register with me either?"

More silence.

"You can't bring anything with you." My mother's announcement shocked me all the way down to the roots of my hair.

"Not even my Jesse Jesus paper doll?" I whimpered in a panic.

"There will be lots of toys and books at the hospital," Daddy reassured me.

"And you *can* bring a comb and brush and your new toothbrush," Mommy added. Luckily my toothbrush had a little dog attached to its handle; this was something of my own I could break off to play with.

I have no memory of our overnight stay at Auntie Bert's. What I do remember is driving to San Francisco the next day and sitting in Shriners large waiting room along with children who had survived polio, cerebral palsy, and spina bifida. Even though I blended in, it was a strange and scary situation and I wanted to sit in my mother's lap, but her hands were busy wadding up her handkerchief.

I felt for the paper doll I had hidden in my underpants. Jesse Jesus was going with me no matter what. I needed something familiar to hold on to.

"Paula Viale to the front desk, please," a voice scratched over the intercom.

My father picked me up and carried me to a nurse's waiting arms. "Your mommy and daddy have to leave now, but they'll be coming to visit you real soon," the nurse promised. Her name tag read "Miss Blair."

Stunned by this news, I looked towards my parents who stared at the floor tiles. From the nurse's arms, I leaned over to kiss my parents goodbye. Mommy stood stiff as a statue. Tears streamed down my father's cheeks. I stroked his face. "Don't cry, Daddy. I'll be alright." My parents handed over some papers at the front desk and then turned away and walked out the doors.

I patted my hip, feeling for my contraband paper doll. Good, still there. Miss Blair put me down and together we ambled into a green tiled bathroom where a large claw-footed tub stood. A frog's head served as the waterspout. Another trick—everything was disguised.

The nurse stripped me down, carefully removing my wrinkled paper doll and putting Jesse Jesus in her pocket. "She'll be waiting for you when you go back home," she guaranteed, bending over the tub to pour in a healthy dose of Hexol disinfectant. The last straw broke. I succumbed to a numbing despair as the nurse lowered me into the hot water. "I'll be right back." She squished out of the room in her sturdy-looking nurse's shoes.

I stuck my big toe into the frog's gaping mouth, spraying water everywhere. Miss Blair was not amused when she returned with some clothes thrown over one arm. She mopped up the mess, washed my hair with a foul-smelling shampoo, swished a washcloth over my body, and rubbed me dry with a rough towel.

Standing naked, at almost five years old, I felt alone and totally abandoned. In a state of shock and misery, I let the nurse pull on a pair of too-big underwear and a worn gray undershirt. She expertly maneuvered my arms through the sleeves of a dark blue dress covered in bright orange marigolds. Nothing felt real. Unable to endure this loss of personhood, my fear turned into dull dread. The abandonment by my parents could only be examined fleetingly, like the tongue's exploration of a loose tooth.

Miss Blair plopped me into a wheelchair and rolled me down a dark twisting maze with pipes overhead and into an elevator. The doors opened onto a brightly lit hall; sunshine streamed through the windows. My heart lifted a little. We passed a huge kitchen where giant cans of food lined all four walls and a big-boned woman loaded dirty trays into an enormous dishwasher. Further down the hall we approached the bedpan room.

Miss Blair wheeled me in to show me the huge steel machine used to sterilize bedpans. "One of the most important things to remember here at Shriners is the bedpan schedule. The pans arrive before and after breakfast, before and after lunch, and before and after dinner. Oh, yes, and right before lights out."

My eyes widened as I thought about the far reach of Shriners rules. "What if I have to go some other time?" I murmured.

"You'll have to wait until the next round of bedpans. Shriners runs on schedules. You just need to practice bladder control. And another thing, no water after lights out and not a drop until morning rounds."

Suddenly my mouth dried out and I had to pee, "so bad I could taste it" as my mother put it.

I had laughed the first time Mommy spoke this phrase. "What's *it* taste like? I asked, genuinely curious. "Beer," she'd joked. "It tastes like beer." Mommy could be funny at times, which I always enjoyed. And I could have really used some of her humor right then.

When we reached an impressive large front desk at the end of the hall, Miss Blair passed me over to a pudgy nurse named Mrs. Schmitt. One word described the woman: *round*. Mrs. Schmitt wore her dark hair in a round bun balanced on her round head and she had a round belly that bulged a little over the belt of her uniform. Her ankles swelled into puffy flesh that spilled out of her shoes.

Pudgy examined me carefully as she wrapped a name tag band onto my scrawny left wrist. "There you go, Paula." She took me by the hand and guided me through another set of doors. Still in a state of shock and awe, I glanced around the ward where eight empty cribs waited. Turning to the right, I noticed two glassed-in cubicles, one of them with my name on it. Polio still cropped up in some states during the summers. Even though I had caught and survived the virus, Jonas Salk had not yet perfected a vaccine. Anyone coming into the hospital from outside was placed in an isolation cubicle for a week.

I beheld the enormous ward, empty except for Pudgy and me. "Where is everybody?"

"The girls are at school now," Mrs. Schmitt explained, setting me into a crib with its sides down.

I felt a hot wave of humiliation spread over me. I was way too old for a crib. I scowled at Mrs. Schmitt. "When do I get a regular bed?" I asked her.

"If and when one of those beds becomes available, but I have to tell you there's a long list of girls older than you who have first dibs on adult beds. They're in short supply so you might as well get used to the crib." I faced a whole lot of things I was going to have to get used to, including a lump in my throat that I couldn't swallow.

Mrs. Schmitt bustled out of my cubicle. "You stay right there and I'll be back in a minute."

Like I had a choice...

When the nurse returned, she carried a brightly colored drawstring bag with her. She emptied its contents onto the bed—my hairbrush, comb, and toothbrush from home along with a small kidney-shaped pan, a placemat with matching napkin, and an ugly stiff-legged five-and-dime store doll. I longed for Jesse Jesus, but just then a noisy clatter of braces and crutches and little girls' voices burst into the ward.

Mrs. Schmitt shook out the bag and attached it to my nightstand. "For your mail," she explained.

Several girls gathered outside my glass house. "How old are you?' a blonde with a leg cast asked.

"I'm almost five."

"Then you belong in the babies' ward," she taunted, eyeing me suspiciously. "What's your name, baby cakes?"

Her words stung, but I sat up straight and stared her down. "Paula. Paula Christine Viale."

"There's no room for her in the babies' ward," Mrs. Schmitt said to the girl. "She'll be just fine here."

A sinking sensation told me I would never be fine again.

My inquisitor was Pam, a ten year old with wild blond hair and a bad attitude. She walked using crutches. The black girl lying in a pushcart was named Erma. She was seven. The nine-year-old girl in traction was Geneva. She had long brown Goldilocks curls. When she went to school, her whole bed went with her. I soon learned Erma had brittle bones; Geneva was getting her left leg stretched so it would match her right one. Sonny sported a body cast that went from under her chin all the way down and over her hips.

By the time lunch was served, I had slipped into an out-of-body state and only remember hearing the loud clatter of dishes and silverware, noisy bickering, and my heart thumping hard in my chest. I pretended to be asleep when lunch trays arrived and one of the student nurses whispered, "She's all tuckered out from the admitting process. Best to let her nap."

Everybody ignored me when they returned to the ward following the afternoon session of school, anxious to finish any homework so they could watch the *Mickey Mouse Club*. Miss Peach, our butterball of a cook, served dinner at 5:30 p.m. She passed out trays of food to us, struggling with the door of my cubicle and stepping inside. She reached into my nightstand and pulled out my placemat and napkin. "Eat everything up," she cheered me on, "because that will help you grow up big and strong."

Who did she think she was fooling? I smiled feebly and swallowed a spoonful of grayish-green canned peas. The food tasted bad, but I gagged it down, doing my best to follow orders.

Erma ran a spoon through her watery instant mashed potatoes and looked over at me. "The slaves ate better than this," she moaned.

After dinner, I lay down and pretended to snooze again while the rest of the girls settled in to watch television. We didn't have a set at home, so I felt a bit of excitement when the *Mickey Mouse Club* theme started playing and everyone in the room fell silent.

I shut my eyes, overwhelmed by the suffocating sadness inside me. I exploded into sobs of childish grief, feeling bits and pieces of me swirling around my glass house. I put the pillow over my head so I couldn't hear Roy Rogers and Dale Evans wailing "Happy Trails" at the end of their program.

The pillow muffled my sobs. I didn't hear the student nurse enter my cubicle and gave a little jump when she patted me on the shoulder. "Roll over sweetie, I have a nice clean nightgown for you." She pretended she didn't see my red eyes and nose as she dressed me for bed. The nightgown remained warm from the dryer. I suspected from its faded condition that by now fifty kids had worn this nightie dotted with tiny blue forget-me-nots. Even so, I loved to stroke the soft threadbare flannel. To calm myself, I rubbed a corner hem between my lips and purred softly into the night.

"Who's making that funny noise?" Sonny's voice called out. In the light from the Big Girl's Ward, I could see her sitting up with the covers pulled under her chin.

"It's coming from the new girl's cubicle," Erma whispered.

"What's she doing?" Sonny asked.

"I'm fuzzing," I snapped, irritated at having my self-soothing ritual interrupted. "I call it fuzzing. My brother sucks his thumb and I fuzz."

A few laughs followed, but I didn't care, even when Pam seized the opportunity to tease me. "Geez Louise, Paula, you are such a baby. Do you wet the bed, too?"

"Look out," Erma warned, "here comes Morton, the witch lady."

A scrawny wire-haired nurse flung the ward doors open ready to attack. She flicked the lights off and on to get our attention. "Good night, girls," Mrs. Morton snipped as she cut the lights again. Her flashlight lit up the glare on her face. "Get on with it and no funny business."

I expected total silence, so the ritual following lights out surprised me.

"Our father," Pam sang out "who art in heaven." The rest of the girls chimed in and reached an impressive crescendo by the time they got to "For thine is the kingdom and the power and the glory forever." They belted out the "Amen" so loudly, I expected Mrs. Morton to race in and put a stop to it.

I closed my eyes and curled up into my favorite safety position. Arms hugging my body, and knees raised up to my chest.

Next thing I knew, Erma sat up and instigated a haunting version of "Day is done, gone the sun," with everyone joining in like before. Another momentary silence.

When Sonny started up the first verse of "Good Night, Irene," Morton stormed through the ward doors. "This is not *Ted Mack's Amateur Hour,"* she railed. "Now get to sleep"

I rolled over on my stomach and thought about the family I had seen in the waiting room earlier that day. A mother and father cozied up to each other smiling down at the two boys seated on the floor at their feet, one with leg braces. I could feel their love dancing around the room, while my parents had sat up stiffly in their chairs not looking at me at all. I imagined the family at home watching television, maybe *Our Miss Brooks* or *I Married Joan.*

I pretended I belonged to them, where, as the only girl, I would be the apple of the father's eyes and a source of pride to the mother. I imagined I would occasionally fight with the two boys, but nobody would get screamed at or spanked, just told calmly, "Now the three of you settle down and be nice." We would obey immediately, smiling at our parents with devotion in our eyes.

It felt like a hundred years had passed since I'd said goodbye to Mommy and Daddy that morning. At least they cared about me more than the doctors and nurses at Shriners who didn't go in for love. As I drowsed towards sleep listening to *My Little Margie* filtering in from the radio in the Big Girl's Ward, I realized I had something almost as good as love. I had safety in the night. I actually felt secure enough to stop playing the breathing game I invented when I got scared. I held my breath while I counted to one hundred. If I reached that number, it meant I won the game and wouldn't die in the night. At Shriners, I could breathe normally until I drifted off to sleep.

My seven days of cubicle life crawled by, but I took advantage of the time to memorize the important facts about life at Shriners. I had given some thought to becoming a writer since even people damaged by polio could handle a pen and paper. Moreover, there were two women who worked at the newspaper with Daddy and they wrote for the *Standard* every day. I could be both a girl with polio and still get a job.

At my request, Mrs. Schmitt brought me a pencil and a tablet so I could keep a record of my four ward mates. It helped pass the time while they were off at school each day. I knew how to print my ABCs, both upper and lower cases, but I hadn't learned to spell many words. Olga printed the names of each of the girls on the top of four separate sheets in my tablet and I began my note taking.

Erma, the only Negro child I had ever encountered, was seven and had brittle bones. "I can break an arm or leg just rolling over in bed," she told me at breakfast the next morning. I drew a picture of her under her name, lightly shading in her skin so you could tell she was black. Her last name was White, which everybody joked about except Sonny. Sonny's last name was Black even though she was white as a sheet. To indicate Erma had brittle bone disease, I drew tiny cracks in her arms and legs. I carefully sketched the bunches of braids sticking up all over her head.

Under ten-year-old Pam's name, I drew a picture of a sort of potato-shaped kid with naturally curly hair. Later, when I could get some crayons, I intended to color her curls a bright yellow. Pam had a clubbed foot that she hated for anyone to see. I couldn't get an up-close view of her misshapen appendage, so I made her barefooted, with her one normal foot and the other shaped into a twisted ball of flesh.

Sonny Black had been part of a set of Siamese twins. She had a big hump on her back where the doctors had cut away her sister who died on the spot. Drawing Sonny took very little time since all I had to do was sketch her head, arms, and legs sticking out of a square-shaped body cast. As soon as she shed her plaster suit, I planned to do a full body profile so her hump would show. I was the only one who hadn't seen it and my curiosity nearly killed me. I also showed Sonny's tongue hanging out with blood dripping from it. When enough of us encouraged her, she would bite the tip of her tongue and squeeze blood out of it. We were all impressed by her courageous display of talent. Sonny would turn eight in a month.

It took me a long time to draw Geneva who had just turned nine. Her long shiny black hair flowed all the way down her back. "I have to be in traction for five months," she told me one afternoon when all the girls returned from school for lunch break. She threw off her quilt, pulled her skirt up over her knees, and pointed to two holes in her cast where ugly steel pins dug into her leg bone to slow down the growth of her good one. Thanks to polio, Geneva's bad leg was three inches shorter than her good one; by slowing down the growth in her good one, they hoped her polio leg would catch up. "That way, I'll have less of a limp when I grow up," she explained between bites of an egg salad sandwich. "The problem is now my good leg will be covered with scars like the rest of my body." I had to draw Geneva in her bed where she was forced to stay flat on her back, her leg suspended mid-air by slings and pulleys. Geneva wore braces on her teeth, but they were too hard to draw, and besides she wouldn't be doomed to wear them for the rest of her life.

At last, my seven-day isolation period ended. I was happy to get out of my glass prison, but then received some shocking news from Pam. She swung on her crutches over to my new spot in the ward. "I see you got a window seat," she noted, referring to my crib being placed in front of a beautiful arched window. From my new vantage point, I could see into the living room of the gingerbread Victorian directly across 19th Avenue. "When are your parents coming, Paula?"

"Pretty soon, I guess. I plan on seeing Mommy and Auntie Bert next Sunday."

"For one thing, Paula, you'll need a pair of binoculars to see them." This was where Pam started to rain on my parade.

"But why?"

"We all line up at the windows of our ward and yell down to our parents because they have to stand on the ground below."

"That's plain stupid." How can we hug them and kiss them hello and goodbye?"

"You throw them kisses like this," Pam demonstrated, kissing the palm of her hand and waving it out the window. "Like Marilyn Monroe. Keeps germs from spreading."

I thought Pam had lied to me, but I found out later that when my mother, Auntie Bert, Uncle George, and occasionally my father made their Sunday pilgrimages to Shriners, they had to stand on the ground below our second-storey windows and wave or shout up the latest news from home.

Although hospital policy changed when the Salk vaccine was discovered, my first hospital stay was rigidly regulated. No polio germs allowed. The two German doctors who headed the staff insisted our hair be cut short or plaited into tight braids and nails be trimmed so the tips of our fingers showed. They worried about our eating habits and bowel movements, which were really none of their business.

Pam declared they were Nazis guards, left over from the concentration camps after World War II. "I think Shriners head doctors were on the Nazis' side during the war because they treat us like Jews or Gypsies most of the time," Pam speculated. "They treated Anne Frank the same way. I'm reading about her in my history book."

"Did she have polio, too?" I asked.

"Don't you know anything about Anne Frank?" Pam sighed with contempt. "She didn't have polio, she had the bad luck to be Jewish. The Nazis put her in a concentration camp and she wrote about it in her diary."

All I knew about Nazis came from a newsreel they showed once before the main feature at the Bell-Air drive-in. Daddy ordered me to close my eyes and not open them until he said I could. I squinted, but I could still see long lines of human skeletons shuffling along with no hair or clothes. That disturbing image never seemed to go away which is the price, I guess, of living with your eyes open.

Erma and I spent a whole afternoon studying the fanciful murals that graced the ceilings of each ward. They depicted gardens of beautiful healthy children running after butterflies and chasing balls or sailing toy boats on a duck pond. "Not one kid with a crutch or a cast," I commented to Erma.

"And not one Negro."

Sonny picked up the commentary from her bed. "It's like crippled kids don't exist. I guess their families hide them in attics and basements or leave them to rot in old folk's home like where my grandma lives."

"Face it," Pam chimed in, "Here at Shriners we're in a ghetto, just like Anne Frank." None of us understood what she was referring to, although it sounded awful. "Only ours is a crippled kid ghetto." Pam laughed out loud at her observation, while the rest of us sank into silent brooding.

My first stay at Shriners stretched out to four months, months that included my fifth birthday, Thanksgiving, and Christmas. During that time, I came to know and like Mommy better because she wrote me a letter almost every day. Maybe my absence made her heart grow fonder of me because she took out time from her busy housekeeping chores to make me little five-by-seven-inch scrapbooks. All letters were opened by Mrs. Schmitt, the head nurse to inspect for contraband. Somehow she overlooked these little scrapbooks when she checked my mail.

My mother cut and pasted paper dolls to the scrapbook pages, barely attaching them so I could peel off Betsy McCall along with the outfits that came with her once a month. Mommy was very artistic in spite of her nerves. I had always thought that it was me and all the trouble I made that caused Mommy's occasional breakdowns, but she actually had one while I was at Shriners so it wasn't just me who rattled her.

At least twice a month Mommy joined Auntie Bert and Uncle George on the lawn below my window, waving up at me and yelling out the latest news from home. Daddy came once, but he started to cry and I saw Mommy glare at him until he waved goodbye to me and went off to wait in the car. Those visits left me sad for the rest of Sunday and it took me at least a day or two to overcome the separation blues and homesickness following these long-distance encounters.

Weekdays weren't much happier times. Shriners offered no preschool or kindergarten, so I sat alone in the ward, but I put the time to good use. Along with gumption, I came by a sturdy little ego that sopped up attention like a dried-out sponge. I finagled my way into the hearts of Mr. Johnson the janitor, as well as Russian Olga and Mrs. Johnson—the two stern but loving nurses' aides, and Mr. Allen, the gardener who kept up the beds of dahlias, roses, and endless plantings of petunias and hollyhocks that graced the grounds at Shriners.

I had been a favorite of Mr. Allen's ever since I had called out to him from my second-storey window, waving my good arm and yelling, "Catch me when I jump." This unnerved Russian Olga, who cautioned me away from the window, but Mr. Allen never tired of telling the story and I never tired of hearing it. Audience was everything to me and I took every opportunity to seek out attention.

I knew I was one of Russian Olga's favorites because she often took the time to wrap my hair in rags so it would be curly when the Shriners came to admire their good works. My other fan, Mrs. Johnson, spoiled me by plaiting my hair into cornrows, which she bobby-pinned flat to my head. "This'll keep those bangs of yours' out of your eyes," she declared the first time she styled my lumps of matted hair. She wove the braids tight enough to give my eyes an Asian slant that I liked, but the touch of her hands, not the hairstyle, meant the most to me.

If Russian Olga caught me pouting, obviously bored and lonely, she wheeled my crib into the babies' ward where I had the company of several pre-school girls. Olga would turn on the TV set to *Howdy Dowdy Time* or *Ding Dong School* with the tubby Miss Francis. I liked being the oldest in the babies' ward, but I was glad I didn't have to go to bed at 7:00 p.m.

In spite of my scheming and socializing with the staff, I passed many a long and wearisome day waiting for Pam, Sonny, Geneva, and Erma to return from school. Erma continued to lay flat in her low-riding cart.

"One time I broke three ribs just laughing," she complained. She looked sad. "Sort of takes the joy out of having a good time."

At least my bones were solid, I thought as I watched the girls troop back to the ward. Pam limped with her clubfoot and all, but doctors predicted it might look as good as new when they removed her cast.

"Didn't work the first time," she complained to Sonny, who, being flat on her back, showed no sympathy for Pam.

"My foot was clubbed even when it was new. I want it to look *normal.*"

"You are *soooo* lucky to be going to Shriners," Great Aunt Bertha had told me more than once. "Lucky, lucky little girl." Her voice grated, sounding all raspy and high-pitched. An ear infection in her teens left her nearly stone deaf; I had to acknowledge my good luck by shouting into a boxy hearing aid Great Aunt Bertha wore pinned to her chest. It had a tiny wire that ran from the box and plugged into her ear.

Rich donors to the hospital paid for our surgeries and any other expenses we incurred during our stays. I never realized that Mommy and Daddy were too poor to afford my stay at a high-class facility like Shriners. Although parents were restricted to the grass lawn below the second floor when visiting, the Shriners, a circus of silly middle-aged businessmen, paraded around the wards on a twice-a-month basis.

Our world-famous Doctor Shultz led the tour, pointing out how Shriners money meant little children would walk and maybe even run again.

This infuriated Erma. "They look like they pity us," she railed. "Well, I pity anyone who has to wear an upside-down red bucket on his head."

Mrs. Johnson looked up from the janitor's broom as she swept the floor. "Now you be nice," she ordered. "That there bucket is what you call a fez," she explained. "Those gold tassels add a bit of glory."

Olga immediately supported Mrs. Johnson. "Ya, I think they look grand."

Erma lay down, careful not to break another bone. "Whatever," she sighed. Like her, none of us was the least bit impressed.

Pam laughed. "They look like a bunch of fuddy-duddies if you ask me."

"*Vell,*" Olga cut in, "Nobody didn't ask you."

The Shriners arrived on Saturdays, right before lunch. Their visits produced a festive spirit, more fun than Easter, but not as long lasting as Christmas. Early Saturday morning, Russian Olga and Mrs. Johnson circled around our ward, wheeling a rack of dresses hand-sewn by Shriners wives; this was the only time we were allowed to choose our outfits.

By the time the rack rolled up to my bed, I could see nothing decent remained in my size. "Can't you get another rack?" I pleaded.

Olga sank into a nearby chair overworked, and definitely out of patience. She blew some silver gray bangs out of her eyes. "Look, there is no other rack. We are running out of time, so tell you what," she said, jumping out of her seat, "I am picking a dress for you."

Before I could protest, she pulled down a garish pink and purple paisley jumper and matching blouse trimmed with rickrack. It looked much worse when Olga took it off the hanger and helped me into it. The jumper hung limply down past my knees. "This reminds me of one of Grandma Ida's flour sacks," I pouted.

Pam wrinkled up her freckled nose. "It sure *looks* like one on you."

My eyes welled up with tears of anger.

Pam rolled her eyes at me. "You are so immature."

I ignored her, unsure at my age, of the meaning of the word. *I bet Great Aunt Bert wouldn't feel lucky in this stupid outfit.* Little did I know that the worst was yet to come.

Olga leaned over my crib rail, holding a wide satin ribbon up against my jumper. "Ya," she nodded, "it's the perfect match." She seized a hank of my hair, tying the ribbon around it into a lopsided purple bow.

I refused her offer of a mirror. "No thanks, Olga."

I surveyed the room of my ward mates. I didn't need a mirror to tell me we resembled a gaggle of Little Orphan Annie's with big and floppy satin bows bobby-pinned to our heads. There *was* a saving grace. We could keep the ribbons as private property after the festivities. We all prized personal possessions.

Once we were dolled up in our finery, Olga and Mrs. Johnson rolled a three-shelved toy cart through the ward, dispensing dolls and stuffed animals for our temporary use.

"Gimme that doll," Sonny implored. "That wooden one." Mrs. Johnson tossed it over to her.

Despite her club foot, Pam bee-lined it to the cart, grabbing a phony makeup bag filled with a compact, pretend lipstick you could roll up and down, and a plastic nail file. "My sister says it takes practice to be a teenager, especially a beatnik teenager," she lectured. She looked well on her way since she'd picked out an orange and black dress with purple zigzags on it. "I'm a cool cat," she added, acting snotty. We all moaned.

I examined the toy shelves closely when Mrs. Johnson parked the cart at my bedside. "I guess I'll take the story book, Mrs. Johnson." I couldn't read many of the words, but I enjoyed the fanciful pictures in *Red Riding Hood, Goldilocks,* and my favorite—*Three Billy Goats Gruff.*

We were encouraged to play with our toys whenever a Shriner stopped by our bed. It helped break the ice.

"Here, Paula, you take this puppet, too," Mrs. Johnson insisted. "You can put on a show for some of the nice men," she laughed. "You sing them 'I'm a Little Teapot.' You were mighty funny when you pantomimed to that record the other day."

Back home, I had been something of a sensation when I took to pantomiming the popular "Little Teapot" ditty. I mouthed the words, moving my lips in an exaggerated manner while balancing my bad arm on my hip to form a handle, and shaping my good arm into a spout. By the time I lip synced the "tip me over" line, Mommy and her friends and neighbors hooted hysterically, sometimes so hard they had tears in their eyes. It felt good to make people laugh, especially Mommy.

Olga liked my act too. She put the wizard puppet on my good hand. "You can make him sing." Olga laughed. "You sure did look like a little teapot that day when you did the song."

"You looked like a little moron, is what you looked like," Pam snorted. "That song is not cool."

I threw the puppet to the foot of my bed, feeling limp like the wizard. "You're just jealous, Pam."

"Am not," she shouted.

"Are too."

"Am not." The argument died there from lack of interest.

I turned to looking at my book, hoping to finish it in time. When the toy cart returned at the end of the day, we had to give our playthings back, but I hadn't finished my picture book. I placed it under my pillow for later.

More than once I slipped a treasure between my bed covers and later asked Pam to stash it in my nightstand. So far, I had hoarded a whistle, two books, and a scantily dressed, stiffed-legged plastic doll, the kind that stands in the middle of a birthday cake. Only Pam knew. I didn't trust her to keep her lips sealed, but I had no choice; nobody else could get out of bed except her.

Shriners visits occasioned hot dogs and ice cream for lunch. They personally delivered the treats to us with great pomp and circumstance. I made sure I smiled and batted my eyelashes to lure a Shriner or two my way. At the very least, I'd get a helium balloon out of my coy performances. Another benefit of these visits was the chance to meet famous people like Roy Rogers and Dale Evans. Hopalong Cassidy even snuck in his horse. Evidently, the Shriners cultivated dozens of important Hollywood contacts.

The Shriners visits broke up the tedious routine of hospital life. Later I came to understand that their joviality was often preceded by the consumption of large quantities of Wild Turkey and Jim Beam. All I knew was that by singing a charming solo or acting like Little Merry Sunshine, I garnered heaps of attention from the revelers; the very first time I did my act, a Shriner dressed as a clown, gave me a stuffed French poodle he'd used as a prop during his performance.

"I saw you eyeing this little pooch," he smiled, handing over the toy. "Do you know why I'm giving you this?" he asked.

I gave him a well-practiced response. "Because I'm a brave little girl?" I whispered shyly.

Tears flooded the clown's eyes, causing his makeup to run down the sides of his face.

I basked in his attention. Although I felt a tinge of guilt as I happily petted Fifi, I discovered I could easily live with that kind of guilt.

Early one Friday as I sat atop my bedpan attempting to produce an overdue bowel movement while Pam made faces at me, Vampire Sally stopped by my bed. We called her that because she came around to take our blood. She looked stiff in her white lab coat, but she had a nice smile.

"When you're done there, I'm going to prick your little finger for some blood," she explained, stepping aside so Olga could remove my bedpan.

I fell back on my pillow, searching my repertoire for a snappy reply.

Sally studied my arm closely. "Hmm," she said, glancing up at Olga, "these veins look a bit flimsy, "We'll just stick with the finger and hope that's good enough."

"Just like the queen pricked her finger sewing in *Snow White*," I stated with a regal shiver in my voice. This clearly amused Vampire Sally and took some of the sting out of the slit she made in my finger. She sucked up the dabs of red with a little hose she held between her teeth. Done with the stabbing, she packed up her tools and returned to her lab in the basement.

I assumed Sally could tell if my blood was good or bad by the taste of it, but Erma straightened me out on that one. According to Erma, Sally never tasted the blood because she spat it into one of the test tubes she carried with her at all times.

Erma White was recovering from a broken wrist, which happened because she clapped her hands too hard. Mrs. White died giving birth to Erma. She rarely had visitors and never any mail, so my mother sent little cards, which pleased Erma no end and made me a little jealous. My mother could be nice, especially to kids less fortunate than me.

Each of the few times Mr. White did come to wave and yell up at Erma, a different beautiful lady stood beside him. Erma said one of them might be her stepmother someday.

Pam rolled her eyes. "R-i-g-h-t. They sure don't look like stepmothers to me." She was always looking for an opportunity to rain on someone's parade.

"Shut up, Pam," I hissed.

She threw a pillow at me, but missed. "No, you shut up."

I did. I mean, why bother?

It started with a mysterious stench permeating our ward. Olga noticed it first, but after a day or two, we could all catch a whiff of something rotten.

"I think it's our lunch coming," Erma suggested to Pam.

Lunch that day was canned spinach, mashed potatoes, a slimy piece of liver and chocolate pudding for dessert. I leaned over my tray and took a deep breath. "As bad as this is," I reported, "it's not our food that's causing the stink."

Eating awful food is part of hospital life so I soon developed a technique that kept me from gagging, at least most of the time. Spinach was the most offensive thing on my tray that day so I shoveled all of it into my mouth, swallowed hard, and then sucked up a big spoonful of chocolate pudding. The mixture nearly lurched out of my mouth. I scanned the ward, noting how everyone left bits and pieces of their meal, spreading stuff around in their trays to make the pile look smaller.

Sonny always did battle with her food, so her empty tray surprised all of us. Olga even complimented her. "Dis food is good for you," she said, looking under the tray to see if Sonny had hidden her food there.

As ward magician, Sonny had one or two tricks up her sleeve. Like biting her tongue or talking Pig Latin, the language my parents spoke when they exchanged secrets. Now Sonny had a suspicious way of making mushy vegetables and slimy liver vanish.

Her trick was exposed when Olga decided the foul smell emanated from Sonny's bed. The nurse called in an intern for a consultation. They immediately rushed Sonny to the plaster room so her body cast could be sawed off. That's when they discovered two days' worth of rotting vegetables stored there. The doctor was hopping mad because it was a lot of work to build a body cast. To top it off, a student nurse, new on the job, vomited and nearly fainted from the strong odor released into the room. Sonny was sentenced to a two-day stretch in one of the hall cubicles for her culinary disappearing act.

Life poked along. I woke up early one Sunday morning and looked at all the lonely helium balloons stuck to the ceiling of our ward. They were leftovers from Sonny's birthday party the day before. Like them, I felt a little deflated.

I rolled over on my side and squinted at a pink slip taped to the top of my nightstand.

Pam read it aloud to me. "Oh-oh. It says no solids, nine a.m. surgery scheduled." She paused a moment. "So that's why Vampire Sally took your blood on Friday." She whistled. "Poor you, you'll be the first patient of the day to go under the knife. I just hope the doctor's awake."

Back in the fifties, the prevailing opinion held that young children should know nothing about any operation awaiting them. Better to keep mum about what was in store to limit the patient's anxiety. Surgeons believed that any child under five would probably have no long-term memories of the nightmare.

When I looked up, Pam smirked at me and ran her finger across her neck as if slitting her throat.

Erma tried to comfort me. "The good part of today is you'll get lots of hard candy to suck on. It's to thicken your blood so you won't bleed to death."

Pam couldn't wait to butt in. "And the bad part is you'll have to drink gallons of water and they'll shave whatever they're going to operate on and give you an enema."

"What's an enema?"

"You don't want to know," Sonny answered, reaching for her hairbrush. She brushed her hair a hundred strokes every day. She planned to sell it to a wigmaker because she read somewhere that hair like hers was much in demand.

"I threw up for two days straight after I got my leg stretched," she continued. "And you were sicker than a dog, as I recall," she added, nodding over at Erma.

Erma winced. "The thing I hate most is waking up in the hall cubicle. They make you stay there until you stop moaning in pain."

"Screaming's more like it," Sonny chimed in. "I couldn't wait to get my pain shots even though they made me hallucinate that I was dripping blood all over the bed."

Erma looked serious. "That's why they put a rubber sheet under you," she explained. "Sometimes kids bleed to death and ruin the mattress."

"Poor *you*, Paula," Pam simpered, as if she cared.

The food cart came rattling through the double doors passing right by me. Mrs. Schmitt came over to my bed with a bag full of hard candy. "This will keep you from feeling too hungry. Let me know if you want more."

"Yeah," Geneva warned, "you gotta thicken your blood or it runs right out of your body and you die."

I lay back down, grabbing my covers in my teeth and pulling them over my head. I had no idea what was in store for me, aside from pain, blood, and solitary confinement in the hall cubicle. Things became worse when an intern and a student nurse wheeled my crib down the hall into an examining room.

"What are you doing to me?" I whimpered, panic creeping into my voice.

"Don't you worry," the doctor ordered breezily. "Turns out Sally couldn't get enough blood from your finger prick and she said your arm veins were too small to stick a needle in." I blinked at him. I didn't even know his name or the student nurse's.

My heart flip-flopped. "But where's Vampire Sally?" I started to cry.

"That's what they call Mrs. Sampson," the nurse explained to the intern. In the midst of my fear and confusion, the student nurse rolled me up in a sheet real tight like a papoose so I'd be still enough for the doctor to stick a mile-long needle into a vein in my neck.

"Stay still and it won't hurt, the doctor ordered impatiently.

Liar.

It was useless to struggle and what made me maddest was that the creeps never told me what they were going to do to me. They shattered the little bit of trust I had in the staff at Shriners.

I woke up screaming in pain. "Where am I...where am I? Why does my chest hurt?" Someone pushed my bangs back out of my eyes with a hand that felt soft and cool. The last thing I remembered was a black mask covering my nose and mouth, then the sickly sweet smell of ether and a wall of darkness. I turned on my side and threw up into a kidney-shaped pan.

"It's all over, Paula," Miss Blair whispered. "Your surgery went well and you were a real trooper."

A *wounded* trooper. I tried to open my dry mouth, but that only made me vomit again. "I'm so thirsty," I wailed, watching as Miss Blair dipped a washcloth in water. "Try and suck on this, Paula. In a while, you can have a sip of water."

I hurt everywhere, but my eyes focused on my good hand. I saw that the doctors had strapped it flat to a board. Miss Blair adjusted the needle that poked into my hand, making me wince. "Hold very still, Paula." She straightened the thin hose that was attached to the glass bottle of blood dripping into my vein. The bottle hung from a pole at the side of my crib. "The doctors performed a muscle transplant on your right arm," Miss Blair explained. "That's why your arm is strapped to your chest."

Muscle transplants were a house specialty and experimental at the time. Nobody knew then if I would be able to move my limp right arm someday. "This surgery has only been performed six times, so you'll be quite a celebrity with our latest batch of interns." Miss Blair placed a flexi-straw in a glass of water. She bent down and poked the straw into my mouth. "Just a sip," she cautioned, but I was way past that, glugging away until I'd emptied the glass.

I almost immediately barfed up the water, leaving only the bitter taste of bile in my mouth. I burst into tears because the jerking I did while vomiting pulled at the stitches in my arm and chest. "Can't you make the pain go away?" I pleaded.

"Not quite yet," she said. I blacked out again only to be awakened by Mrs. Schmitt jabbing me with a needle. A warm wave of relief spread though my body and again the sweet darkness came. I stayed in the hall cubicle next to Mrs. Schmitt's desk for three days, eagerly awaiting the stab of her needle. On my last day, the pain shots stopped.

"But it still hurts," I moaned.

"Life hurts," the pudgy one replied. Then she brought her radio into my cubicle so I could listen to *Our Miss Brooks* and *The Life of Riley*. My pain subsided and I even felt a little bounce in my heart.

Everyone seemed glad to have me back on the ward, even Pam, until my repeated accounts of the rare muscle transplant that I had survived started to get on the girls' nerves. "Enough with the cut-and-stitch stories," Pam ordered. For once, I complied with her wishes.

Although the transplant was my very first operation, I gradually stopped thinking about it, at least during the day. However, the surgery did become a rich source of material for my nightmares. Where had I gone when they filled me with ether and cut me up? Was I almost dead during the operation? For the six hours before coming out of the ether haze, where had I been? Nowhere? Was being dead like being nowhere? Those questions haunted me in the lonely spaces of the night.

When two weeks had passed, it was time to take my stitches out. A student nurse rolled my gurney down to the plaster room. "I've never seen stitches removed before," she announced a little too eagerly for my taste.

"Me neither," I mumbled as she wheeled me into the part of the plaster room where sutures were yanked out. A Dr. Berg carefully unwrapped my arm, easing it apart from my chest. We both stared at the ugly red scar running across my chest up under my arm and over my shoulder. He snipped fifty nasty black stitches and one by one yanked them out like pieces of thread. I cried out fifty times.

10

DOCTORS' ROUNDS

My first experience with doctors' rounds started early on a Tuesday morning. Even though Pam and Erma had described this ordeal, they barely scratched the surface when it came to capturing the humiliation and helplessness involved.

"At least we don't have to go to school," Pam told Sonny. "You ought to be happy about that"

Sonny frowned as she ran a comb through her matted red hair. It was only shampooed every five weeks when they replaced her old body cast with a new one. "Nobody asked for your opinion," she snapped.

"Drop dead," Pam yelled back. Before Sonny could reply, Mrs. Johnson and Olga hurried in to interrupt our breakfast. We suffered through hasty bed baths and were dressed in white hospital gowns that flapped open in the back. The worst part was the "tee-binder" that took the place of underpants. It was a sort of bikini that went between your legs and tied at both sides of the waist. Doctors and nurses could simply untie them without having to tug underwear over braces and casts.

"This one is three times too big for me," Pam protested, pulling the strings of her tee-binder as tight as she could. The ward filled with the spirit of rebellion.

Erma waited until the nurses left for the Big Girls' Ward before throwing hers into a used bedpan, yelling, "I am not wearing that thing."

Olga appeared out of nowhere. "Yah, you sure as heck are!" She whisked the bedpan away and returned with a new tee-binder for Erma.

Mrs. Johnson stopped at my bed, lowering the rail. "Lean forward, Paula, so I can tie up your gown." I slumped over, relieved to feel the touch of her warm brown hands. They contrasted sharply with the stark whiteness of my examination gown.

Pam put on a thin line of lipstick and examined her reflection in the window. "Well, I'm going to make a good impression; not all of the doctors are creepy like Dr. Ramsey and Doctor Shultz," she insisted. "The new ones are smart and cute." Pam batted her eyelashes, satisfied with the pretty blonde image looking back at her. She grabbed every opportunity to test out her pre-teen wiles on the newest shipment of interns. "They're not real doctors yet," she theorized. "So that means they're still pretty young. I'm almost as old as some of them."

We did the math and agreed that Pam's was a bit off. "Are you telling me some of those guys are teenagers?" Geneva laughed.

Pam resented the challenge. Taking another reassuring look at herself, she declared lots of people thought she was much older than she looked. "Plus my sister dates a boy who's nineteen," she protested, "and she's only fourteen."

We rolled our eyes in unison. Pam lied with such ease that we never actually knew if she was telling the truth or not. We let the subject of Pam's beatnik sister drop.

A loud rustling came from the hallway where a herd of doctors crowded together, preparing to invade our ward.

"The blonde guy who looks like Tab Hunter is mine," Pam announced right before the young interns crowded around our beds.

Dr. Shultz introduced each of us by our disease or how we came to be crippled. He stopped at my bed, read over my file, and started rambling. "This five-year-old Caucasian female is something of an anomaly.

She contracted polio six weeks after her birth, so doctors first diagnosed her with encephalitis. As you know, newborns usually have an immunity to polio, but because her mother chose not to breastfeed, Paula didn't benefit from the colostrum antibodies present in the first milk of the mother. We believe that explains why the virus took hold so early, perhaps immediately. An older boy in the hospital where Paula was born also came down with polio when he was having his tonsils removed. Most probably the nurse who looked after both of them transmitted the disease."

I had no intention of taking all this mumble-jumble lying down. I swung my good leg over my head, bringing it back down to gain the necessary momentum to sit up. "At least I lived to tell about it," I declared. "And I'm five and a half."

"That's amazing," an intern named Dr. Bilboa exclaimed, stroking his pointy brown beard. Can you do that again?" His hair curled around his head like a dead animal.

"Do what?"

Dr. Bilboa frowned, his eyebrows crawling together like two furry brown caterpillars. He put his hand on my chest, pushing me down without even asking my permission. "Now do that thing with your leg again," he demanded. He turned to his fellow interns with the enthusiasm.

I remained motionless, refusing to perform the trick. Dr. Shultz winked at me. "Can you show Dr. Bilboa how you did that? Let's get it on film," he directed, pointing to an intern with a movie camera in his hands.

For once, I didn't want to be captured on film. "Sorry, but I can only do it once a day. Maybe you can come back some other time."

Dr. Shultz fumbled with my file and resumed reading my life story. "This patient is recuperating from an experimental muscle transplant," he explained, abruptly sitting me back up, untying my nightgown, and yanking it down to expose my chest.

I shut my eyes, pretending it was Mrs. Johnson's hands poking and prodding me.

"As you can see here, we took muscle tissue from her breast and transplanted it into her arm and shoulder, here and here," he continued, twisting my arm around to expose my railroad track scars to the gawkers. "We're hoping she may regain some use of this arm. It's only an experiment," he added, patting my shoulder.

An unexpected rage filled me as I jerked my arm away and pulled my nightgown up, using my teeth. I turned my back to them so I couldn't see the wolf man's eyebrows shooting up and down.

"Wow, would you look at that?" he whistled. "It's amazing to see how she substitutes her teeth for hands and uses her leg to compensate for her stomach muscles to sit herself up."

I wanted to demonstrate how I could substitute my foot for my fist and punch him in the stomach. I lay there numb down to my toes, listening as the crowd of white coats shuffled over to Erma's bedside.

"This ten-year-old Negro female has brittle bone syndrome..." Dr. Shultz blabbed on.

I heard him give the lowdown on Geneva and Sonny, opening my eyes again when the doctors arrived at Pam's bedside. "This ten-year-old white female has what most people refer to as a clubbed foot. Of course, her leg casts prevents us from seeing the foot, but you can observe the extent of the malformation here in her x-rays."

Pam batted her eyelashes and smiled beguilingly. Dr. Shultz whisked her out of bed and onto the floor, letting her go once she gained her balance. "Can you show us your current gait by walking back and forth?"

Startled to find herself upright, Pam did her best to strut across the ward. That's when the back of her hospital gown fell open and everyone could see her tee-binder slipping down her legs and onto the floor.

Pam reached around struggling to close her gown. Tears streamed down her checks while her face reddened.

So much for impressing the interns... My smugness evaporated when Pam caught my stare. I looked away, ashamed of myself. Not even a snob like Pam deserved to be stripped of what little dignity we were granted.

That night at dinner, Pam refused to clean her tray and as a consequence had to spend the night in one of the hall cubicles. I think she appreciated the alone time.

No one ever mentioned the incident and Pam returned to us the next day, cheered up by a letter from her sister. "She's going to show me how to apply makeup the next time I come home," she read. "Says here that beatniks use a lot of purple eye shadow and thick black mascara," Pam exclaimed, having regained most of her attitude.

I smiled. It felt good to have her back.

11

CHRISTMAS AT THE SHRINE

It was beginning, as the song goes, "to look a lot like Christmas." As a kid in the hospital, you learned to live from one holiday to the next. We anxiously awaited anything that broke up the routine. Halloween disappointed everyone. We all got to pick one of three masks to wear and the nurses, dolled up in their own costumes, doled out a small bag of hard candy to each of us. I wore a black eye mask and pretended to be the Lone Ranger.

Thanksgiving was nothing to write home about either. First, we watched a boring movie about the Pilgrims, but the film broke halfway through so we were spared the ending. Miss Peach served turkey, mashed potatoes, and stuffing, with pumpkin pie for dessert, but it still tasted pretty much like the turkey-a-la king we had on most Thursdays.

Everybody held high hopes for Christmas. On holidays and Sundays, Father Neal, a very handsome priest, sermonized to us about God and the suffering little children He loved so much, gradually working around to the stable birth of baby Jesus and the true meaning of Christmas. Mrs. Johnson, who was Southern Baptist, lamented that Father Neal's calling was such a waste of his good looks.

"A pretty man like that would make some woman a fine husband and that's a fact," she moaned, shaking her head.

As for me, I thought the priest would make a good daddy for a suffering little girl such as myself.

Pam told me the Shriners went all out to stir up our Christmas spirits throughout most all of December. "They haul in a live Christmas tree and we all get to make decorations."

"The Shriners bring the tree the first Saturday of December," Erma added. "I outta know," This will be my fourth Christmas at the hospital."

Pam sneered at Erma. "Yeah, it's cheaper to keep you here because then your daddy-o doesn't have to buy you any presents." Pam's teenaged sister had been writing her letters using beatnik talk and now Pam practiced it all the time.

Our parents weren't allowed to send us presents, even at Christmas. Russian Olga pointed out "This keeps things fair and square. Nobody gets no more presents than anybody else."

"You need to write a letter to Santa and tell him *exactly* what you want," Pam continued, pretending she still believed in Santa Claus. "Otherwise, you can end up with stuff like yo-yos and Slinkys." Like Pam, I was a nonsubscriber to Santa propaganda since our house had no brick chimney or fireplace, only a woodstove with a pipe that even an elf couldn't squeeze down without being burnt.

"I didn't get the roller skates I asked for," Sonny whined, still in pain from her latest torture session in the plaster room that morning. She had just been fitted into another new body cast. They took off the old one with a buzz saw. The doctors claimed that the whirring blade couldn't cut you, demonstrating this fact by running the blade across an open palm. Still, the saw could definitely scratch tender young skin, leaving little red lines and nicks if the doctors weren't careful.

I'd been in the plaster room having my polio arm attended to and witnessed Sonny's torture. While an intern removed the sling I'd been wearing since my surgery, I watched doctors balance her on a narrow strip of cloth that stretched out and fastened at both ends to a rack. She was held in place with a strap under her chin and a sort of garter belt that attached around her hips. A doctor turned a wheel that pulled her head up and her hips down, stretching her out until she screamed for them to stop.

"Well, you might as well have asked for a dog sled," Pam piped up, eyeing Sonny's tormented face.

"Drop dead, Pam," Sonny ordered with contempt.

"No, you drop dead, daddy-o," Pam snarled back.

"Nobody's dropping dead," Olga interrupted, nipping their fight in the bud. "Take these," she insisted, handing out packets of shiny colored paper strips. She demonstrated how to lick one end and then stick it to the other, making a circle. We made chains to hang on the Christmas tree when it arrived.

I had a hard time doing this with only one good arm, but with the help of my teeth and gumption, I succeeded in looping together three long chains. "Good girl," Olga said, making it totally worth my trouble.

"*Ya* now, we have these egg cartons which we shall turn into bells." Olga cut the cups from the carton, turned them upside down and—presto! She'd created ornaments. We painted them red, blue, and green and then fastened each with a little bell attached to a pipe cleaner. Our decorations looked very handmade like the kind you'd see in an orphanage or something Mary and Laura might construct in *Little House on the Prairie.*

As promised, a dozen Shriners marched in on Saturday morning wearing gold ribbons across their chests and those stupid red hats. It took a lot of sweat and a few cuss words, but two men named Bud and Charlie managed to drag a six-foot pine tree into the sunroom just off the ward. For once, the San Francisco fog lifted and a golden light streamed through the large arched window on one side of the wall. We lacked only a manger and some sheep.

While Bud and Charlie anchored the tree in a stand, two other Shriners—Mort and Mike—wrapped it in lights. Olga kept us busy stringing popcorn and dried cranberries just like in the olden days.

"You're eating more popcorn than you're stringing," Sonny tattled.

It was true. I ate most of my popcorn since it was too hard to poke the needle through the kernels.

Olga topped off the decorating by tying red gingham bows on every one of the tree branches. Mr. Johnson, the black janitor and Mr. Allen, the gardener pushed in an upright piano and a tall and goofy-looking Shriner named Ed started to play Christmas carols.

We had just finished "Silent Night," when out of the blue, a television camera crew burst through the double doors and into the ward. At first, they just followed around a bunch of the Shriners, asking them about the money they raised to pay for our operations and braces. Every New Year's Day, the Shriners sponsored the East-West football game with all the money going to the hospital. The Shriners loved the publicity.

Then the cameras turned on us. Here was my chance to be famous. Caught off guard, most of the girls stared blankly into the camera while they recited their names and ages.

I had bigger plans. I zeroed in on a reporter with a microphone, carefully slipped off my bed, and hobbled over to him smiling my sweetest movie star smile. With the camera rolling, I told him I could sing "You Are My Sunshine," a perfect crippled child's song, though not very seasonal.

"Hey, Al, this little cutie has a song for you," the reporter called out. He carefully posed me in front of the piano and waited until I had my balance. With cameras rolling, I sang through all three verses, accompanied by Shriner Ed who had abandoned the piano for his snazzy accordion.

"I'm up for singing more," I offered, but Ed shook his head. "That's enough, honey."

Pam glared at me because I was using up all the film and time ran out before she got to say anything but her name.

A swanky lady reporter from the *San Francisco Chronicle* snapped a picture of me and Erma in front of the Christmas tree.

She took out a notebook and wrote something in it. "What's your name, honey?"

"My name's Paula and I'm five. Also," I rambled, "I may be the youngest baby ever to get polio and not die from it." That didn't get printed, but I did make the six o'clock news.

There was no sound in the TV footage where I was singing "You Are My Sunshine," but you could see my lips moving. The camera showed Pam frowning with no Christmas spirit at all in her eyes.

I felt a little bit famous even though Pam said I looked like a fish when I mouthed the words.

"You're just jealous," I countered. "At least I didn't look like I was going to murder Santa Claus." The camera had captured Pam's dull glare perfectly; she actually did look like she had murder on her mind.

During that week's Sunday visiting hours, I yelled down to my mother about how I was on television and Auntie Bert and Uncle George yelled back that they had seen me. Auntie Bert waved the picture of me that was printed in the newspaper, but she was too far away for me to see as it fluttered in the wind.

We girls were restless on the ward that Christmas Eve and after we sang out the "Lord's Prayer" and "Day is Done," we vented our energy by running through an impressive medley of holiday carols.

The overhead lights flashed off and on. Morton stood in the middle of the ward like a bad Christmas troll. "Santa just landed on the roof," she reported in a hushed tone. "One more 'Jingle Bells' out of you and I'll tell him to go away and take your toys with him."

I hated Morton. I guess that hate along with the spirit of Christmas gave me enough spunk to say, "Be careful not to fall off the roof, Mrs. Morton."

A few snickers passed between the girls. The troll was at my bedside in half a second, shining her flashlight into my face. "You think you're so smart, don't you, you little weasel?"

I looked shocked before I said quite solemnly "It's just that my grandpa fell off a roof and had to be in a wheelchair for the rest of his life." I gazed into her spotlight, all pious and teary-eyed like any good weasel.

Morton scanned my face looking for any indication that I was lying. The phone in the hallway started to ring, and much to everyone's relief she flicked her flashlight off and ran out to answer it.

"Must be Santa Claus," I whispered, "wishing her a Merry Christmas."

After four or five minutes, the giggles died down and we fell quiet, all snug in our beds.

I lay there peacefully recalling the lighting of the big spruce that took place earlier that night. The nurses had placed us in wheelchairs and rolled our holiday parade outside. They parked us in a circle around a giant pine tree as the countdown began.

Mr. Allen did the honors. "Everyone ready?" he belted out into the starry night. "Three, two, one." He plugged in the long black extension cord.

In a rush of magic, strings of dazzling lights burst into colors winding all the way to the top of the tree. The display left us speechless. Soon, Erma, Sonny, and Geneva sang a round of "Deck the Halls" and eventually Pam and I chimed in.

To my surprise, Christmas at Shriners was turning out to be a lot more relaxed that it was at home. "I just hate Christmas," Mommy proclaimed the moment she flipped the Feed Store calendar over into December. Her wacky nerves and the way she stalked around our Christmas tree, grim and tight-fisted, made it hard for David and me to be festive. "It's lopsided," she inevitably complained to my father after he had spent all day Sunday scouring our property for the perfect pine.

A dark cloud rolled across his face as he sputtered, "It will be just fine when I add some more branches." I'm sure he had better ways to spend his only day off than drilling holes in the tree's trunk and shoving in branches. Once we recovered from Mommy's foul mood, we were always proud of her efforts. In spite of the high drama, her Christmas trees were the best decorated in the neighborhood, mostly because she put the icicles on one strand at a time.

I felt a little pang in my chest for Mommy who hated holidays so much. I wished she loved Christmas and all the trappings that went with the season. That year at Shriners, I learned that holidays could be fun, even joyous. Without the fear of Mommy having a nervous fit because of the stress, I soaked up the Spirit of Christmas like never before.

Once I had the spirit inside of me, no one could take it away from me ever again.

A ground fog stole in at dawn on Christmas day, long wispy tendrils of white snaking around the Victorian houses across the street. In lieu of snow, Jack Frost had iced the whole scene, setting rooftops to sparkle as the sun peeked out. I sat up in my crib, the first person on the ward to see the net stockings hanging on each bedpost. Mine bulged with mysterious boxes, a paper fan, Chinese handcuffs, and an orange.

I scooted down to the end of the bed and poked my big toe through the loop at the top of the stocking. I tore a sizable hole in the mesh, but I managed to drag it through the bars of my crib before anything spilled out. I was too lazy to use my hands.

Suddenly, my eyes landed on something that took my breath away. There, at the side of my bed, was a miniature set of bunk beds, each one occupied by a doll. A white kewpie doll sat on the top bunk while a black doll sporting a wild crop of tiny braids occupied the bottom bed.

My heart sank. Surely, the bunk beds were meant for Erma because the Negro baby matched her to a tee. Maybe my present was the bright red enamel trunk, the blue wicker buggy or the baby's high chair propped against the door of the sunroom. Still I couldn't take my eyes off the bunk beds.

A scream from Sonny solved part of the mystery. "Hooray, I got the baby buggy I asked for," she sang out.

Just waking up, Erma emitted her own delirious cry of joy. "Santa brought me the official Gerber Baby high chair." A black doll matching mine sat in the chair patiently waiting to be fed the glob of plastic mush cooling in a bright pink dish on the tray. "Look, she's even got jars of fake baby food to eat and a bottle of milk. The kind that empties when you turn it upside down and—"

"We know," Pam interrupted carelessly. "Miracles of miracles, the bottle fills back up when you set it upright."

"I know that," Erma shouted at Pam. "You didn't have to steal my story. It was mine to tell."

Pam shrugged. *"Sor-ry,"* she said, though we knew she wasn't. She busied herself riffling through her Miss Revlon cosmetic bag complete with a phony compact, nail file, and a lipstick that actually left a light tinge of pink on her lips.

"Hey, pipsqueak," she called to me. "Look at my tortoise shell brush and comb set with the matching mirror."

My eyes remained riveted on the dolls and bunk beds. Through the process of elimination, I realized they must belong to me.

Pam slipped out of her bed and waddled over to me. In a show of supernatural good will, she picked up the two dolls and tossed them over the rails of my crib so they landed on my lap. They were dressed in identical nightgowns and fuzzy white slippers.

I watched as Pam examined the sheets, pillows and quilts that came with the beds. "Looks like the Shriners Sewing Club ladies have been busy," she muttered, unimpressed with the handmade bedding.

"I think it's beautiful," I answered dreamily, fingering the real lace on the border of the blanket and the hearts embroidered on the pillowcases.

"Hey, there's a box here at the foot of one of the bunk beds," Pam noticed. She threw the brightly wrapped box to me, hitting the corner of my eye with it. "You did that on purpose," I winced, but I recovered and tore the wrapping paper off with my teeth.

"Don't eat it, shrimp legs," Pam laughed. "There's real candy in your Christmas stocking."

I barely heard her—I'd managed to remove the lid of the box and dumped out its contents. I counted three matching sets of party dresses and bonnets trimmed with lace, two beautifully knitted sweaters, dainty undergarments, and two woolen coats with real pockets and buttons.

"How come your dolls have matching outfits?" Erma asked, dressing her own in a flashy skirt and sweater. "They sure enough ain't twins."

"They're sisters under their skin," a soft voice answered. Mrs. Jaspers had entered the ward dispensing candy canes. "Can I see your dollies?" she asked as she lowered my crib's railing. "Looky here, this one's a Madame Alexander baby," she explained, obviously impressed with the white doll's lineage.

I lifted up the nightgown of the Negro baby doll and showed the writing on her back to the nurse. "Made in Occupied Japan. That's about right," she said a little sadly. "That's about right."

Geneva's delirious scream came from across the room. The bright red doll trunk turned out to be for her. She opened it to display a rack of store-bought doll dresses hung on little hangers. An official Betsy McCall doll looked out from a sort of sleeping bag attached to the other side of the trunk.

We all felt a little woozy from the excitement and candy we had ingested. Miss Peach looked disappointed when so many of us left food on our breakfast trays. She had gone to the trouble of making us green and red pancakes for our Christmas treat. I felt sorry for her so I ate as much of mine as I could. Even though they tasted okay, I had a hard time swallowing the pancakes, especially the green ones.

The Shriners reappeared for New Year's Eve Day, accompanied by the football players set to play in the East-West game.

I ended up being paired with one of the coaches. Mike was over forty, had lost most of his hair and lacked the pizazz of the athletes, but I got my picture taken with him handing me a football. Pam was livid when they ran that photo in the *Oakland Tribune*. Her mother clipped it out and sent it to her with a note that read, "I bet this little girl Paula is one of your best friends." *Ha!*

Russian Olga rescued the clipping before Pam had a chance to rip it to shreds. Pam managed to wad it up in a tight little ball, but after Olga wrestled it from Pam's fingers, the nurse took it home and ironed out most of the wrinkles.

Just after Easter, Mrs. Schmitt told me I was on the going home list. Pam had already left with her modified clubfoot. The doctors said she needed two or three more surgeries before she could fit it into a high heeled shoe, her main goal in life. They released her anyway so she could catch up with family life back home.

The sun woke me up on the day of my departure. I hadn't seen Mommy or Daddy for weeks and weeks so I was thrilled about my impending release.

"You awake?" Erma asked, carefully sitting up so as not to break any bones.

I smiled at my first black friend, memorizing her face so I'd always remember her. "Yep. I can't wait 'til Mrs. Schmitt brings me my going-home clothes. No more tee-binders or flour sack dresses for me," I sang out. "I'm sorry you have to stay here until they track down your Daddy, Erma."

She shrugged. "Oh, they know where he is," she muttered, rummaging through her mail sack to retrieve a tattered postcard. "This came from Texas and that's where we lived before. It says here I should stay put until he gets back on his feet." Erma sighed.

"He sure has trouble standing up," I noted.

Erma nodded in agreement. "Sometimes I think he'll never find a place for me." Erma had developed a growing cynicism about her father and his so-called intentions to settle down with some nice lady who would help him make a real home for Erma. She was becoming a lifer at Shriners, no doubt about that.

"At least you're not being electrocuted," Geneva said in an attempt to cheer up Erma. A hush fell over the ward. Mrs. Schmitt and Olga had been listening to the radio all week long, following the details surrounding the Rosenbergs who had just been executed for spying.

"This is none of your business, little girls," Olga scolded, unplugging the radio she had set on Geneva's nightstand.

The idea of electrocution obsessed my thoughts. I had nightmares about it. In my dream, I was strapped on a gurney, waiting to be operated on, only it turned out that instead of putting a gas mask over my nose and mouth, the surgeon attached a funny helmet to my head.

"This will only hurt for a minute," he explained "and then you will be on the other side."

"What other side?" I cried, waking myself up. For years afterwards, dreams of my impending execution continued to haunt me, making the prospect of surgery more terrifying than ever. What scared me most was not knowing where I went once I breathed in the sickening smell of ether. *What if I couldn't return from the other side?*

But for now, I was going home. I forgot all about the Rosenbergs when Olga bustled in with a big box containing my brand new wardrobe. Taking off my nightgown, she put me in a new set of Carters' underwear, with pink roses covering the undershirt and pants.

Mommy always bought me Carters' underclothes because they were union-made and very sturdy. Olga pulled my arms through a lacy pink slip and stood back to look at me. "Yes, you're ready to go."

I glanced up at her, relieved that she was just pulling my leg. Carefully, she removed a low waisted turquoise dress with white daisies embroidered on the collar. It was very starchy and made crinkling noises when she buttoned up the back. I wished it had been a fancy party dress, but it was new and all mine. Olga strapped a new knee brace on my bad leg. It had a built-up sole on the shoe so I wouldn't limp so much and when Olga stood me in front of the sunroom door, my reflection pleased me.

Mrs. Schmitt danced into the ward, placing a polka dot box on my bed. "Let's hear the cheer," she sang out as I opened the lid to reveal an official Madame Alexander Queen Elizabeth doll dressed in her coronation outfit. Fortunately, the doll looked nothing like the Queen.

"Two, four, six, eight," Pudgy counted out to get the ball rolling.

"Who do we appreciate?" Geneva, Sonny, and Erma chimed in.

For some reason I couldn't look at them as the "Paula, Paula, Paula, hip, hip, hooray!" refrain followed me out into the hall.

Mommy and Auntie Bert waited for me in front of the elevator. They both had red and watery eyes. Nothing felt real until Auntie Bert scooped me up in her arms and practically hugged me to death. When she put me down again, Mommy took my hand in hers and gave it a little squeeze. Reaching into her coat pocket, she pulled out something and handed to me.

"My Jesse Jesus paper doll," I yelled, holding it to my chest as I pushed the button for the first floor with my chin. I wanted to show Mommy my can-do spirit. I felt very grown up and full of gumption, at least for the ride down.

Uncle George waited for us in his brand new gold Plymouth, merrily honking his horn. Mommy pushed the front seat forward so I could get in the back. "Can I sit on the hump seat?" I begged, referring to the armrest that pulled down from middle of the back seat.

Mommy arranged the armrest and helped me mount it. "I'm going to hold on to your arm so you won't fall off your horse." Mommy sat back and gazed out the window at the red brick Shriners Hospital for Crippled Children shrinking in the distance. I was learning to be content with the few moments when I felt connected to my mother. Something inside her was broken and I gave up on my attempts to take more of her love than she had to give. I leaned my head against her shoulder and let out a big sigh.

12

HOME AGAIN, HOME AGAIN

My brother and I huddled under a scratchy old army blanket in the living room, mesmerized by the test pattern flickering on the screen of our new television set. Mommy was sold on the TV once she saw it came inside a fancy maple cabinet with doors you could shut. "I don't want an ugly screen staring back at me," she told my father.

Promptly at six a.m., the test pattern turned into an American flag flapping in the wind while the Marine band played our national anthem. David threw off the blanket and helped me stand up, placing my scrawny hand over my heart. Since Uncle Robert and Uncle Raymond had perished in WWII, we felt it our patriotic duty to display our allegiance to the red, white, and blue even if it was black and white on our Motorola.

"It's my turn to pick the channel," I said, forgetting that we only received one.

"There's nothing good on until five," my brother scoffed.

A television announcer verified the fact. "Good morning, television friends," he chirped in an amiable voice. "You're watching KIEM T.V. Channel Three in Eureka, California. Regular programming will commence broadcasting at 3 p.m. this afternoon. Tune in then to watch the Army's *Big Picture* followed by *Industry on Parade*. At 4 p.m. gather the kids around for the *Uncle Bill Show* featuring the Funny Bunnies and their puppet friends."

Daddy bustled into the room with an armload of wood for our stove. "What are you kids doing up so early?" he asked.

I limped over to him, anxious to warm my hands and feet. "We wanted to watch them putting up the flag. Is it true they can see us through the television, Daddy?"

He smiled. "No, honey."

I glared at my brother who had convinced me to brush my hair when I got up so I'd look presentable when the Marine band played "God Bless

America." He thumbed his nose at me as he left to get dressed for school. He had been nice to me for the first week after I came home from the Shriners, but now we were back to our regular kiss-or-kick relationship.

Things had changed while I was away. Along with the TV, Mommy had a new ringer washing machine and Daddy had added two goats to our barnyard menagerie. Much to my regret, David had changed too, developing an independent streak that put more distance between us. At eight, he had begun to count the days until he would be old enough to drive and escape our tumultuous household.

Each Sunday night I watched him put seven X marks across the previous week of the calendar with a bright red crayon. "Can I go with you?" I pleaded, already anticipating that day in the faraway future when he would abandon the family homestead and quite possibly me.

Sometimes he said "Ah, sure," but if we'd had a fight, he might reply, "Not in a million years." This emotional blackmail hung over me, making fight or flight decisions hard.

Like every weekday morning at 6:45 a.m., Daddy and David drove off in the pick-up. David stayed at Momo's until it was time for school while Daddy, dressed in his black work clothes, manned the presses down at the newspaper.

Looking through the picture window in the dining nook, Mommy and I watched them drive down the hill. I dreaded the lonely hours until their return, although there had been a change in Mommy. She seemed a little brighter since she had suffered her last nervous collapse and gotten some of the panic out of her system. From the scary way David described the episode, I was happy I'd missed it. Still, Daddy never left for work without making me promise to be a good girl and not upset Mommy. Nothing new there...

My daily routine of looking at books, playing paper dolls, or visiting with Sharon continued, punctuated by Mommy's occasional meltdowns. Every week or so a door-to-door salesman would show up to break the monotony. Even though Mommy had a brand new vacuum, the Hoover salesman still came by to see if we needed additional attachments.

I sat beside Mommy on the Chesterfield, engrossed in the latest demonstration the Hoover man performed. I especially enjoyed watching him pour sand and ball bearings onto our braided rug and then demonstrate how the Hoover sucked both of them up with equal gusto.

It took three or four years of visits from the encyclopedia salesman before my mother, with a go-ahead from Daddy, broke down and bought us a set of the *World Book Encyclopedia*, but until then, Mr. Nash kept showing up, letting me look at the art pages and the transparent insets illustrating the anatomy of the human body. Each time he rewarded my attention with a beautiful colored bookmark with his name and phone number printed on it.

Of course, no month went by without a visit from Mr. Guy Trindle, the happy-ever-after Fuller Brush Man who opened up his fat suitcase filled with cookware, knives, soaps, scissors, and shoelaces.

Mommy and I examined all the items carefully. "I think I'll order a broom and dustpan," she told Mr. Trindle who cheerfully recorded her every wish. "And I'm all out of lavender cologne so put me down for a bottle."

I ogled the bath powder that came with a huge pink powder puff, but Mommy said it was for grown-up ladies. I wasn't too disappointed, knowing what came next. After repacking his case of merchandise, Mr. Trindle always winked at me. "And here's a present for the little lady." He handed me a tiny sample bottle of perfume.

Even though nobody living on Pigeon Point had much money, salesmen constantly trawled our neighborhood. One time I was at Sharon Barnhart's house when a salesman with a giant book of carpet samples interrupted our lunch. Given the Barnharts still had tarpaper on their roof and clear plastic sheets covering most of the windows, I hardly expected Mrs. Barnhart to jump at the chance to buy something as fancy as a Persian rug.

Ever the optimist, Sharon pointed to a sample of a blue and white rug sprinkled with purple flowers. She practically drooled over it. "Oh, Mama, can I have this for my bedroom, please, pretty please?" She caught her mother's frown out of the corner of her eye. "I mean when Daddy builds me a bedroom," she added a bit forlornly.

Even though it seemed pointless to me, the salesman left the sample book with Bernie. "I'll pick it up tomorrow when I finish my rounds in your parts. You and your hubby take a second look."

Before she could say, "Don't bother, mister," the man was out the door.

"Well, I got to get the washing done." Bernie heaved a weary sigh. "You two let me know before you go running off somewhere."

We promised, but forgot it in our hurry to get back to my house. Sharon lugged the book of samples with her. "I want to look at them again," she panted, stopping every three feet to catch her breath and get a better grip on the massive collection of rug strips. "Especially all the ones with roses."

We headed straight to my clubhouse where we could study our plunder in private.

I pointed to the little tieback curtains Mommy had made for the windows. "Aren't they pretty, Sharon?" In one of her rare cheerful moods,

Mommy and I had made a list of decorating plans to spruce up what was essentially a shack. The curtains had been the first upgrade.

"Well, yes, they're nice, but now the rest of the clubhouse looks kinda run down."

We both studied the dirt floor with childish disdain. Sharon gave her golden curls a sassy shake. "We need a rug. That's what we need."

I smiled. "Just what I was thinking." We sat down and opened the sample book until we both agreed on a pink and blue swatch that matched the curtains. I leaned over and pulled off the square of material using my teeth.

Sharon wiped my spit away and held the swatch up against the curtains. "Perfect match," we sang out in unison.

"We can take any of these we want." I told her. "They're free samples just like the perfume bottles from the Fuller Brush Man."

Sharon squinted dubiously. "Really? How many can we take, I wonder?"

"As many as we want, I guess." I thought a moment. "You know, we could carpet the whole floor with about twenty or thirty patches."

Riding high on my enthusiasm, Sharon exclaimed, "then we can sew the pieces together. I can use the sewing machine I got for Christmas."

"And even though they won't match, they're free!" I yelled gleefully. I knew that would please our parents for sure.

With complete abandon, Sharon ripped samples from the book until we covered the dirt floor in a crazy-quilt pattern. "This will look great once we sew them together."

Fatigued by our decorating spree, we left the book in the clubhouse and traipsed inside to get a glass of Kool-Aid. Mommy set down two tumblers full and put a straw in mine. "What you kids been up to?" she asked. "Bernie just called to say you'd better bring that rug sample book back before you get it dirty."

"But we can keep our samples. Right, Mommy?"

She shook her head. "Absolutely not. Those are only to look at."

I choked and some of my Kool-Aid went down my throat and squirted up and out my nose. "Don't drink so fast," Mommy chided.

"Let's go back to the clubhouse," I suggested to Sharon, eager to make our getaway and try to restore the sample book to its former pristine condition.

Sharon eyed me nervously. "Yes, let's…"

Neither of us spoke until we were back in the playhouse.

Sharon picked up a piece of red carpet, shaking some dirt off it. "I thought these were free samples, Paula."

"Me too." I sorted through the rug remnants. "Gosh, they look kind of used up now."

Sharon frowned thoughtfully and then lit up. "I know…we can wash them in my toy washing machine."

Problem solved. We loaded me, the book, and a bagful of samples we'd torn out of it into my brother's wagon and Sharon pulled it all back to her house.

"*Now* what are you two up to?" Bernie mumbled around a mouthful of clothespins. Her back was to us, so we hurried by.

"Nothing," we sang out in sweet innocence, parking the wagon around the back of the house beyond any prying eyes. Luckily, Bernie had lots of wet laundry to hang, so she left us to our project.

Sharon ran inside to get her battery-operated Little Sweetheart Wringer Washing Machine. It had cost $5.95 so it counted as two regular Christmas presents. She poured two cups of water into the tub, adding a capful of Brecks's shampoo before jamming in the first load. Much to our dismay, Little Sweetheart could only hold two rug samples at a time. Sharon pushed the 'on' button. We held our breaths as the toy emitted a satisfying hum. "Darn it," she cried, "this will take forever."

Unfortunately, we didn't have to wait that long. Little Sweetheart shimmied, shook, and finally produced a sad pintsized wail before toppling over on its side. It died before it finished a single cycle.

Sharon gave her toy machine a hard kick and then ran back into the house, emerging with of big bowl in her arms. While I ran water into it from the hose, Sharon squirted shampoo in until she had a decent head of frothy bubbles. All of the pieces of carpet fit in and looked much cleaner when we set them out on the picnic table to dry in the sun.

It took no time at all. "Gosh, they sure swelled up," I remarked, laying a rug square out on the table so I could flatten it with my chin.

Sharon held up a blotchy lump of wool for my inspection. "And some of the colors ran."

Undaunted by the fiasco, she hurried into the house yet again, this time bringing out a bottle of Elmer's glue. As we baked in the sun, we set to pasting the samples back onto page after page.

We had difficulty closing the book because all the samples were so puffed up. Sharon and I took turns sitting on the giant volume and after it flattened out a little, we managed to shut it.

"Good as new," Sharon proclaimed with relief and delight. She looked over at me and shrugged her shoulders. "Well, almost as good."

Without wanting to put Bernie on alert, we tiptoed back inside and put the book on the kitchen table before Sharon pulled me home in the wagon. The next morning Sharon told me that Bernie had placed the book outside on the back steps with a note that said: NOT INTERESTED. The salesman retrieved it without a word. Fortunately for the little home improvement twins, we never saw him again.

On Saturdays, cousin Debbie and I often stayed overnight at Grandma Ida's. Even after fighting all day, we pleaded with our parents to let us sleep over. We made a tent in the living room by draping a sheet over the backs of three kitchen chairs. We crawled inside to inspect my new Davy Crockett doll made by Madame Alexander. Davy wore a brown buckskin shirt and pants and a tiny coonskin cap. We spent several minutes undressing him. We had to carefully peel off his underpants because they were glued on. We could hardly wait to see if he was anatomically correct.

We were disappointed that he had the same empty space between his legs as all of our girl dolls. "My brother sure doesn't look like this," I told Debbie, who was still an only child. We gave a little jump when Grandma Ida lifted a corner of the sheet and caught us red-handed, inspecting Davy's non-existent genitals.

"It's time for you cowpokes to get into bed," she said, ignoring our prurient interest in Davy's crotch.

We giggled hysterically, following Grandma into a small bedroom off the living room. "Now you two go straight to sleep," she ordered, turning down the bed. The sheets, made out of rough muslin, felt like sandpaper on your feet.

"Night, Grandma," we said, cuddling next to each other to get warm. We were exhausted after hours of make believe and let's pretend. First, we had pretended to drive in Uncle Bill's old Model T, taking turns at the wheel and honking the horn. We didn't see our moms when they crept around the back of the car and gave it a hard push forward.

We'd both screamed while Mommy and Auntie Dot bent over and laughed. Debbie leaned out the window, red with embarrassment and rage. "That's not funny, Mommy," she had wailed. Not to us, at least...

"It *was* pretty funny," I admitted as we lay there in the dark recalling our antics.

"Go to sleep girls," Grandma called from her bedroom.

But we still couldn't.

Debby rolled over on her side of the bed.

"Does your stomach still feel icky, Paula."

"Not anymore," I whispered. "But I'm never going to try smoking cigarette butts again."

"Me either," Debbie agreed.

Like all genuine cowpokes, we needed our smokes and had gathered up several butts from Grandma's driveway. Since we weren't allowed to play with matches, we lit our ciggies on the little flame from the gas heater in the kitchen. The real cigarettes scorched my throat, so I experimented with rolling up a piece of paper and substituting it for the real thing. I leaned over the heater. A flame blazed up the roll of paper and singed my bangs before I dropped it on the floor. Luckily, Grandma never noticed the burn in the linoleum.

"Burnt hair sure smells bad," Debbie complained sleepily, ending her observation with a snore.

The next morning Daddy arrived to pick me up. Debbie was still asleep so we tiptoed out to avoid disturbing her. Daddy hoisted me up into his truck and laid a bag from Stanton's Grocery in my lap. I shook it until a small box fell out. "Oh, Daddy, my own cigarettes! Thank you." The brand he purchased was made of mint candy with a pink blob painted on one end so it looked like it was lit.

"No more smoking butts from Grandma's driveway, promise?"

I took in a long drag on my Camel and blew out pretend smoke. "It's a deal, I promise."

After that, Debbie and I bought and sucked on candy cigarettes at every opportunity. We found the glamour of drawing in each phony breath and then exhaling it in exaggerated sighs impossible to resist.

Daddy patted me on the knee. "So, are you happy to be home from Shriners?"

His questions shocked me out of my smoking reverie. "Of course I'm happy. Who wouldn't be?"

He smiled as I continued to consider his question.

For all that I rejoiced in my release from Shriners, returning home took weeks of adjustment on my part. In those heady first days of my homecoming I'd felt like a princess; even Mommy gave me the royal treatment for a while. Almost as soon as I had stepped into our living room after the long drive back from San Francisco, I encountered a backlog of birthday and Christmas packages waiting in the corner where the Christmas tree had stood. I ploughed through the goods in no time, ripping off wrappings with my teeth, even though I knew Mommy preferred to save the paper to reuse.

Several minutes had rushed by before I noticed the major change in my sleeping arrangements. Daddy had taken down some walls in David's and my shared bedroom and reconfigured it into two separate bedrooms, one for each of us.

I loved my new room, but I missed sleeping in the same bedroom as David. Daddy still read to us each night from *Mother West Wind's* storybooks, my brother listening at the foot of my bed before retiring to his own room. It just wasn't the same. It felt strange and awfully sad to me.

Sleeping alone was a change I hadn't anticipated. My first night home, I repeated the Lord's Prayer and sang "Day Is Done" after Daddy kissed me good night, but I missed the girls on the ward chiming in. Before long, I resumed my old habit of holding my breath and counting to one hundred to make sure I wouldn't die in my sleep.

"You're afraid again, aren't you?" David remarked after story time.

I nodded, swiping at my eyes.

A smile lit up David's face as he ran into his bedroom and returned with his old white radio. "I got a new radio for Christmas so you can have this one. It'll keep you company," he consoled me. And it did. At night, I'd stare at the bright orange light coming from the radio dial and pretend that I was the daughter in *The Life of Riley* or the teacher's pet in *Our Miss Brooks* until I fell asleep. If I woke in the night, I'd kick off my blankets and holler for Daddy to come cover me up. Back at home again, nestled in the crook of his arm, I'd drift off feeling peaceful and safe until morning.

13

ACADEMIA

Just before I turned six, the dull routine of home life gave way to days of shopping for my first school clothes, finding me a lunch box, and a visit to my brace man, Mr. Hawkins. Daddy had to take off work to drive us there because my mother just couldn't see herself behind the wheel of a car with her bad nerves.

"You're going to have to see yourself there and soon," Daddy said, "because I can't keep taking off from work to drive you and Paula everyplace."

My mother poked around in her purse to dodge my father's frown. "Watch the road, Jack. You're making me nervous."

Daddy jerked the car up in front of Mr. Hawkins's office.

"Bess will be picking us up, so you can get right back to work. Jack—" She snapped her fingers "—like that." She dragged me out of the back seat and slammed the door shut. The tires screeched as my father spun out into the street.

I smelled the fresh new leather and glue as soon as we walked into the tiny storefront office. A tall man with black hair and wearing a green handyman's apron greeted us. He twisted around on his stiff legs and smiled as he bent over to study me.

I liked Mr. Hawkins because he knew what it felt like to have people stare at him the way they stared at me. He was a war hero, having no legs and only one and a half arms to show for it. He wore a hook to take the place of his missing arm part and a glass eye, which seemed to be headed in the wrong direction.

"So, who do we have here?" he asked, as if he didn't remember me. "No, wait a minute, it's right on the tip..."

"You have Paula," I blurted out, wincing when my mother pinched my arm, I guess because I had rudely interrupted him. Also, I think my father had put her in a bad mood.

"Looks like we're going to have to fit you with a bigger leg brace," Mr. Hawkins observed, lifting me up onto a wooden table to examine my old orthopedic relic. He placed a large sheet of paper under my bad leg and traced around it with a fat pencil. He wrote down measurements and notes on the paper.

"Do I still have to wear these brown high tops on my brace? They look like old people's shoes and kids don't wear them in first grade."

"As a matter of fact, I've got something else for you." Mr. Hawkins winked at me as he disappeared into his shop in the back.

I got excited, imagining myself finally getting to wear a pair of Mary Janes, made of shiny patent leather. Maybe in red.

Mr. Hawkins returned, handing me a small shoebox. I struggled with the lid, finally opening it with my teeth. I carefully folded back the tissue paper, exposing bright white leather. Oh, well, so they weren't red Mary Janes, but at least they weren't brown. Maybe they were sandals. Sandals would be okay, I told myself.

What I pulled out of the box was nowhere near okay. Tears stung my eyes and clogged up my throat. "But these are baby shoes," I whimpered. "High top baby shoes."

Mr. Hawkins smiled. "But look, they're not that ugly old brown color."

Mommy poked me. "What do you say?"

I glared up at my mother. "I say they're high top baby shoes," I hissed, pulling my arm away before she could pinch it.

My next big disappointment came when I learned that I would be going to a different school than my brother or the other kids in our neighborhood. My mother and I caught a ride with Auntie Bess that opening day in September 1953. Franklin Elementary School offered special classes for crippled kids like me. The long, L-shaped yellow building had real oak floors that smelled clean and were slippery. Mommy gripped me under the arm so I wouldn't fall and wreck her day. Her high heels clicked on the shiny surface, a sound I knew well and found comforting.

I have vague memories from that morning of listening to the radio coverage about Russia exploding an atomic bomb and causing the start of what they called The Cold War, but my main focus centered on the new shirtwaist dress I was wearing. I loved it!

The top glowed a bright orange while the skirt was brown and covered with ABC's and addition and subtraction problems with the answers. This took some of the pressure off me because I figured I could copy whatever test answers I needed with a quick glance at my dress.

Over my protestations, Mommy stuffed me into a stiff plaid coat with a velveteen collar. It looked nice, but I could barely bend my arms, encased as they were in the heavy woolen sleeves.

"You won't be bending your arms all that much," my mother responded when I complained. "Besides, you'll be taking it off when you get in the classroom."

I had some notion of what school was like because I had accompanied my mother to David's third grade class when it was her turn to be a room mother. This meant she had to bake and bring thirty cupcakes to school to celebrate my brother's birthday. My mother hated to bake and the idea of having to come up with the cupcakes made her nervous and cranky. The only dessert Mom made was Jell-O, which we ate right out of the little tin molds.

When Mommy and I entered my classroom, I saw it was nothing like my brother's. First, there were students of all different ages, from teenagers to four-or five-year-olds. I spotted a boy about my size who wore a leg brace and seemed pretty normal, but a majority of my fifteen classmates were jerking around in their seats, some drooling, others babbling and making weird noises.

It was my first experience with shame, which flooded over me when I looked around the classroom. *I am not one of them, I am not one of them*, I repeated to myself.

A tired-looking old lady introduced herself to my mother and me. "I'm Mrs. McGill," she said, pushing a thick pair of glasses up on her nose.

She pointed at clothes hooks in one corner of the room. "All our boys and girls hang up their wraps here," she explained, pointing to a row of jackets and sweaters dangling haphazardly from hooks in the wall.

My mother helped me off with my coat and much to my dismay, told me that she and Auntie Bess wouldn't be back to pick me up until three o'clock. Mommy vanished. It was almost as bad as being left at Shriners. My throat knotted up while tears stung my eyes.

"Now let's act like a big girl," Mrs. McGill chirped, taking my hand and steering me over to a desk between Timmy Wilson, who had polio and Robby Dames, who smiled at me as he jerked and waved his arms around. Robby's body moved in short spasms.

"After we get you settled, Paula, it will be time for lunch," the teacher explained. She opened up the lid of my desk and pointed to a *Dick and Jane* reader, a box of fat color crayons, a pad of paper, and two large black pencils. I was momentarily overcome by the sight of my very own school supplies, but my enthusiasm faded when Mrs. McGill shut the lid and announced that following lunch we would get out our navy blue cots so we could take a nap. I'd never been a napper and the idea of using school time to sleep was stupid. I could see I wasn't going to fit in here either, but for the most part, that was a relief.

"Boys and girls, let's go quietly to the table and get out our lunches," she cooed. I pulled a chair from under a big wooden table and sat between Timmy and Robby. Timmy had a Roy Rogers lunch box while Robbie brought his sandwich in a brown paper bag. No one but me had a stupid kid-sized wicker fishing basket. Mommy insisted it was lighter and smaller than a lunch box and I would be able to carry it myself. I unfastened the little hook and took out my favorite meal, a peanut butter and mayonnaise sandwich on puffy white bread. I smashed it flat before taking my first bite.

The next day, a tall thin teacher named Mr. Beebe drove me to school. He was paid to cart around crippled and mentally retarded kids. He drove a smelly old station wagon with candy wrappers and apple cores on the floor. By the time he reached our house, the car had already filled up with Robby, Kathy, Benet, and Owen. I squeezed into the back seat and slid below my window so nobody could see me. I remained in that uncomfortable position for all the years Mr. Beebe drove me to and from Franklin School.

When we reached school, my day traveled downhill fast.

Mrs. McGill caught me at the door. "Before you sit down, Paula, you need to hang up your coat." She pointed to the black hooks along the wall.

"I can't," I mumbled. "My hands don't work all that good."

The teacher wagged her finger at me. "'Can't' is a word we never use in here."

I searched my limited vocabulary for another word to express my current dilemma. None came to mind.

"Sometimes 'can't' means 'won't try,'" Mrs. McGill admonished me. "When you decide to hang up your coat, you may take your seat."

I smiled weakly. I eyed the buttons of my coat, willing them open. No such luck.

"Fine then," Mrs. McGill huffed. "You can just stand there."

And I did. Until lunchtime when Mrs. Smith, our teacher's aide, saved me. She waited for Mrs. McGill to leave the room before helping me slip off my coat. "Just between you and me, Mrs. M's an old fuddy-duddy," she joked. If only Mrs. Smith were my teacher.

It came as no surprise when Mr. Beebe's wreck on wheels broke down forcing Daddy to pick me up that afternoon.

He lifted me into the truck. "How was your second day of school?"

"I hate it, Daddy. You didn't tell me I'd be in a class for weirdoes."

My father scooted me over closer to him. "Listen, Sweetheart, some of those kids have what's called cerebral palsy, but most of them have as good a noggin as you do." He tapped my head, but I pulled away from him.

"Not Robby's head. He jabbers and shakes and makes snot come out of his nose *on purpose.*"

Daddy sighed. "Well, some of the kids are mentally retarded, Paula, but you should feel sorry for them and thankful that you're not."

I felt nothing of the sort. "Don't you see? Everybody's going to think I'm retarded too."

Daddy patted my knee playfully. "Look, Paula, Franklin is the only school that accepts handicapped children. Unless you want a home teacher, it's all you've got."

A vision of long days spent at home with Mommy stopped me in my tracks. For the rest of the ride, I sat in silence, listening to the comforting purr of the truck.

During dinner, I broke down again, tearfully explaining to my mother how long I had to stand around because I couldn't hang up my coat.

"Don't be such a moaning Mary," she pooh-poohed.

"Don't be such a moaning Paula," David mimicked.

"Make him shut up, Daddy."

My father whacked my brother hard on his shoulder, making David's spoon fly out of his hand.

Both of us ended up crying. I hated David for teasing me and I hated myself for making my father hit him. I regretted saying anything. Mommy calmed Daddy down before he could do any more damage to my brother.

Before bed that night, she took me into the kitchen and showed me some of Daddy's oldest work shirts. "Pick one."

A bit confused, I chose my favorite, a soft brown fabric that still smelled like Daddy.

Mommy slipped it on me and grabbed a pair of scissors, cutting off all the shirt's buttons. "Now then," she said, posing me in front of her. "Problem solved." She smiled when she rolled up the sleeves to expose my hands.

If only all my problems could be solved so easily. When I arrived at school the next morning wearing Daddy's shirt instead of my heavy coat, all I had to do was shimmy back and forth until the shirt fell off. Then I bent over, grabbing the shirt collar in my mouth and hung it over a hook. Mrs. McGill didn't think much of the solution, but as long as I could hang the shirt up, what could the fuddy-duddy do to me? Best of all, having Mommy on my side, helping me resolve an issue I was too young to handle, relieved and comforted me almost as much as if she had picked me up in her arms and hugged me. *Almost.*

Left to my own devices, drawing and printing came easy for me during my first half-year at school. By threading my pencil through the fingers of my good hand and pressing down on it with my chin, I scribbled along with the best of them, but Mrs. Beck, Franklin's physical therapist, was determined to have me write like a normal kid. She fitted me with a thumb and pointer finger cast that poised my hand in the correct position for holding a pencil. As if that wasn't enough, she also dragged a special chair into the class, rigged up with slings, pulleys and weights. She put my arms through the loops, letting them hang there to give me, as she put it, "free range of motion."

It did nothing of the sort. Hampered by a finger cast and arms strung up above my waist, I could barely manage to hit the paper with my pencil. For two or three days, I made many attempts to print, paint, and paste words and numbers into my workbooks. Finally, I'd had enough, so I threw down my pencil in an act of rebellion that felt a lot like gumption to me. Mrs. Beck abandoned her attempts to alter my unorthodox grip on a pencil and allowed me to return to my own method of printing out my assignments.

As the winter months passed, I continued to share my school days with an ensemble of crippled, jerking, drooling classmates. I wanted to be in the real first grade, but that was going to take some doing.

Miss Asselstein, an elderly brute of a principal with wiry white hair, took a shining to me because of my get-up-and-go. Most kids feared Miss Asselstein and her wooden paddle. She was especially hard on the sixth grade boys from the wrong side of town. If she caught any boy running in the hallway, she would grab him by his collar and tear it clean off his shirt. Too much gumption can backfire if you're not careful.

Miss Asselstein worshipped neatness and cleanliness, which was why Cathy Kurkindall disgusted her. Cathy looked and smelled like a pigsty and Miss Asselstein wouldn't let the girl anywhere near her. I thought she acted mean-spirited when she avoided Cathy like some piece of garbage with cooties. The teacher reminded me of one of the ugly stepsisters who tormented Cinderella.

At rest, the features of Cathy's fair-skinned face settled into a recognizable six-year-old girl, but wide-awake, Cathy drooled, laughed a not quite human laugh, and jerked every which way when she walked down the hall. Cathy took a liking to me and since I couldn't run the other way when she careened into the classroom, I kept her at bay by promising to read to her during naptime after Mrs. McGill left for her lunch break. Cathy gradually understood how easily I tipped over and stopped throwing her arms around me until I sat down.

Cathy rode to school with Mrs. Smith and a carload of my fellow classmates, so at least I didn't have to worry about normal kids seeing me in the same station wagon and assuming I was like her. Cathy had a foster mother who sent her to school smelling of dirt and sweat and urine. Her blonde hair clung to her sticky forehead and when she bent over, you could see that her underpants had more elastic than cloth because of the big holes. I felt sad for Cathy and agreed with my mother's observation that some mothers weren't nearly so fussy about clean clothes and brushed hair as my mother was.

My mother always rambled on about how lucky I was to be kept clean and smelling fresh. I needed no reminding that I *was* better off than the kids whose parents neglected them or boarded them out. Foster care meant you only had to be fed, clothed, and sheltered. Regular kids had it bad enough, but if you were crippled and mentally retarded on top of everything else, in most cases nobody but the dregs of society picked you out to take home.

One afternoon as I prepared to read to Cathy from my *Dick and Jane* reader, she presented me with a bunched up piece of paper containing a barrette she wanted me to have. I unwrapped a little plastic kitten with one ear chipped off. I oohed and aahed over it, which pleased Cathy. "I do this for you," she drooled.

Before I could stop her, she had clipped the broken kitten to a hank of my hair. I didn't want to hurt her feelings, so I left the barrette in place as I read about Dick running and Jane jumping and their dog Spot barking bow-wow-wow. I used a gruff voice when I barked, sending Cathy into fits of laughter.

I discovered an amazing thing about Cathy during our reading sessions. Once when I stopped mid-sentence in the story, Cathy continued mouthing the words to herself. *She could read!* I just hadn't been able to comprehend what I thought was mindless chatter. After that, we took turns reading aloud, and little by little, I began to understand Cathy's speech. She could talk as well as I could, it was just in a language I couldn't understand yet. Now, not only did I feel badly for Cathy's having a rotten foster mother, but it hurt even more to see her mind trapped in a body over which she had little control.

Two of the older boys in the class, men actually, were also trapped in their bodies by cerebral palsy. Owen and Danny were taking a typing course in case someone hired them as secretaries. Once they turned twenty-one, their schooling, what there was of it, ended and if they were lucky, which didn't seem to be the case, family and friends would take care of them.

For the most part, people like Danny, Owen, and Cathy were placed in institutions at birth and lived out their lives there. It would take a social revolution sparked by the disability movement to change things, and that was still years away.

14

A STEP AHEAD

I handled all the first grade work so successfully the faculty decided I could go to the real first grade at Franklin and mix in with the normal kids during read-aloud time. Miss Hamilton was the teacher for the upper first grade. She stood tall and graceful like a giraffe, even though she had to wear a neck brace. I'd begun to notice that people with no legs or who wore braces could hold down real jobs, which made me think maybe I could too when I grew up.

My brace squeaked when I walked over to the reading circle. My ugly white high-top shoes had already captured everybody's attention. A bony kid with red hair and freckles scooted out the chair next to him and motioned for me to sit down. Brad Brisbon towered over the rest of the first graders, making him stick out like me. I liked him right away.

"Paula will be joining us for our reading circle," Miss Hamilton explained. "Please make her feel at home."

"Is she a retard like those other kids in special class?" a freckle-faced girl named Laura asked. She eyed me with contempt while she pulled at one of her long brown braids. I imagined leaning over and pulling the other one right out of her stupid head.

My face burned red hot. "Polio does not affect my brain," I stated emphatically. "I have weak arms and legs, but I am," I thought a moment, "sharp as a whip." This became my standard response when kids called me mentally retarded.

Not the least bit impressed, Laura stared at my high-top baby shoes, scrunching her nose like they smelled funny. When I caught her eye, I gave her a murderous look and she shut up. Gradually I learned how to use my glares and words to defend myself against kids like Laura.

Right from the start, I could read far better than she could. When I read aloud, I made my voice sound very grownup and professional. Laura just squeaked and stumbled over easy words like *could* and *should*. Why did God give snotty girls like her pink leather Mary Janes?

In the regular classrooms, they had ball monitors and book monitors and at Miss Hamilton's suggestion, I was assigned a monitor of my own. Susan Lewis volunteered to be my first monitor. "What do you want me to do?" she asked politely.

"Mostly just carry my fishing basket lunch pail and make sure nobody knocks me down at recess."

If I did fall, Susan could help me back on to my feet with lightning speed so no teachers, or worse yet, my mother, ever knew I'd fallen. Mommy became furious whenever I fell down. If I fell at home, she'd pick me up and give me a good shake. "See what happens when you hurry or don't look where you're going?" She said it took ten years off her life every time she saw me stumble. If I did cry, it wasn't over the bump or skinned knee I incurred; it was because I didn't want her to yell at me for being careless; I felt bad for taking so many years off her life.

With my first taste of what would later become "mainstreaming," I begged my parents to let me stay all day in Miss Hamilton's class. The school officials balked at the suggestion, but in a turn of luck, I did become an all-day student, thanks to my father's quick thinking.

Like the other kids in my special education class, I had physical therapy every day with Mrs. Beck. She taught me how to walk straighter and to fall the right way so I wouldn't hurt myself too badly. I learned to fall on an inch-thick soft gray mat: knee first, hip second, elbow, and finally shoulder. If I was lucky, I kept my head from hitting the ground too hard and cracking open.

One day, when I was getting into position to fall on the mat, Mrs. Beck lost her grip on me and I landed hard on my elbow. I heard a little crack and then a searing pain raced up my polio arm. I had trained myself not to cry too loud when I fell to avoid upsetting my mother's nerves, but she was the last thing on my mind as I opened up my mouth and emitted a long gruesome wail.

This had a very negative effect on Mrs. Beck. After helping me sit up, she raced around the room until she found some cloth to use for a sling. As I continued to scream in ever-increasing decibels, Mrs. McGill ran into the room and surmising an emergency, hurried to the office phone and placed a call to my mother.

Mommy still hadn't learned to drive and since Auntie Bess was out of town, she called my father.

Daddy raced over to the school, still wearing his inky work clothes and driving his green Studebaker truck. Mrs. Beck tried to explain what had happened, but my father yelled at her to get out of the way. Lifting me into his arms, he ran back to the truck.

Daddy never got mad at me when I fell, so I was glad he was the one to drive me to the hospital. All the way there I kept screaming, "I'm dead, I'm dead. Daddy, I'm dead." And I wished I were.

At a loss for how to comfort me, my father made up three or four stories featuring me as the main character and for a time my arm hurt a little less.

Dr. Ely sent me straight for x-rays and when he came into the office, he stated I had broken my arm in two places. A nurse wheeled me into another large room where I was fitted with a cast. It had a big loop across the top of the lower arm so you could pull a sling through it. This was a new technique, which rapidly fell out of favor with Mommy because nothing fit over the loop and she had to sew three special blouses and skirts for me to wear to school.

That first night of my accident, I slept with Mommy and Daddy, even though it wasn't Sunday morning. In a way, I liked being wounded because I got very special treatment. Better yet, since Mrs. Beck, not me, had been the careless one, Mommy wasn't mad at me for falling. When she came home from her Friday night shopping with Auntie Bess, she presented me with two sets of paper dolls. I hadn't received any new ones since I'd had the mumps and stayed with Auntie Bess to give my mother a rest.

My broken arm proved to be a lucky break. In return for not suing the school and Mrs. Beck, my father arranged for me to be in normal classes full-time. I still had to ride with Mr. Beebe and the rest of the kids in Special Ed, but from first grade on, I attended regular, everyday school. I was laugh-out-loud happy that no one would take me for a brain-damaged child, just a crippled one.

I insisted on participating in all the recess activities. Gradually, my left arm gained enough strength for me to spin it around like the blade of a windmill. By tying one end of the jump rope around my wrist, I could rotate my arm in perfect timing with the girl holding the other end. Susan paired up with me for this game since she knew to drop her end of the rope if a kid tripped over or stepped on it. Otherwise, I would be pulled down flat on my face. Then I'd have to dream up some story about how I got gravel burns on my nose and chin.

I also loved tetherball, and while other playmates batted the ball with their hand, I hit it with my head. This became a popular alternative way to play unless a recess supervisor spotted us and stopped the game. "It's not good to hit your head like that, Paula. Doesn't it give you a headache?"

"Not so far."

"Well, I want you to stop it right now. You can sit on the bench and keep score."

I would obey the supervisor's directions until she disappeared to hound the rowdy kids on the other side of the yard.

"Your turn, Paula," Susan or Mary Elroy encouraged me and I started head-butting the ball again. Accommodating my needs so I could play with them, my friends invented new strategies for hopscotch and kickball. I could send the fat bouncy ball quite a distance with my strong leg while a designated runner covered the bases for me.

Part of the motivation for the kids to include me in playground life were the highly imaginative "let's pretends" and fantasy dramas I created. The prettiest girls loved my made-up rags-to-riches sagas featuring them as unappreciated princesses or damsels in distress. I liked playing one of the offspring of a wicked stepmother. Sheila, a stout ruddy-faced girl with a bad temper vented much of her anger and frustrations about life through her role as the vengeful stepmother. She had a switch and whipped my stepsister and me at the slightest provocation, leaving more than one scratch or welt that had our parents puzzling over the mysterious wounds.

"If I switched you that hard," my father noted while applying a Band-Aid to my minor leg injury, "you would be screaming your head off."

It was true to a point, but Daddy's anger over one of my sassy remarks was one hundred times scarier than Sheila's huffing and puffing. Plus, we could call an end to our playground scenes if they got too violent, something not possible when Daddy got on a roll—my brother still the focus of Daddy's blowouts. I would stand screaming, "Daddy! Daddy, stop!" while Mommy fluttered around ineffectively, calling out "Calm down, Jack." Never once did she step in to shield David from one of my father's slaps or ear-boxings.

15

THE CATAPULT

David and I slouched in the back seat of the Ford as we accompanied Mommy and Daddy up the winding dusty road to Uncle Kite's and Aunt Letha's house. Uncle Kite was one of Mommy's nine brothers, the father of our cousins Mike and Steve.

Daddy looked at us in his rearview mirror.

David squirmed restlessly and pushed me over to my side of the car. My father shook his head and pounded on the horn. "Get out of my way," he yelled at a little old lady driving a monster Buick. Daddy rarely swore at little old lady drivers, but he had just finished a long tirade at David, which put them both in a bad mood.

"I want no repeat of the shenanigans you and Steve pulled last time," he smoldered. "Do you understand?"

"Yes, Daddy," David said, followed by a big sigh.

I was practicing silence. I found our last visit to Stevie's and Mike's quite entertaining. Actually, I admired my brother for his ingenuity. He had the best ideas about how to make go-cart racers, came up with amazing original Halloween costumes, and added a touch of intrigue and semi-violence to the pretend games Debbie and I played at Grandma Ida's house. My brother loved to create fly-by-the-seat-of-your-pants projects and had a well-deserved reputation for building the best forts on Pigeon Point. On our last visit to Uncle Kite, David had surpassed himself, coming up with his best-ever idea: a catapult.

"What's a catpull?" I had asked from my vantage point on the front steps. Since there was nobody my age to play with, Daddy told David he had to let me tag along with him and Stevie. "Does it hurt the cat?"

My brother smacked his head with an opened palm. "No dummy, it's a *catapult*. It sorta works like a big slingshot that knights used to knock down castle walls." He observed my puzzled expression. "Just sit there and watch," he ordered. "I'll show you how it works. Come on, Stevie, let's get started."

Stevie blinked in the bright sunshine, rubbing his head to make sure his buzz cut was standing up. "What do you want me to do?" he'd asked. I don't think he knew much more than I did when it came to making a catapult. David dragged Stevie over to where an old inner tube rested against the side of the barn. He rolled it until satisfied that it would be perfect for his project. He looked around warily before taking his Cub Scout hunting knife out of his jacket pocket.

"Mommy said you can't use that for a toy," I scolded, happy to find a familiar role to play in the enterprise.

David picked his nose and threw a booger at me. "Just keep quiet or we won't let you watch."

I returned to my former role as silent observer.

"Get those big garden shears over there," David directed Stevie. "We need a bigger blade to cut this rubber." They worked their tongues as well as their hands and after a long passage of swear words and grunts, they succeeded in cutting the inner tube into long, wide pieces.

Steven stared at the rubbery strip in his hands. "I don't get it. How's it supposed to work?"

"Here, gimme it," David demanded. "You just hold it and stand by your tree while I take my end and tie it around this tree trunk. Stevie watched David walk over to the second scrawny apple tree, a twin to the one Uncle Kite was nursing back to health after our wicked winter of sleet and hail.

David tied his strip firmly around the trunk. "Now you do the same with your end."

Stevie looked lost. Never a patient kid, David strode over to our cousin, grabbed the end of Stevie's strip, and gave it a hard pull until he could reach Stevie's tree and secure it firmly. "See, you take one end and tie it to your tree and then stretch it out like this and tie this end to my tree." David moved between the two trees. With both ends secured, he gave the rubber strip a hard twang, smiling when it snapped back into place.

Next, the boys searched around the yard for an appropriate object to serve as the missile. David picked up a big round rock the size of a baseball. "This outta do it," he said with the confidence of any good inventor.

Giving no thought to the possible trajectory of the rock, David and Stevie positioned it into the rubber sling and pulled it back as hard as they could. "Ready, set...go!" David ordered.

The catapult worked perfectly until the rock was stopped in mid-flight by the door of Uncle Kite's brand new second-hand car. One of his two apple trees suffered collateral damage as well, its trunk snapping in two.

David and Steve's momentary taste of triumph dissolved as they inspected the large dent in the car door. "Ah, gee, Dad's going to kill me," Stevie whimpered. He gave David a snarly look. "You and your big ideas." Stevie pulled out the tail of his t-shirt, spit on it and frantically tried to rub out the scratch that accompanied the dent.

David and I looked at each other hopelessly. We knew Uncle Kite wouldn't kill his offspring, but he'd be cutting off a whipping branch to use on him.

I hobbled over to try to comfort Stevie while I examined the wounded vehicle. "Look," I pointed out, "you can tell the car used to be red." I patted my cousin's limp arm. "You're right Stevie, your Dad *is* going to kill you."

"Us," he yelled at David. "He's going to be killing both me and you," Stevie cried, wiping a clot of snot from his nose.

The three of us trudged back into the house and stood around nervously, waiting for something to happen. Uncle Kite glanced up from the card table where our parents played another round of Crazy Aces. Daddy slapped two cards down, heaved a sigh, and declared, "I'm out!" He helped pick up the cards and slipped the deck into its box. Mommy and Aunt Letha got up to do the dinner dishes.

Uncle Kite remained seated, eyeballing Stevie suspiciously. He motioned for him to move closer. "What's wrong, son?"

Stevie shrugged. "Nuthin'."

"Did you show David our new car?" he prodded.

"Yep."

Uncle Kite smiled at Daddy. "Come on, Jack, let me show you the car. She's a real beauty. Got her for a song." He put his hands on Stevie's shoulders and steered him out to the yard.

David and I hung back, watching the three of them out the living room window. We could only wait and observe from afar.

Uncle Kite's smile slowly transformed into a row of gritted teeth. "Holy shit!" he bellowed. David and I exchanged glances, happy that we'd remained in the house. We watched Uncle Kite stare at the side of his car, stroking the dent in disbelief.

He whacked Stevie on the side of the head. "Damn it, did you do this?"

Stevie turned to see us standing at the window. "David helped me," he confessed, pointing at the window. "It was all his idea."

Now Daddy turned, frowning at the two of us as we stood in the safety of our vantage point.

"I bet you're going to get in trouble too, David," I said. He nodded.

And he did. Trying to remain calm and collected in my uncle's company, Daddy called out to my brother. "You," he yelled with a pointing finger. "Out here. Pronto."

"Stevie's a big fat tattletale," David grumbled, slowly moving through the front door and down the steps to join his partner in crime.

Following Uncle Kite's lead, Daddy whacked David's head. I couldn't watch the rest. I went into Stevie's bedroom and got on his rocking horse, which was actually a swan. I rocked back and forth for a long time, soothing myself every time I heard yelling and crying coming from the living room where Uncle Kite continued to rant and rage.

David and Stevie each had to stand in a corner and miss out on the lime Jell-O dessert topped with whipped cream.

"It wasn't all that good," I told David on the drive home. "It had carrots in it."

David leaned against the backseat, poking his shoe into a hole in our car's floor mat.

"I don't care," he said, smiling to himself. "I can't believe I finally got a catapult to work. Wait 'til I show the Barnhart brothers," he reflected, a faraway gleam in his eyes. "It's the best darn catapult I've ever seen," he boasted proudly.

I had to agree. "If only that stupid car hadn't got in the way," I told him. "I bet that rock could have gone another hundred miles."

My brother grinned. "Easily. Oh, no doubt about it, sister."

True to his promise to Daddy, David refrained from wrecking anything on our next visit to Uncle Kite's. And for the first time ever, my brother and Stevie let me join in on two rounds of Monopoly.

16

THE SHOOT-OUT

The porch thermometer registered a sweltering sixty degrees in the shade on the day of the shootout. That in and of itself seemed a good omen, since most mornings Eureka lay swathed in a dense fogbank. I scanned the bedroom until I spied my new cowboy outfit draped over the chair: jeans, red checkered shirt, chaps, holster, vest, sunglasses with Colt 45's adorning the corners, and a hat. A solitary cowboy boot stood in the corner. I had to wear a white high-top shoe on my brace leg, which spoiled the whole effect.

Mommy looked in. "Jesus, I forgot I had to get you ready." I felt as if I were a big rock chained around her neck. It wore her out always having to do so much for me.

Still, I did make, as my mother pointed out, "Quite a picture" in my get up. The reason I was allowed to wear my cowboy outfit was that we were heading to Sequoia, birthplace of my father and one of the few places where Mommy thought cowboy gear appropriate. The flat lay miles from any town where I might stand out more than usual.

Days earlier, Dave Hoppy had dropped by our house to take my picture for the *Humboldt Standard* to publicize the upcoming county fair. Mr. Hoppy and my father worked together at the newspaper and one of the benefits of being a child of an employee was you sometimes got your picture in the paper. This served as my introduction to small-town nepotism.

The way the photo turned out disappointed me. The caption read "Six-year-old Paula Viale anxiously awaits a day at the fair with her pony, Sweetheart." I stood at rigid attention in my cowboy gear, holding Sweetheart, my new pony, by a rope and looking half-crazed with terror. Sweetheart was a nipper and I had the scars to prove it. Still, it was good publicity and gained me extra attention from the students in my class. Up until then, nobody knew of my intentions to be a cowboy and maybe marry the Lone Ranger. Roy Rogers already had a wife.

Our family adventure started with a bumpy ride in Daddy's new pick-up. This one was pink and white because it had been an ice cream truck before he bought it second-hand. The drive to Sequoia meant two hours of twisting and turning down a serpentine road to the old homestead. I always got carsick and my mother usually had a bad case of nerves, but today it was really worth it. We'd been invited over to Charlie Harms's to pick peaches and make ice cream.

Charlie was a genuine cowboy who wrangled cattle up and down central California for a rich rancher. I couldn't wait for him to see my new outfit...but that was not to be. We came to a sudden stop on the dusty road—Charlie's log cabin ablaze in the meadow as he tried unsuccessfully to put out the flames with a kinked-up garden hose.

As my father ran over to give Charlie a hand, something whizzed by his head. He stopped dead in his tracks. There were popping sounds all around and before I realized what was happening, Daddy grabbed hold of me and my mother, dragging us behind a stand of old-growth redwoods.

"Stay back," he yelled when I tried to peer around the tree, my heart thumping with excitement. Just then, something hit a nearby redwood, exploding pieces of bark everywhere.

"Jesus Christ, Jack," my mother screamed, "was that a bullet?"

My father nodded and my mother glared at him. She had a habit of blaming my father for most of the ill fortune that plagued our family.

Charlie, it turned out, was a gun enthusiast who had stored several rounds of live ammunition in his cabin. It made quite a spectacle. For a child with no sense of mortality, it was a dream come true. Here I was at a real shootout! (Or almost...) And I was wearing my cowboy outfit for the occasion. This was even better than having my picture in the paper.

After the fire burned out, the adults stood around the smoldering embers, commenting on how lucky it was that no one took a bullet. "I guess this means no ice cream," I ventured, poking at the dust with the toe of my cowboy boot. Nobody said much to the contrary, and I had to be content with a Fresh Freeze sundae on the drive back home.

"Did we narrowly escape being killed today?" I asked Daddy that night as he tucked me into bed. My heart pumped pure adrenaline every time I replayed the dramatic shootout in my head.

Daddy started to chuckle, but then turned serious. "Yes siree. We escaped death by the skin of our teeth. Now go to sleep and thank your lucky stars." He switched off the light and closed the door behind him.

I smiled. First I had conquered polio at only six weeks old. Today I had dodged real bullets and lived to tell about it. If I kept at it, I could become a legendary crippled child.

17

PARTY ON, OH HEATHENS

David's and my birthdays came only ten days apart, so Mommy always tried to convince us to celebrate them on the same day and, "Kill two birds with one stone" as she put it. Dead birds or not, David and I insisted on having our cake and ice cream on the real days.

We changed our minds the year Mommy promised us that we could have a genuine go-for-broke party and invite all our cousins, friends, and neighbors if we'd agree to celebrate on the Saturday that fell between our seventh and tenth birthdays.

Who could refuse such a tempting offer? Neither my brother nor I had ever experienced a full-blown birthday party, although we'd attended a slew of them what with our twenty-two cousins and all.

Mommy was pregnant, expecting a baby in April, but she assured my father that her nerves were up to the task, so my brother and I sat down at the kitchen table with our Big Red giant tablets to compose our guest list. Naturally, I would invite Debbie and my cousin Janet and best friend Sharon, while David selected Ronny and Doug Blazina and Sharon's brothers, Barney, Keith, and Mikey. We agreed not to include Gary and Richard Harris because they smelled funny, but since they lived next door and could see over the fence into our yard, Mommy said it would be impolite to leave them out.

"All the more presents for us," David told me.

We returned to our work with fresh enthusiasm.

"Look, I've got fifteen kids on my list," David showed me. This attracted Mommy's attention right away.

Wiping her dishwater hands on her apron, she picked up my list and frowned. "And Paula has fourteen," she muttered. "I think you'd better narrow it down to five or six each." She set the paper down in front of me. "I really doubt if the garbage or mail man could come anyway."

That Friday night before the great event, Daddy drove us to Jones' Variety so we could buy a 'Pin the Tail on the Donkey' game and some cheap party favors. David decided on Chinese handcuffs while I chose paper dolls for the girls. Mommy picked up a bag of balloons and some party hats to round things out.

"What other games should we plan for, Mommy?" I mused, watching Daddy place the $5.11 on the counter.

Mommy thought for a moment. "Well, we can set up 'Drop the Clothespins in the Bottle' and you can play 'Mother May I?'"

"By then it'll be time for cake and ice cream," Daddy added before we could think of anything else to add to the bill.

David and I exchanged glances and grins. We had two other games in mind, but were sure neither Mommy nor Daddy would approve. Sometimes it was better not to ask. We called one game 'The Dentist' and the other 'All You Can Drink.' My brother's genius brain invented both of them. Excitement made sleep impossible. I crept into David's bed and we talked about our plans far into the night. It felt like old times.

The next morning, Mommy whipped up an angel food cake—the only kind she knew how to make—and spread on the butter cream frosting. My brother scooped up any batter left in the bowl while I licked the beaters from the mixer.

We followed the Swedish tradition of opening our presents before getting out of bed. We arose at 6 a.m. before Daddy left for work. He still worked on Saturdays even though the union had set a limit to mandatory overtime. Daddy took advantage of extra hours offered so we could afford luxuries like parties and electricity.

"Wow," my brother exclaimed as he spread out a football game that you played by drawing cards and advancing from one end of the board to the other. He barely hid his disappointment over 'The Cootie Game' where you threw dice and took as many body parts as the dice showed. The player who assembled a complete cootie first won. It took forever.

I received a Miss Revlon teenaged doll who came with three outfits, plus a hat, and real high heeled shoes. I liked her better than my other present, Mr. Potato Head. This popular pastime of the fifties called for a real raw potato to serve as the base. The kit came with a bag of plastic eyes, eyebrows, nose, mouth, and three hats that you were supposed to stick into the potato. Because it was our special day, Daddy played the football game with David and helped me assemble a full-featured potato person before he left for work. David and I decided that the extra time Daddy spent with us qualified as a present unto itself.

The party kicked off at 1:30 p.m. so Mommy wouldn't have to serve lunch. Janet, Sharon, and Debbie all wore pretty dresses made out of the scratchy material Mommy hated. "You'll be uncomfortable in a nylon dress," she warned when I showed her the outfit I wanted to order from the *Sears* catalog. "And I think nylon looks cheap."

"Well, I'm real uncomfortable in my brace and I put up with that," I muttered. I despised my dowdy lavender birthday dress made of cotton with a union label poking into my neck. "Maybe kids would stare at the dress instead of this stupid thing," I grumbled as she buckled up the leather and steel weight I had to drag around on my leg.

"That 'stupid thing' cost seventy-five dollars and you don't even appreciate how hard Daddy had to work to buy it for you."

Mommy got that right. I felt no appreciation, although the price of my stainless steel legging both shocked and outraged me. For that much money, I could have owned a hundred scratchy cheap looking outfits and felt like a princess instead of a crippled kid with a brace and a frumpy dress.

"Let's see what you got," Debbie insisted when the party had split up into sets of boys and girls. I escorted my guests into my room. I waited momentarily, closing my eyes and soaking up all the shrieks of delight as Debbie passed Miss Revlon down the line of enthusiastic admirers.

"She's the most beautiful doll I ever seen," Sharon whispered reverently. Debbie, Janet, and even Judy Lermo agreed. For a moment my brace and useless hand vanished.

Everyone agreed that I had every right to be disappointed over Mr. Potato Head. "I put mine together and set him out by the window," Janet lamented. "A week later he wilted away into a shrunken head with slimy shoots crawling out of him."

"Roots," Judy clarified. She knew because she had received the vegetable wonder last Christmas.

We dressed Miss Teen Revlon in all three of her outfits and strutted her up and down my bed, a plastic model prancing on a lumpy runway. David and the boys played touch football in the backyard, tripping and shoving and knocking each other down like boys do. Later, we all went outside and gathered around the card table.

Mommy had placed a bouquet of flowers in the middle of the cake so you couldn't tell that it sloped a little. She arranged seven candles on one side of it and ten on the other. David and I blew them out together. Mommy served up both chocolate and strawberry ice cream to go with the cake and handed out the paper dolls and Chinese handcuffs.

The paper doll fairies included lots of clothes decorated with flowers and moss. The Chinese handcuffs consisted of tightly rolled up cones of paper. You inserted a middle finger in each end and shoved your hands together as hard as you could. When you tried to pull your fingers out, the cone unrolled, stretching and pinching your digits even tighter. The struggle to escape the paper trap really hurt, which made for a popular party favor.

The angel food cake pleased everyone. After licking the frosting from our sticky hands, David and I divided up our loot.

I struggled to open my first gift, always challenging because I had only my left hand to tear paper and unseal tape.

"Hurry up," Sharon cheered me on. "Try using your floppy hand."

I did my best to hold back tears. I wanted to chop off that hand and get it out of the way for good.

"Here, Paula, let me help you with that," David offered. "Otherwise we'll be here all day." He grabbed the package I held in my teeth and ripped the paper off easy as pie.

Sharon gave me a set of bathroom furniture for my dollhouse. The toilet seat actually went up and down, and the sink had cabinets that opened and shut. Janet also got me furniture, a card table with folding legs and chairs that matched it. Cousin Debbie bought me a set of dominoes, which I could use to build houses for my western town. The Blazina boys gave David a set of twenty-five baseball cards, each with a flat piece of bubble gum inside. The Barnhart boys gave him a cap gun that popped loudly and released a puff of smoke when he shot it.

The best presents came from Richard and Gary Harris. They gave me a small goldfish bowl completely decorated for the tiny fish inside swimming in frantic in circles.

"I won that at the carnival," Gary boasted with pride as he carefully placed the gift on the table. "I had to shoot off the heads of six ducks to win it."

"But it's from both of us," Richard explained, handing David a complete marble set with a beautiful shooter marble.

David and I congratulated ourselves for including the brothers who didn't smell that bad after all.

"Time to drop clothespins in the bottle," Mommy called out from the other side of the yard. She handed cousin Janet five clothespins. Janet had spindly legs, which made it hard for her to balance on them. Everybody laughed at the way she teetered and tottered.

"Oh, darn, I only got one in. I want to do it over."

"No way!" Richard pushed her aside so he could go next. Mikey won the prize even though he was allowed to hold the clothespins about an inch from the milk bottle. Mommy said that was only right because he was the littlest. She and the other mothers went inside to have a cup of coffee and rest their weary bones.

Like most children of the fifties, we acquired our knowledge of biology in bits and pieces by playing the doctor-and-nurse game. Whenever we found ourselves out of our parents' sight, we took the opportunity to expose our private parts to each other, puzzling over the differences in the equipment of boys and girls. Without ever being told why, we knew our parents frowned on this sort of game. It was definitely out of the question for our birthday party.

That's why David and I convinced our group of party animals to participate in "The Dentist Game." This could be played in the full light of day without arousing our guardians' suspicions that we were up to any hanky-panky as we checked out each other's teeth. Little did they know the full extent of a dental check-up.

We lined up the folding chairs and threw a bed sheet over the clothesline to serve as a makeshift office where the kids awaited their turns in the dentist chair—a half broken piano stool that still spun up and down.

David was the dentist and I was his dental assistant.

Being the oldest, Barney went first. "Now open your mouth really wide," Dr. David ordered. "I need to use my flashlight to look for cavities. Aha, here's a loose one," he exclaimed to the squirming patient. "Butter knife, please." I handed him the instrument and he gently hammered the loose filling back into place and sent Barney on his way.

"Now it's your turn," David called to little Mikey who looked like he was being summoned to join a death march.

David turned to me. "Dental pick," he demanded as I handed him one of several toothpicks. He cleaned Mikey's gums until they bled.

For the grand finale, David convinced his last patient, Ricky Lermo, to let him tie a string around the boy's wobbly front tooth. In one quick move, he jerked the tooth out. He had to pay Ricky a quarter so he wouldn't tell his mother.

'Pin the Tail on the Donkey' came next. What a waste of Daddy's hard-earned money. We got bored with it after a while and took turns putting on the blindfold and spinning around until we fell on the ground. Judy managed to keep spinning the longest, winning a magic slate and pencil.

"Look," I explained to her, making a jagged mark on the plastic sheet that covered the black board. "See? When you lift up the plastic, the mark I made disappears."

Judy shot me a bored stare. "I already got one of these," she complained, her voice full of scorn.

"Here then, give it to me," I demanded, remembering my own worn out magic slate.

Judy held it up away from me. "No, I'll keep it. I can probably trade it for something more stylish at school. Maybe a ring or bracelet."

I couldn't see that happening, but I let her keep her dream of trading a thirty-five-cent slate for some classy jewelry.

Mommy came out occasionally to check on us, but returned to the house as soon as she concluded nobody had been stabbed or blinded by our birthday games.

We saved our drinking game until last. This was a contest to see how much each of us could drink from the garden hose without stopping to breathe. Naturally David had come up with this brainstorm.

Richard won by a long shot. Some of us had to lie down and roll on the grass because we were so waterlogged. The Blazina boys, who according to their teacher were on the road to becoming juvenile delinquents, took the hose and squirted everyone, even little Mikey, who was howling because he couldn't free his fingers from the Chinese handcuffs.

"I warned you not to let your fingers swell up," Keith told him, cutting his little brother free from the paper roll with his pocketknife.

Like every kid in America in those days, we roughhoused until somebody got hurt. That happened when Gary socked his brother Richard's waterlogged stomach so hard, Richard threw up and ran inside to tattle on Gary.

We had disassembled into a motley crew of exhausted partiers by then so nobody fussed much when Mommy ended the free-for-all. The Barnharts followed their mother across the field to their house and Mrs. Blazina threatened to slap her boys silly if they didn't get into the car. I could see them beating up on each other from the rear window as they drove down the hill.

David and I agreed it was the best birthday party ever.

18

AND BABY MAKES THREE

On April 18, 1956, my world shifted on its axis…but this time in a good way. I was heading to Jones' Variety with Auntie Bess after spending the night with her. Mommy had landed in the hospital, but not for a nervous breakdown. She was there to have a baby. I wanted to buy my brand new sister a welcome home present with the two dollars I'd saved from my allowance.

After searching through the infant section of the store, I purchased a pack of three flannel receiving blankets. Two would go to my new baby sister, Jeanne Louise, and one to my baby doll, Teresa June aka TJ.

Teresa June—a Christmas present from my parents— came straight from the *Sears and Roebuck* catalogue. According to the catalogue, "Bannister Baby is a life-like replica of a newborn." I could definitely tell her apart from a real live baby, but as advertised, she came with a bottle and two diapers for when she peed after a feeding. Best of all, my mother, who by the holidays was "showing" her protruding stomach, promised to make TJ a layette, exactly like the one she was sewing for the baby inside her.

I have sweet memories of my mother sitting at the dining room table, bent over her rarely used Singer Sewing machine, busily creating two identical sets of baby clothes. I think Mommy wanted to fend off any resentment I might hold against the baby when it arrived. She whipped out soft flannel tee shirts and nightgowns, one set for the baby to come and one identical set for Teresa June. I was in heaven, not just because of TJ's new layette, but also in anticipation of a new sibling. I felt close to Mommy, the way I did when she made all the clothes for Jesse Jesus. I still longed to be hugged and cuddled by Mommy, but spending time together helped lessen the distance between us.

Up at the cash register in Jones', I proudly announced "I'm buying all these things for my new baby sister. She's only two days old so I haven't got to see her yet."

"Aren't you the nicest big sister," the clerk commented as she bagged the baby blankets.

"I'm going to earn money babysitting for her," I explained, eager to claim my new and important role. "Her name is Jeanne Louise." I continued to express my delight as Auntie Bess nudged me through the exit turnstile.

For the past few months at school, I had used up most of class "sharing time" announcing the stages of my mother's pregnancy. Some of the second-graders were so sick of hearing about my mother's expanding stomach and her new wardrobe of maternity clothes that they made little booing sounds when I wobbled to the front of the class.

"We got a baby crib and a tailor tot and three stuffed animals at Jones' yesterday," I bragged, still glowing from the blissful time my mother and I spent shopping.

"We've already heard that," Mark Fieg protested to our teacher, Mrs. Center.

"Well, I also bought this new pin," I rambled on. "It's a silver fork and next time I'm going to buy the spoon and knife."

"Let's give somebody else a turn," Mrs. Center prompted. Clearly, the purpose of sharing escaped me.

The General Hospital frowned on juvenile visitors. I waited two more days before my father drove my mother home from the hospital to Auntie Bess's. Mommy quietly tiptoed into the living room and laid Jeanne down on the sofa.

"Want to have a look at your new sister?"

I nodded. "But first, you have to open her present. I bought it with my own money."

My mother smiled as she examined the set of blankets. I could tell they were a hit. "Now, why don't you look at the baby you've been wanting for so long?" She and Auntie Bess returned to the kitchen, leaving me alone in the room.

I walked over to the bundle and gently uncovered her face.

I nearly caved over in shock. This was no Gerber or Bannister Baby. She looked nothing like my roly-poly cousin Debby I once held in my arms. I stared down at a bright red wizened-faced infant, covered in downy black hair. My precious baby sister resembled the spider monkey at the Sequoia Zoo.

I poked the head of Jeanne Louise hard and prepared to order a different baby. Disturbed by the rude awakening, Jeanne flailed her arms in the air, opened up one fist, and then curled her baby fingers tightly around my big sister finger. An overwhelming love welled up inside of me and escaped in a little sob. My days of boredom, rejection, and loneliness had come to an end. I loved my new baby sister and I could tell she loved me back.

"She'll lose that body hair in a few weeks," my mother explained to me later as I watched her give Jeanne a bath in her little pink bathtub.

"Will she still be red and crinkly?" I asked. "Not that it matters to me," I whispered to Mommy, even though Jeanne couldn't understand my words yet.

Cousin Debbie had a new baby sibling too, a blonde, blue-eyed baby girl named Becky. We argued over which baby sister was the cutest, but after a while we got tired of having to babysit them and keep quiet during their frequent naps. Once our baby sisters were old enough, we dressed them in our hand-me-down clothes and wheeled them around in the big baby buggy parked at Grandma Ida's house. When either baby started bawling or pooped in her diaper, we exchanged them for our better mannered dolls.

The moment I returned from school each afternoon, I pulled up a chair next to Jeanne's crib, feeling a love that was new to me. I held her in the rocking chair, singing her to sleep just the way I wished Mommy had done with me. My heart overflowed with happiness when her face lit up whenever she saw me. Love given, love returned. For the first time ever, I felt I was the most important person in somebody's life and a premature mantle of motherhood settled over me.

I told Jeanne fairy stories and read to her long before she knew what I was doing, but when she wrapped her little finger around mine, it hardly mattered. I would be a heroine to my sister, not a Moaning Mary or a crippled kid with few prospects.

Even Mommy commented on my daily attention to Jeanne. More than once I overheard her bragging on the phone about me. "Honestly, Bess," she told my aunt, "I don't think she has a jealous bone in her body. She even rinses out Jeanne's diapers in the toilet and puts them into the soaking pail."

I enjoyed caring for TJ, but my laughing, crying, pooping sister Jeanne set my heart on fire. As soon as she learned to talk, I imagined us having long conversations about fairies and our fears about Mommy's stability and Daddy's job security. I hoped that she wouldn't have to see Daddy beating up on David—that was too sad for a baby to witness. We would be a constant consolation to one another as we struggled to survive family life at home.

19

SHRINERS AGAIN

Returning to Shriners for the second time proved to be even harder than my stay when I was five years old. Not only would I be leaving my brother behind, but also Jeanne to whom I was so bonded. Mommy taped a picture of me onto the inside of Jeanne's crib so she could give me a good night kiss and not forget me while I was held captive in the hospital.

The admitting nurse refused to let me bring in a picture of Jeanne, so I couldn't repeat the nightly ritual kiss from my side of the world. "Honey, that's just going to make you miss her more," she said, snatching the photo out of my hands. "It'll be waiting for you in your locker when you go home." This hurt my heart a lot, much more than when they took away Jesse Jesus during my first visit.

A few of the worst rules had changed at Shriners since my previous stint. I think the Nazi head doctor had quit because they used less Hexol in the pre-admission baths and our fingernails weren't cropped so short. With the Salk vaccine campaign up and running, the fear of polio's contagion had lessened. No longer would I have to yell down to my visitors from a second-storey window while they stood below, sometimes under umbrellas, other times sweltering in the rare humidity of San Francisco, while we exchanged smiles and gestures.

Shriners now allowed face-to-face visits every Sunday afternoon from two until four. My father couldn't take off work more than once, but my mother came every other week when possible. Back then, the 350-mile trip from Eureka to San Francisco took up to nine hours, even longer when the construction workers were building the new interstate highway 101. Auntie Bert and Uncle George never missed a Sunday.

Only one visitor at a time could be on the ward with you. I knew when my mother had made it by the clicking of her high heeled shoes echoing from the hall. *One-two-one-skip. One-two-one-skip.* Mommy always looked pretty when she came. We didn't talk much, but she massaged my hand the whole time she stayed. As promised, she'd had Jeanne kiss my picture each night at bedtime.

"She won't forget me, will she Mommy?"

"Not in a million years."

The best thing about my second stay turned out to be advice I received from an intern when he found me crying in the cubicle. It was my second day at Shriners and I was still angry and upset over having my sister's picture ripped out of my hands. Kids only had to be quarantined for five days now, not for polio, but run-of-the mill stuff like measles and pinkeye. They used the cubicles on the ward instead of the ones out in the hall. The glass didn't reach the ceiling and my germs could have floated over the top, but I guess it didn't matter.

"What'cha doing over there by the window?" the tall blonde intern asked as he entered my cell. Dr. Shaw was very handsome and he knew it. I watched him admire his reflection in the glass cubicle.

"See that girl sitting at the kitchen table in the house across the street?" I pointed out the window. "We've been waving at each other."

Dr. Shaw moved closer to the window and squinted. "Looks like a vase of flowers to me," he shrugged, picking me up, and carrying me over to my bed. He unbuttoned the front of my dress and pulled up my undershirt so he could examine the railroad tracks running across my chest and up over my shoulder from my muscle transplant. "Looks like a complete success," he exclaimed. "Bravo."

I started to cry, angry at his intrusive actions with my dress and flustered that I'd been waving at a stupid vase of flowers for the past hour.

"So, why all the tears?" He stepped closer and listened to my heart with his stethoscope. Could he hear it breaking?

I collapsed into sobs, pushing the instrument away. "I'm lonesome and I'm homesick," I coughed out. "I miss my baby sister. It hurts my heart."

"A big girl like you shouldn't be homesick."

I stared at him while he stared back. He was right. I was too old to be homesick and it hurt to keep on missing my sister. I shut my eyes, trying to feel dead. I would learn to feel nothing whenever pain threatened to swallow me up. I imagined I had control of a big light switch that I could turn off and on. I practiced for a long time until something in my chest snapped like a rubber band and my homesickness disappeared along with the doctor.

In therapy some thirty years later, my counselor caught me in the act of shutting down over a painful memory and pointed out that I used this strategy as a major psychological defense.

"Where did you go just now?" she asked during a particularly difficult session.

I was back there in that cubicle, a little girl of eight who learned how to shut down her feelings in the face of abandonment.

When I proved to be free of any deadly virus, Russian Olga moved my bed out of the cubicle and under the big arched window in the Middle Girls' Ward. Olga's familiar face reminded me that I could survive. Mrs. Johnson, the nurses' aide, Mr. Jackson the janitor, and the gardener Mr. Allen all remembered me, which was nice because I didn't know any of my ward mates.

The newly formed Middle Girls' Ward housed eight to twelve-year-olds. I just made the cut. Olga introduced me to Jenny, age eight. Beverly and Justine, both eleven-years-old, were eager to move into the Big Girls' Ward which overflowed with teen-aged girls who flirted with the interns and made a lot of racket once lights were out.

Unfortunately, Mrs. Morton—that mean old stick of a night nurse—still reigned over our sleeping hours. On my first night out of the cubicle, she came tearing into the Big Girls' Ward to get everyone to settle down. "Quiet," she ordered. "I don't want to hear another peep out of anyone."

The room settled down, but as Morton started to leave, somebody whispered, "Peep" and you can bet Old Big Ears heard it.

Morton went ballistic. She flicked the lights on and off to get everybody's attention. "Who said that?" she belted out. Nobody volunteered an answer.

"Fine. Until someone confesses, this ward is on restrictions. No television and I'm moving lights-out up to seven-thirty." A group moan followed before everyone fell silent.

I sat up in bed, trying to hear the drama unfolding in the other room.

Suddenly, Morton's flashlight turned on. I hadn't heard her creeping up on me. "You're supposed to be asleep," she hissed. "Now lie back down."

No wonder Mrs. Morton had night duty. No one on the day shift would put up with her.

After three nights of no television and the early bedtime curfew, a pretty girl named Donna caved under peer pressure and fessed up to Morton. "I made the peep," she admitted unapologetically.

For her punishment, Donna spent three days on *our* ward. I walked over to her cubicle to introduce myself the very next morning before breakfast. "I think you're very brave," I told her. "How old are you, anyway?"

"I'm seventeen." I stood there dumbstruck. I had no idea they could still put you in Shriners when you were that old. A sense of doom flooded over me until I switched it off.

"How old are you, Paula?"

Flattered by her interest, I told her "I'm eight…and a half." I stressed the point, looking as mature as I could.

"Is this your first time at this dump, Paula?"

"Second," I told her, adding, "I was only the sixth kid to have a muscle transplant," to impress her even more.

Donna rolled her eyes. "Lucky you. Well, I practically live here at Stalag 19. They call it that cause it used to be run by Nazis and it's on 19th Avenue. I've been a Shriners guinea pig seven times and have the scars to prove it." She rolled up her sleeve to show me some ugly marks running down her arm. "I was the second one to have a muscle transplant."

"What do you mean—guinea pig?"

"We're all guinea pigs, Paula. That's why our parents have to sign us over to Shriners when we get admitted. Our parents agree to let interns practice on us; that way all our surgery and stuff is provided for free."

"You mean they *own* us?" My voice trembled. My parents forgot to share this information with me. I flashed back to my mother and father signing a lot of papers when we'd arrived at Shriners. That must have sealed my doom.

Russian Olga overheard us as she swept by pushing the food cart. "Get over to your bed, Paula. And get out your placemat and napkin. And don't worry, only God owns you. Not the Nazis."

She set down a tray with segments dividing the mush and fruit cocktail. I loved fruit cocktail, but I had lost my appetite, even after Olga explained that Shriners provided the best medical treatment money could buy. Just not my parents' money…

I felt like a poverty-stricken orphan owned by God.

20

UNDER THE KNIFE

My four months at Shriners in 1957 are more a blur of images than distinct memories of faces and events. I gained near-celebrity status when my parents donated a new record player and a bunch of 45s to the ward. Everybody loved "You Ain't a Nothing but a Hound Dog." I pretended to, just to go along with the crowd.

All of us Middle Ward girls joined the Big Girls Ward any night Elvis Presley appeared on the *Ed Sullivan Show* and swiveled his hips. The studio audiences nearly drowned him out with their screams. I liked the jugglers and magicians better.

I made friends right off the bat with Jenny. She told very funny dirty jokes, most of which flew right over my head. She amazed me by blowing bubbles with her spit. We laughed a lot and shared stories about life back home.

Jenny's father, who visited regularly, reminded me of the little old winemaker from those commercials in the fifties. From the way he would merrily waltz onto the ward, I think he drank some of the little old winemaker's product.

"Your dad is a hoot," I told Jenny one Sunday afternoon. Visiting hours had just ended. "Is he Italian?"

"'No, he's Russian."

My mouth dropped open. "You mean he's a Communist?"

"Of course he's not," Jenny snapped. "Better dead than red is what Papa says."

I remained a bit sketchy on global politics so I let the matter drop. What interested me most about Jenny was her medical history. She was recovering from the same surgery I was scheduled for in the coming week. After they removed her stitches, she informed me, the doctors encased her in a body cast from her neck to her hips. Now I knew what my future held in store for me after they fused my spine.

"Do you still get presents after surgery?"

"Yep." Jenny leaned over, no small feat in a body cast, and fished out a pair of sunglasses from her nightstand. Big purple ones with rhinestones in the corners. She put them on and pursed her lips. "Don't I look just like a movie star?" she asked, removing them and batting her eyes.

She did look stunning. Even wearing a body cast. I nodded my approval, eager to focus on the thought of exotic surgery presents, forgetting what I'd have to suffer through to earn those pretty things.

I didn't forget for long. The next morning, I spied the dreaded "Liquids only" pink slip taped to my nightstand. I knew the routine. I'd get some hard candy to suck on so I wouldn't starve, then an enema, and maybe they'd shave my back where they made the incision. It took eighty-five stitches to sew Jenny up. From what I remembered of my muscle transplant, it hurt when they yanked the stitches out one by one.

Justine arrived on the ward a few days before me. She hobbled over to my bedside after breakfast...all three feet of her. She wore her blonde hair in a beehive to make her look taller. She wasn't a midget, she explained, but had stopped growing at about five. Plus, she had a clubbed foot, which seemed doubly unfair. Sometimes I hated God. It was getting to be a habit.

"What do you want for your surgery present?" Justine asked between spoonsful of sticky gray mush. "You're bound to get some kind of booby prize."

"I dunno." I shrugged, too scared and depressed to consider the possibilities.

Miss Pearl, a new nurses' aide, came to walk me down to the examining room. It was right across from the kitchen where they cooked our food. Just like my last time at the hospital, the giant cans of corn and string beans lined up on the shelves captivated me. I can't say the same for the meals.

Miss Pearl sat me down on a chair and put a towel over my shoulders.

Doomed again. I just knew it. "Now what?"

"I'm going to cut your hair so it will be easier to manage when you're in a body cast."

I stiffened. My hair had just begun to look good again after my latest Toni permanent. The only good thing about a Toni perm was the paper doll included in the kit.

"How short are you going to cut it?"

"Short, just like Amelia Earhart's." Miss Pearl whisked out a pair of scissors she'd been hiding in her pocket. "I noticed you were reading a book about her."

I liked Amelia's haircut, so I relaxed a little as I watched my locks fall to the floor. "Now hold still and bend down your head and tuck in your chin," the nurse ordered.

In less than a minute, Miss Pearl had shaved my neck and halfway up the back of my head. "We wouldn't want nasty hair to get into your incision," she explained

I hated the phony "we" nurses always used. I shed a few tears and then allowed a steely indifference to overtake me. It was time to turn myself off.

"I didn't know Amelia got her head shaved," I quipped, trying to be chipper.

Miss Pearl was too busy sweeping up my hair to hear me. She bent over and picked up a handful of my curls, studying them carefully. "Such pretty hair," she mused, looking as if she might shed a few tears herself. "It's okay, Paula," she soothed. "By the time you get out of here, it will have grown back."

"But it'll be straight as a stick," I ranted, not feeling in the least soothed.

Miss Pearl shrugged and we walked back to the ward in silence.

Nobody mentioned the scalping I had just endured. "Why didn't you warn me about this?" I demanded of Jenny during lunch.

"I'm sorry," she apologized. "I didn't want to get you all worked up."

I turned my back to her. Then I felt the prickles on my neck and head and rolled over so my buzz cut wouldn't show. "I hate God," I mumbled.

Jenny gasped and crossed herself like a good Catholic; later I discovered she was Russian Orthodox. "You shouldn't say that about God," she scolded. "Especially not before surgery."

I burped loudly and we both started laughing. Then Jenny farted and we were hysterical.

"You did that on purpose," I snorted, trying to catch my breath.

"Made you feel better though," she pointed out.

It did…until Dr. Shaw and a student nurse showed up before bedtime snack. I wasn't used to seeing them at night so I got a little nervous. A lot more so when they parked the gurney they were pushing next to my bed. The doctor let down my bed rail, lifting me onto the gurney. He and the nurse wheeled me out of the ward and down the long hall.

I could tell Dr. Shaw was mad at the nurse by the way he bumped up against her when he leaned over to press the basement button in the elevator.

"Cat got your tongue?" he said in a whiney voice.

"Well, he speaks," the nurse hissed back as the doors opened and we moved into a semi-darkened hall.

I studied the musty-smelling pipes that zigzagged across the ceiling and made loud clanking sounds. Dr. Shaw steered me next to a boy just outside the plaster room. "We'll be back for you in a minute, Paula."

"Not if she murders him," the boy said.

The boy and I exchanged smiles. I had only been to the Boys' Ward once for an indoor picnic so I felt a little shy. He introduced himself. "My name's Tony, what's yours?"

"Paula." I waited a minute before asking him, "Do you know what's going on, Tony?"

"I think Dr. Shaw broke off his engagement to that nurse."

"Not what's going on with them, what's going on with *us*?"

"They do all the creepy stuff down here at night," he whispered. "Top secret stuff. And this is where they bring the alien baby," he continued. "They usually keep her in hiding."

I grinned and started to make a snappy reply when he nodded over to a curtained-off room. "No lie. Just wait and see."

I didn't believe him until a nurse slipped behind the curtain and came out wheeling a gurney. My bones froze up as I watched the toddler pass by. She had a gigantic head. Way too big for her poor little body. I hated it when people stared at me, but I couldn't take my eyes off the freak baby when the nurse pushed her by.

The nurse frowned at me, but I kept staring until the alien baby was out of sight.

"What happened to her, Tony?"

"Water on the brain, my dad says. They have to keep draining it off to keep her head from exploding."

"She's not really an alien though, is she?"

Tony shook his head. "Still, my dad says she'd be better off dead."

Better dead than red.

We fell into our own private ruminations and I didn't even say goodbye when they wheeled Tony's gurney down the hall. I knew I would never get the image of alien baby out of my head.

A girl from the Big Girls' Ward arrived in the plaster room ahead of me. They came for her, and the next thing I knew she was screaming bloody murder.

With good reason. When my turn came, two nurses rolled me over on my stomach and pulled up my undershirt. Dr. Shaw came at me with a giant hypodermic needle which he promptly shoved into my spine. I didn't have time enough to numb myself before I yelled, "You're hurting me! It hurts, it hurts," I cried, finally giving up.

"X marks the spot," he joked. "I just shot some dye into your back so the doctors will know where to cut during surgery."

"Does your mouth ever consult with your brain?" one of the student nurses asked. Her name tag read 'Miss Brite.' The doctor smiled through gritted teeth. "It's a good thing you're pretty or I'd put you on notice," he kidded.

The not-so-pretty student nurse stared at her feet. I couldn't read her name tag, but I appreciated the pat she gave me on my arm. "Ready to go?" she asked, waiting while I pulled myself together. I just nodded and wished I were dead.

Once I got back to my bed on the ward, I started to feel real again. This time, Jenny couldn't even look me in the face.

"I know, I know. I should have told you, but I totally forgot about them shooting dye into my spine."

I didn't believe her, but I accepted her apology.

Sleep eluded me that evening. Jenny had filled me in on some of the gory details she'd remembered about her surgery and I could see why she hadn't told me about them before. Now, instead of having no idea of what was about to happen to me, images of knives and needles and stitches and doctors in bloody gowns haunted me through the night.

I fantasized about taking a hypodermic needle and stabbing out Dr. Shaw's eyes. "X marks the spot," I'd scream at him. When Morton did her 2 a.m. bed check, I pictured myself using her stupid flashlight to beat her on the head until she conked out.

I remembered Jenny telling me that thinking about doing something bad was almost the same as doing it. It struck me that so far I'd stabbed out Dr. Shaw's eyes and bashed in Mrs. Morton's head. I must have said I hated God a hundred times, even though I never spoke my feelings aloud. After I thought about it, I remembered I actually *had* repeated that I hated God out loud to Jenny.

I finally came up with the perfect solution. Instead of asking for a diary for my surgery present, I'd put in a request for a Bible. This would probably please God no end and save me from Hell. Sighing contentedly, I shut my eyes and slept the sleep of the nearly innocent.

21

LAYOVER IN HELL

"Paula, it's time to rise and shine."

Rise and shine my foot. I opened my eyes and swallowed the pill Miss Brite popped in my mouth.

"Just sip a little water," she cautioned.

The nurse pulled me onto a gurney as the rest of the girls on the ward slept. She wheeled me out into the hall, parking me next to the wall. She left, returning with a white gown and cap—my wardrobe for surgery.

For the next few minutes, I concentrated on shutting myself down. Given the threat of the impending operation, I failed to do so. I memorized my body as it was now and wondered how it would be after the surgeons performed their "magic."

Miss Brite rolled me over on my side and poked a needle into my butt. Within minutes, the hall started spinning and Miss Brite looked flat and then wavy. I envied the kids who fell asleep after the shot. I remained semi-alert; awake enough to experience the panic flooding my body; awake enough to see the white-robed and masked figures that rolled me down the hall and into the elevator. I nodded off for a second, but came to again to realize they were lifting me off the gurney and onto a thin aluminum table that felt icy cold.

Dr. Shaw's familiar face hovered above me. The very next second, he placed a mask over my nose and mouth and repeated softly, "Breathe in deeply, Paula. This will all be over in no time."

I tried to wriggle free from the suffocating mask, but it was no use. After holding my breath as long as I could, I sucked in a lungful of the sickly sweet smell of ether. My body buzzed all over. I blew up like a balloon, and then fizzled down to the size of a pea. The story of the princess and the pea rolled around in my brain until the lights dimmed and

I fell into the seat of a Ferris wheel, spinning around and around in empty space.

My body slammed to the ground. Pain occupied every part of my consciousness. I lay on my side so I could throw up into the pan Miss Brite held close to my mouth.

"I hurt," I cried out, stunned that even vocalizing made barbed arrows shoot up and down my spine. "Help me, Miss Brite." Sobs cut me off. "Make it stop hurting."

She brushed some sweaty hair off my forehead. "That's just what Mrs. Schmitt is going to do," she said, stepping aside so Pudgy could jab me with a hypodermic needle. I watched her waddle off as the pain began to subside and I melted into the bliss of morphia coursing through my veins.

A spasm of pain jolted me awake. Mrs. Morton hustled around my room, so I knew it was nighttime. "I need to throw up," I announced, though I couldn't imagine my body heaving vomit into the pan. How could I hurt so much and still be alive?

Morton thrust a thermometer into my mouth, hindering my attempt to vomit or beg for more pain medication. "You came through your surgery, lickety-split," she said, looking at her watch as she took my pulse. "Knew you would because you're a spunky little kid."

Morton's comment immediately caught my attention. "Am I dying?" I mumbled, working my words around the thermometer. Maybe that was the reason for her being so kind.

"Didn't I just say you came through your surgery, lickety-split?" she bit back, writing down my temperature in her little black notebook. She straightened her red cardigan sweater and patted down her hair as if she were going somewhere. Shriners hospital staff appeared and disappeared leaving no hint of their private lives once they removed their uniforms.

"See, your temp is normal."

Relief swept over me as her voice returned to snippety and her face to its usual scowl. Even so, I caught a smile in her eyes.

"I don't feel normal and I definitely don't feel lickety-split," I moaned. "Can I have another pain shot, please?"

Morton shook her head. "Too soon. You have another hour to go before your next one." Back in the fifties, doctors believed pain management would lead to a life of addiction and debauchery.

"I'll be back then," Morton called over her shoulder. She returned to her nightly rounds, the bright beam from her flashlight guiding her way.

An hour of grueling pain stretched into eternity as I lay in the darkness whimpering. I tried to roll over onto my back, but a sharp throbbing and a mountain of bandages prevented that. I scanned the room, my eyes stopping on a drawstring bag propped up against a thick black book. My surgery presents awaited me. The minutes moved a little faster.

The next morning, excitement tempered my pain as Miss Brite helped me empty the gift bag. My haul pleased me: one pretty Madame Alexander storybook doll, a jigsaw puzzle of the Eiffel tower which I planned to visit if I ever got out of Shriners, a coloring book and a box of thirty-two crayons in a flip-top box with a crayon sharpener on the back.

"What's this?" the nurse asked, placing the big black book next to me on the bed. "Oh, for heaven's sake, what a thing to give a child."

I was no child. I felt very mature and smart for my age as I prepared to take on the Gideon version of the Holy Bible.

I remained in the hallway cubicle for the next three days so as not to disturb the girls with my moans and groans.

"You would have kept us up all night," Jenny explained.

"Yeah, and wrecked our beauty sleep," Justine chimed in. She flashed a toothy smile my way. "Of course, it'd take half a century for you to wake up beautiful," she snorted.

Within a week, I improved enough to return to Shriners school and resume memorizing the exports and imports of Central America. I rode to class flat on my back in a low cart like the one Erma White had used.

Once my stitches healed and the doctors ripped them out, they whisked me down to the plaster room, balanced me on a thin strip of canvas, tied a cloth belt around my hips and put another strip of canvas under my chin. Finally, they turned a crank to stretch me out, so they could wrap me up in rolls of dampened plaster of Paris. Each layer had to harden before they slapped on the next. To allow the plaster to dry as fast as possible, they kept me naked except for a small quilt thrown over my legs. The repeated torture took hours.

Back on the ward, everybody left me alone, knowing I wouldn't be up for a chat until the cold, damp plaster had dried into unforgiving full-body armor.

Two weeks later, I sat rigid on a chair in the physical therapy room. Nerves made my hands break out in tiny little bumps as I waited to hear my name called by Miss Rosewood, the physical therapist assigned to me. An energetic sturdily built woman pushing a wheelchair bustled over to me.

"Ready, are you?"

I nodded and before I knew it, she had picked me up in her strong arms and hoisted me into the wheeled chariot. She had her thick blonde hair styled in a Dutch-boy cut and I half expected her to be wearing wooden shoes instead of a pair of canvas sneakers.

"So, you are Paula," she smiled. "And I am, of course, Miss Rosewood. Today is a big day for you. We are going to teach you how to walk in your body cast."

"But my legs are too weak to hold me up while I'm in this cast," I protested. "Even with my leg brace on."

"That is why we are going to do exercises to strengthen them." Miss Rosewood, who actually turned out to be Dutch, rolled my chair in front of a ramp with handrails. "First I will stand you up. Don't worry, I'll hold on tight."

Before I could object, she had me upright. I felt dizzy and my legs buckled.

"Grab on to the hand rails," she instructed, "they will help support you and give you balance."

"I can't use my arms," I explained, frustrated tears squirting out of my eyes.

Miss Rosewood caught me before I fell and sat me back in the wheel chair. "I can see that," she replied in a calm, soothing voice while adrenaline pulsed through my body and made my head swim.

Miss Rosewood pulled over a chair next to me, studying my medical file while shaking her head with annoyance. "The doctors should have noted your inability to brace yourself with the hand railings. I am so sorry. But we will start over," she announced "and pretty soon you will be walking without using the handrails."

I studied my skinny wasted legs.

"Will you trust me if I stand you up again, Paula? Can you be brave for me?"

Since she had caught me before, I figured I could trust her, so I tried again.

This time when she stood me up, she held me under both arms, which shifted some of the weight of the body cast off my weakened legs and provided balance.

"Great," she cheered me on, "soon you will be walking all by yourself."

We stood on the ramp for a few minutes, my underused legs buzzing with pins and needles. My back surgery hadn't completely healed, so I could feel the skin around my scar stretching painfully. "That's all I can take," I groaned in misery. "I can't take it anymore."

"No, you can take just a little bit more," the therapist encouraged, keeping me upright for another whole minute.

"There, you see, you must push a little beyond what you think you can do. That is how you will develop the strength to walk out of here."

The thought inspired me. If learning how to walk while carrying a ten-pound body cast would earn me a ticket home, I would use my gumption to push myself as hard as I could. I put fear and pain behind me and by the end of the week I could stand on my own and even take a few steps. I glowed with enthusiasm when Miss Rosewood praised my dedication.

In no time, she pronounced me ready to walk unassisted. I had enjoyed her company, and for the first time I realized at least somebody knew I was doing my best. Mommy doubted this much of the time, so I blossomed under the sincere praise and excitement Miss Rosewood heaped on me. She'd make a great mother.

"This will be our last session," the therapist announced on a Friday. "You have worked hard and been very brave."

Her encouraging words and obvious affection left me giddy. "I'm going to miss you," I told her. "You helped me a lot."

"But that was you, helping yourself. Keep up that spirit and you will go far in the world.

Your teacher, she tells me that you are a good writer and that you love reading. I can just see you writing lots of good books."

In spite of my sadness in parting with the therapist, I glowed from the inside out. We separated in tears and I was too upset to return to school after our session.

The girls were still in their class when Miss Rosewood reappeared at my bedside. "This was my favorite book when I was your age. I want to give you my own personal copy."

The book, written by Ruth Sawyer, was called *Roller Skates*. On the frontispiece the name Aida Rosewood had been penned and below it a dedication to me:

May you fly through life on the spirit of your invisible roller skates. Love, Aida Rosewood.

"Thank you so much," I beamed. "I'll always remember how you taught me to push a little harder to get where I'm going."

Miss Rosewood kissed my forehead and vanished through the ward doors.

Justine studied my gift that night before lights out. "You could get in trouble for having this," she warned, jealousy withering her voice. "And Miss Rosewood could get fired for giving something personal to you."

I looked up from the page I was reading. "Don't trouble your little mind about it."

"All you do is read books," Justine pouted. "You're just not fun anymore."

It was true. I had begun my lifelong love of reading, especially stories about strong girls and women who never got married. I imagined I'd lead a solitary life and write poetry and novels. If I couldn't get a man to fall in love with me, I would look to the outside world for love and affection. If I could be famous, I'd forget about falling in love and getting married.

I would never admit to being lonely or depressed, but I carried those feelings inside of me most of the time, even though I fooled people into believing I was a funny, spunky kid with not a care in the world.

22

HOME SCHOOLING

A week before my going-home date, Mommy sent me a picture of the outfit I would wear. The navy stripped dress had puff sleeves and a bright red pinafore just like Anne of Green Gables.

Our neighbor, Doug Harris, drove down with Mommy in his flashy new Nash Rambler station wagon to pick me up. The back seat folded down so I could ride home flat on my back as the doctors had ordered. My eyes hungered for the outside world and gobbled up the tops of houses and trees and anything else I could see while lying in the back of the car.

Doug turned up the radio to listen to the news with Gabriel Heater. "The Cold War has taken a turn for the worst," Heater informed us, noting that America's testing of the first aerial hydrogen bomb over an island in the Bikini Atoll last year hadn't helped. "It had the force of ten million tons of TNT," the newscaster added for emphasis.

"Guess the girls on that little island won't be wearing bikinis this year," Doug joked with Mommy.

Mommy avoided risqué conversations about intimate apparel, especially with Doug Harris who fancied himself a lady's man. "He reads *Playboy Magazine*," I overheard her tell my father in disgust.

Doug turned up the radio a notch so we could hear about some general's call for more bombs and bomb shelters. I figured my body cast would prevent me from blowing up in the case of nuclear war.

The other big news was the attempt by Negro students to attend white colleges. "Now, I just don't know about that," Doug interjected. "I think Ike may have to call on the National Guard to fix that problem."

Again, Mommy seemed uncomfortable with the topic. "All I know is I usually sat by a Negro girl on the school bus. Louisa was a nice girl and I hated seeing her there next to an empty seat. I can tell you that riled up my brothers though, seeing me chatting with, a—I think they called her a 'darkie.' What a bunch of idiots."

Mommy and Daddy practiced what they preached to us. Daddy voted to let a Negro join the Pressmen's Union even though most of the guys at work blackballed him.

"One of my best friends at Shriners was Erma White," I stated from the back of the car. "She was black and sometimes she said that was worse than having brittle bones."

Gabriel's newscast went on and on, listing all the problems of the Cold War. The eight-hour drive to Eureka crawled by and I sighed with relief when Doug switched the station to one that played Country-Western music.

I was in for a big surprise when upon arriving home, Daddy had me close my eyes as he carried me into my bedroom and plopped me on the bed.

"You can open them, now," Mommy said.

I had a newly decorated room, painted in pink with a white trim. Mommy had spruced up an old table from Grandma Ida's, sanding out the dents and hanging a pretty scalloped mirror over it. Auntie Bess donated two bookshelves to hold my ever-growing library.

"It's beautiful!" I raved. "Oh, I have new tie-back curtains too. I love this room."

Which was fortunate given the fact that I spent the next three months in it, flat on my back, before I returned to Shriners plaster room. When that time arrived, the doctors put me in a new cast that allowed me to sit up and walk around like Miss Rosewood and I had practiced.

The school district refused to let me return to third grade, so rudely interrupted by my confinement at Shriners.

"But that means I won't see any of my friends, Mommy. I miss them." We sat together on my bed, mesmerized by CBS' presentation of *The Wizard of Oz* on the Sunday Night Movie.

"That's true, but it also means you won't have to go back and deal with Mrs. Killmore. That should be a relief."

I nodded in agreement.

Mrs. Killmore's name fitted her perfectly. She hated eight-year-old girls and crippled ones in particular. She wasn't that fond of eight-year-old boys either. To prove that she would treat me just the same as the normal kids in her class, she flunked me in both math and handwriting. Because our math tests were timed, my inability to write fast meant I failed most of them and my wobbly handwriting looked like "chicken scratches" according to her.

When I tearfully presented my report card to Mommy and Daddy, they were furious...but at Mrs. Killmore, not me. Daddy immediately called up the principal to complain while Mommy tore up my report card and tossed it in the fireplace. I appreciated my parents coming to my defense, but I didn't look forward to facing Mrs. Killmore the next morning.

She greeted me frowning and standing stiff as a broom handle next to my desk. "Our principal, Miss Asselstein, has instructed me to write you out a new report card," she glowered. "And from now on, I've been directed to give you an extra five minutes on timed arithmetic tests. I don't think we're doing you any favors by giving you special privileges. That's not what the real world will do."

She slapped the new report card onto my desk. After she marched up to the blackboard, I turned over the card. My math grade had risen to a C+, while my handwriting mark shot up to a D+. So much for Mrs. Killmore's refusal to overprotect me from the real world. Mommy was right. I'd be better off without her.

When the academic year began, the school district assigned a home teacher to me named Mrs. McCord. I thought she must be about eighty years old, what with the hairnet she wore over her graying bun, the fuzz on her chin, and her old lady shoes, but Mommy guessed she was more like fifty-five.

"I think we'll have a jolly time working together," the tall graceful teacher announced at our first meeting. She grew up in the Midwest where they used words like 'jolly.' She informed me that she would visit three times a week, and keep me current on all things relating to the third grade.

Mrs. McCord had several tricks up her sleeve. "Now don't go reading this Nancy Drew mystery until I return Wednesday," she warned, knowing full well that I would have finished off *The Mystery of the Tapping Heels* by our next session. Mrs. McCord gradually weaned me off Nancy Drew and her sidekicks Bess and George. One day she arrived with a copy of *The Secret Garden,* a book that was not available at the grocery store.

"I think you'll enjoy this because it involves a mystery." So began my introduction to good literature, a cut above the novels we had at home. Books offered me my great escape into worlds beyond Eureka's city limits and family life on Pigeon Point.

Mrs. McCord took a liking to me and went out of her way to make third grade interesting. "We must work hard to expand your horizons," she proclaimed early on. True to her word, she loaded me, body cast, wheelchair and all, into her car and treated me to the first of many field trips.

"Being stuck for months in Shriners leaves a lot for me to catch up with, you know, Mrs. McCord." I stuck my head out the window, letting the wind rustle through my bangs.

Mrs. McCord shifted the car into high gear and laughed. "Well then, we'd better hurry up and get started."

I liked the way she gunned the car engine, not like a little old lady at all. She drove faster than Uncle George did, a fact I never revealed to Mommy.

Our initial stop was the library where Mrs. McCord rolled her car's back wheel up over the curb. "I've never got the feel for parallel parking," she huffed and puffed as she unfolded my chair, plopped me down in it and pushed me through the red brick building's doors into this side of heaven. Like so many other small towns, we had an official Carnegie Library. I fell in love with the rows of books, the polished oak floors, and long honey-colored wooden tables. I proudly applied for my very own library card, and when Mrs. McCord dropped me off back home, she recommended to Mommy that someone take me to the library every two weeks. To my delight, this became one of the father-daughter rituals Daddy and I looked forward to. I'd bring sister Jeanne along and find her books that were genuine classics instead of Little Golden Books. I had missed a lot of literature for younger kids; reading the classics to Jeanne introduced me to an amazing collection of beautifully illustrated stories I'd never heard when I was her age. I had the chance to savor *Wind in the Willows, James and the Giant Peach,* and the original *Pinocchio,* a much scarier account than Walt Disney's version.

Mrs. McCord had retired from classroom teaching so she could bring the world to kids like me, trapped at home, and she did. "For your next science project, we're going to build a bird feeder and learn the names of all our local birds," she proposed one afternoon after correcting my messy sheet of math problems. I still hated math, but loved most anything to do with the natural world.

"For inspiration, we'll visit the Clark Museum. I can't wait for you to see the extraordinary displays of birds' nests Miss Clark donated. Believe it or not, they still have their original eggs." When she caught my disturbed expression, she added that the yolks of the eggs had been carefully blown out before chicks had a chance to develop.

"That's good, because once I left an Easter egg in a bottom dresser drawer and it took forever to find out where the stench came from."

My teacher's excitement electrified me with anticipation of the discoveries waiting for us. I stood ready at the front door when she picked me up early on a Friday morning and we headed to the Clark Museum. Together we explored the wonders of bird life that filled the shelves. I couldn't help touching the colorful and patterned eggs nestled in their beds of straw, moss, and bits of twine. They took my breath away.

"Next we'll have to attract our own birds," my teacher promised on the drive home.

"How are we gonna do that?" I pumped her eagerly.

"That, my dear, is your science project." Sure enough, Mrs. McCord appeared at our next session with a birdhouse kit and my very own copy of *American Birds in Your Backyard: The Pacific Coast Edition.*

Borrowing a hammer from my father, she and I nailed together all six pieces of the bird feeder and painted it green to blend into the shrubbery outside my bedroom window. The kit also included a cheap pair of binoculars and a notebook for recording my sightings. That simple science project inspired my lifelong love of birding.

"Aha! I see you spotted a junco and three chickadees," she commented after studying my notes. "Your descriptions are excellent."

I couldn't wait to tell her about my latest experience. "But, there's more," I gasped. "I sat with my bedroom window open and put some seed on my desk and a little junco hopped in from the bird feeder. It was only an inch away." I sighed, still savoring the moment when the bird lingered next to my hand and I touched the feathered wonder.

"You're a born naturalist," Mrs. McCord declared with heartfelt delight. Her love of nature was contagious. I'd never met a grown-up so brimming with the pleasures of the world and so anxious to share them with me.

Although I didn't realize it at the time, Mrs. McCord was just one of the many adults who inspired and nurtured my curiosity during those five months of home schooling. Auntie Bess' husband, my Uncle Marsh, gave me his old pair of good binoculars and pointed out the starry constellations to me. Aunt Mattie, the eighteen-year-old beatnik wife of my Uncle Don Viale, presented me with a small but authentic microscope that I dawdled over for hours, slicing up butterfly wings and looking at all the things swimming around in my spit.

I adored Aunt Mattie and her fun-loving spirit. We saw a lot of each other because she and my Uncle Don Viale rented what had once been our garage. Daddy had remodeled it and had dreams of becoming a landlord. Eventually, he turned every shack and chicken coop on our property into a rental.

Aunt Mattie majored in art in high school and as a welcome-home present, she drew me a complete set of Disney characters to hang up in my bedroom. She was my first adult best friend, a status symbol of my adolescence. Mattie included me in frequent visits to her mother's house where Mrs. Krinowski fed us big dishes of exotic ice cream. We went on lots of joyrides in the country, and visited the Eureka City Zoo. We checked out art books from the library so she could introduce me to the works of famous painters not even mentioned in our set of *World Book Encyclopedias.*

I had no idea that Mattie was a lesbian. What attracted me to her were her black and dark blue shirts and tight, peg legged pants, her dismissal of men as pointless, and her heavy use of eyeliner that added an air of mystery to her heart-shaped face. I did wonder why she preferred my mother's company to my Uncle Don's, but who wouldn't? My uncle had a worse temper than Daddy did. More than once, Mattie had to wear sunglasses to hide the black eyes Uncle Don gave her.

I had my hair cut like Mattie's, short with a ducktail in back. I slathered lots of goop on my bangs to keep them out of my eyes, happy at last to have the perfect hairdo for a kid in a body cast.

Then there was Auntie Mae, a sassy Mae West kind of floozy. She and her husband, Uncle Carl, lived down the hill from us in a fairytale-like log cabin. I made many short afternoon visits to Auntie Mae after Mrs. McCord had finished with my lessons. With practice, I had learned to use my foot to propel my wheelchair to Auntie Mae's cabin on my own. Of course, she had to push me back up the hill when I needed to return to finish my math work. "It's a good way to get my exercise," she huffed and puffed all the way home.

Like Mattie, Auntie Mae accomplished things no other women I knew would have dreamed of doing. While Mattie stood out as an artist and beatnik, Auntie Mae served as a WAC in France during WWII. Once she dressed up in her uniform and marched around the cabin, saluting, wiggling her hips, and waving a small American flag, just to show me how she looked in her heyday.

Her stories about life in France enthralled me. She gave me a big box of her souvenirs from Paris, complete with postcards you could view in 3-D through a stereoscope. I made up my mind then and there to visit Paris as soon as I was old enough to fly overseas without an accompanying adult. I could feel my humdrum world expanding and I knew if I could just make it to eighteen, I would figure out a way to leave the streets of Eureka in the dust.

23

SPUTNIK FEVER

As promised, Mrs. McCord kept me up on all my third grade subjects so that I easily passed into fourth grade at Franklin without a hitch.

A tired and worn-out teacher named Mrs. Baxter greeted the upper fourth grade on our first day of school. "Good morning, class," she said breathlessly, as if she'd run all the way from home. "Let's begin by taking attendance so we can get to know each other." She smiled nervously as she opened up her big black grade book.

After calling or mispronouncing the thirty-six names of her baby-boomer students, Mrs. Baxter organized a seating chart alphabetically and waited as we milled around the perimeter of the room, seeking out our designated desks. The combination of our loud voices, disruptive trips and shoves exchanged by the boys and the obviously rehearsed dropping of textbooks at exactly 9:15 a.m. made it hard to hear yourself think.

Worse yet, Mark Fieg, who had shut his eyes and was hopping backwards on one foot, knocked into me and I fell to the floor, hitting my head on one of the radiators and leaving a few drops of blood smeared on it. A chorus of gasps followed.

Mrs. Baxter raced over to me. She sank to her knees, tottering on the edge of incoherence. My new monitor Marilyn had reached me at the same time, sitting me upright and back on my feet before our teacher had come to her senses.

"I'm okay," I assured Mrs. Baxter, patting her on the shoulder. "Some days are like this."

"Good to know," the shaken woman muttered. "Now, please return to your seats and open your readers to page sixteen. This seems to be a perfect time for silent reading." Mrs. Baxter followed suit and the class fell into a restful calm.

The recess bell rang. I locked my brace, stood up, and caught Marilyn Robert's eye. She moseyed over to my desk to escort me out to the playground.

"You look like something hurts," she remarked, noticing the obvious grimace on my face. "I think your perm came out nice."

"That's not the problem. It's my new brace." I winced. "I have to break it in. Mr. Hawkins designed a different ring for the top of it where I put the most pressure. Right now, it's pinching me plus I'm getting a bloody heel blister from the ankle strap." I sat down on a nearby bench and hiked my skirt up far enough to display a new locking device. "But watch this." I brightened up a bit as I stuck my leg straight out and pressed a lever. Like magic, my brace bent at the knee.

"Guess that's progress," Marilyn shrugged. "Hope it's worth the pain," she added with sympathy.

Throughout that September our main academic curriculum fit into a fourth grade reader and three giant textbooks entitled *California Yesterday, California Today,* and *California Tomorrow.* That changed in October. Earlier that summer, the Russians tested an intercontinental missile, capable of reaching the United States and wham, everybody's attention focused on the Cold War, which was taking the place of WWIII. We were, it appeared, way behind the Russians in science and math.

Then on October 4, the Communists lurched ahead of us again by sending up *Sputnik 1,* the first artificial satellite. The American press treated *Sputnik* as a major humiliation, and blamed the low quality of math and science instruction in the public schools. Fourth grade California history took a back seat to updated versions of science and math books.

Poor Mrs. Baxter took the criticism personally. She had just become a newly-licensed teacher after years of working in the home decorating section at Ace Hardware Store. I overheard her telling Mrs. Killmore she feared she lacked the skills and training to handle this abrupt shift in fourth-grade subjects. Mrs. Baxter's fears were well founded. Rumor had it that after failing a series of math and science tests, the Board of Education required her, along with several other outdated teachers, to spend weekends attending workshops for the math and science challenged.

Russia's achievements terrified many Americans. As the *Standard's* editorial put it, "If they can send a satellite into space, they can blast us off the face of the earth." I immediately renewed my campaign for a bomb shelter, although most rocket scientists claimed that nothing would protect us from the blast of the newly upgraded atom bombs.

"Look, don't start pestering me about bomb shelters," Daddy warned, showing me the editorial. "Maybe they'll invade us instead of blowing us away. How's that for a brand new catastrophe to dread?"

Just before Thanksgiving, I had the satisfaction of waving a hot-off-the-press evening newspaper in Daddy's face. The headlines screamed "Reds Launch Dog Laika into Orbit around Earth." The Space Race had been declared.

"Next the Russians will be bombing our backyards, Daddy," I moaned. "You know it's still not too late to build us that bomb shelter," I observed, attempting to sound more cheerful.

Daddy shook his head. "How about I build us a dog house shelter in honor of Laika?" he teased.

I stamped my foot, not the least bit amused by his blasé attitude which placed our very lives at risk. Meanwhile Russia continued beating us in the Space Race.

My cousin Debbie had no better luck convincing Uncle Bill to carve a shelter into the clay bank located behind the back of their house. "I even promised to donate my allowance and help him start digging," she told me.

We had spent the afternoon together drooling over the December edition of *Sears and Roebuck*. I shut the catalog and let it drop to the kitchen floor. "A lot of good this will do us." I sighed.

Debbie retrieved the catalog, hugging the sacred book to her chest. "What do you mean, Paula?"

"Think about it. They're atheists. The first thing the Communists will do when they invade America is cancel Christmas."

24

COUSIN LOVE

The Russians had yet to invade our shores by the time fourth grade ended. Luckily, with my new bendable brace, I managed to sprawl under my desk during "duck and cover" exercises, which I hoped would save my life.

Developments on the Cold War front continued to haunt me. Russia successfully sent up another dog-driven Sputnik satellite, prompting the US to call for keeping Strategic Air Command (SAC) bombers in the air at all times. Our military planned to hide long-range missiles in underground silos. A flood of Civil Defense pamphlets outlining a massive shelter program to protect civilians in case of a nuclear war arrived in the mail.

As if that weren't enough, America failed to launch its first satellite. I had the TV on when the satellite burst into flames on the launch pad. We couldn't even get *into* the space race much less win it.

Despite the dire state of our world, Cousin Debbie and I shared many long lazy summer days together. Since I continued to attend Franklin School, a majority of my friendships developed and deepened there. Unfortunately, I lived miles from Franklin's school district and surrounding neighborhood, which meant I rarely saw my classmates on weekends or over the summer. All my old friends in the Pigeon Point gang attended Freshwater Elementary located in our area's school district. Without the bonds of school to hold us together, I gradually lost touch with Sharon Barnhart, Judy Lermo, and the rest of the gang.

Cousin Debbie remained my closest playmate and confidante. As with many large, multigenerational families, our tribe tended to be clannish and confined relationships to first and second cousins, aunts and uncles, brothers and sisters-in-law. We had so many flesh-and-blood relations that we needn't stray far from the pack to form friendships.

Debbie and I took turns staying overnight with each other during the summer. We especially treasured our overnights at Grandma Ida's. After thirteen children, Grandma had exhausted all her anxiety and left us to ourselves unless serious fighting broke out. The two-and-a-half-year edge I had on Debbie slowly disappeared with her advancement to second grade. I could no longer trick her into taking the smaller half of the cookie or candy bar we shared.

I still set the stage for our hard luck pretend dramas, but Debbie wanted more say in their scripting.

"Let's pretend that we're pioneer orphans who are—"

"I know, I know," Debbie interrupted me, "orphans who were left alone when cattle rustlers killed all the grownups in our wagon train," she finished, pouting in protest. "No! I don't want to be a poor orphan any more. Let's be grownup dance hall girls." Debbie aimed for a much more lucrative lifestyle than me and had the beautiful looks necessary for such an occupation.

I relented. "Okay, but I'm going to be a *widowed* dancehall girl."

Debbie scowled at me. "What's a widow?"

"A lady whose husband got killed, probably in some gold mine cave-in or shootout."

"Well, I'm going to be engaged to Matt Dillon like Miss Kitty."

"What else can I be?" I ruminated. At almost ten, I craved some new role to experience, possibly as a CIA spy. I shared my proposal with my cousin.

"I never once saw a handicapped spy," Debbie snapped, "not once."

"Fine," I yelled back. "We can be two strong widows who inherit our dead husbands' farms and make them prosper."

Without realizing it at the time, we came face-to-face with the limited options open to our mothers and aunts in the 1950's.

"Well, I know one thing, for sure. I'm never going to be a housewife like Mommy."

This surprised Debbie. "Why not?"

"Because she hates her job and I don't blame her. Having to work her fingers to the bone. Iron our clothes, even my Dad's boxer shorts. At least being handicapped means I'll escape chores like that."

"Well, I like playing with the broom and ironing board and iron Santa brought me."

I couldn't fathom how she still believed in Santa. "See, even Santa is preparing you for a life of drudgery. He leaves you a broom and an ironing board instead of real toys like dolls and hula hoops. No thank you to that! I'm going to be a teacher and a writer," I boasted. "And I'm never getting married." I had come to agree with Daddy. I probably would remain single due to the lack of men's interest in crippled women.

"Let's try and think of the jobs that ladies could do in the olden days," I proposed, anxious to get off the depressing topic of nobody wanting me for a wife.

Debbie pondered a moment. "My Aunt Shirley is a nurse. She doesn't want a husband," she mused thoughtfully. "I think they had nurses in the olden days."

"True. Auntie Mae works in a beauty shop," I noted. "She joined the WACs during the war. She showed me her old uniform with arm stripes and everything. She has scrapbooks filled with pictures of her visits to the Eiffel Tower and famous art museums." I sighed. "But that was before she married Uncle Carl and settled down."

"Some women are cleaning ladies. And lots are actresses," Debbie added, gaining momentum. "Once I saw a lady bus driver and you can always work as a telephone operator, can't you?"

"They didn't have buses and telephones back in the olden days, stupid."

Debbie stuck out her tongue and pinched my arm.

Clearly we needed some food in our stomachs before we got irritable and started pounding on each other. Debbie got up, brushing off her jeans. She spat in both hands, rubbing them together before putting them under my arms and struggling to lift me up. We didn't need grownups now that she could perform this task.

School was only days away when Debbie and I had our last summer sleepover at Grandma's. We'd spent a sunny morning rolled up in a sleeping bag, pretending we were camping out on the prairie. After a long argument over how much of the sleeping bag was her half, Debbie got up and unfurled herself. "It's too hot on this prairie," she announced, taking off her Davy Crockett coonskin cap and swinging it in the air by its tail. "I'm going to put the sleeping bag away," she announced, "so get out of it."

Unaccustomed to her authoritative air, I resisted her attempts to drag me out before my time. "I'm going to stay right here for now," I challenged. She gave my arm a hard pull, but didn't have the strength to remove my gone-limp body from the bag.

"Move," she shouted, her tone more threatening than it had ever been. I shut my eyes and curled myself up into a ball.

The next thing I knew, Debbie had zipped the bag closed and began rolling it up with me inside.

She gave a wicked little laugh and plopped down on top of me.

"Get off me, I'm suffocating in here," I ordered, but Debbie maintained her position.

"Say I won and I'll let you out."

"No way," I told her, asserting my own diminishing authority. "You didn't win," I argued. "I'm staying here until I'm good and ready to get out."

Debbie started bouncing on me, at first gently, but soon with growing pressure.

"You're squashing me. Get off or I'll tell on you."

"Not if you can't get out of the bag," she taunted.

She had a point. The balance of power in our relationship shifted some that day with me losing a little ground and Debbie increasing the size of her territory. I knew I could get Debbie in trouble by being a tattle-tale, but I also realized doing so would cancel out any hopes we had for staying overnight at Grandma's. "Okay, you win," I surrendered.

Debbie opened the top of the bag and nestled her head next to mine. "You'll have to say it again 'cuz I can't hear you, Paula."

"You win," I said a bit louder.

Debbie got off me, unzipped the sleeping bag, and helped me out and up into a standing position. "But you didn't win fair and square," I added, once I had my balance.

Debbie gave me a little shove and watched me teeter back and forth. "Say I won," she demanded, folding her arms across her chest. I realized she could push me down and leave me there, but we both knew such abandonment would be frowned upon, possibly putting any prospect of a sleepover that night at risk. Debbie enjoyed these times as much as I did.

"Okay, you win," I told her," adding "but I didn't lose."

We stood, eyeballing each other in a nerve-wracking stalemate before she replied, "Okay."

Detente established, we left the sleeping bag out on the prairie and ran back to Grandma Ida's house to snatch a big round sugar cookie from the jar. As I dusted some cookie crumbs off my lap, I noticed that the time I had spent confined in the sleeping bag had taken some of the starchiness out of the brand new outfit Mommy bought me. Mommy said I had to save it for the first day of school, but once I'd learned that Debbie would be wearing her brand new Davy Crockett coonskin hat to Grandma's that day, I begged Mommy to let me wear my own new purchase. Everything had to be even-steven.

The blouse had stripes and the circular blue skirt came with a poodle appliqued on it. The dog wore a ruby-studded collar for an added touch. The poodle's stripes matched the blouse and my stiff can-can slip made my blue skirt flare out around me. "I just hate itchy things," Mommy reminded me, when I showed her the multi-colored, multi-layered can-can slip modeled by a teenaged mannequin at Dalys "Just feel how stiff this is." She grabbed my hand, rubbing it up and down the netted material.

"It's not *all* that scratchy, Mommy, and besides I need a stiff slip to make this poodle skirt flare out right. Debbie has one just like this," I lied, "and she's way younger than me."

Mommy helped me undress in the changing room, tucking the striped blouse into the waistband of the blue skirt. Sighing loudly, she pulled up the stiff netted slip. I smiled at myself in the mirror, turning this way and that to make the poodle dance.

"Oh, Mommy, I just love it. Please, please, please can I get the slip?"

I held my breath and watched while Mommy did some mental math. "You can get it, but the slip costs as much as your skirt and blouse, so it will have to count as one of your new outfits."

"Agreed," I sang out.

Debbie wiped off her milk moustache and the circle of sugar clinging to her mouth "I love your new poodle skirt," she complimented me after our cookies and milk interlude had resolved any tensions from earlier on. In return, I told her I thought her coonskin cap set off her long golden brown ringlets which I envied far more than her hat.

Grandma Ida took away our empty glasses and joined us at the table. "I like it when you two treat each other nicely," she smiled approvingly. She plopped down a new *Little Lulu* comic book in front of me. It was the big fat summer edition. She looked over at Debbie. "So, do you think Grandma has forgot about you?"

Debbie knew she hadn't and gladly accepted the summer edition of *Tom and Jerry*.

"Now why don't you two settle down on the couch and read them," she suggested. "Grandma's going to take a little cat nap." She yawned.

"Thanks for the comics," Debbie said politely.

"And have a good nap," I added. "Take some weight off your weary bones like Mommy does."

We retired to the living room to enjoy our comics. After twenty minutes or so we got restless. We tiptoed to the half-closed door of Grandma's bedroom where she snored away, looking peaceful. "Let's not disturb her," I suggested, quietly closing the door. "Let's think of something we can do without having to wake her up to ask permission."

"She needs her rest," Debbie agreed, her voice full of phony concern.

Neither of us could think of anything we could do without adult approval so we considered activities that, if not actually forbidden, would get us in the least amount of trouble.

Debbie brightened up. "I know, let's go down to the pond and count fairies. That's not too dangerous." We exchanged guilty grins.

The pond had a bad reputation in our family mythology. Although it couldn't have been more than two feet deep, all of my twenty-two cousins

146

and I had been warned off the site unless accompanied by a teenager or adult.

To Debbie and me, the real draw of the pond was its location in a shady mysterious place surrounded by giant rhododendrons and wild azaleas. Eucalyptus trees ringed the property and the massive woodwardia and sword ferns served as a lush green backdrop when we pretended to be explorers fighting our way through the jungles of South America, like the ones featured in Grandma Ida's copies of *National Geographic*. The drawback to the scene lay in its close proximity to Uncle Charlie's cabin. "You keep away from his private property," Grandma warned us a hundred times. She came up with interesting taboos that sparked our imaginations, but the truth of it was this only made the off-limits cabin more tempting.

With Grandma still catnapping in her bedroom, we quietly gathered up an old bag of bread crusts to lure fish and fairies into our make-believe world. Debby took my arm as we maneuvered our way down the three front steps and set off for the slippery path to the pond. With any luck, we might see some frogs or dragonflies there.

"I gotta be careful not to get my new school outfit dirty," I reminded Debby, decreasing my pace so I wouldn't fall. When we arrived at the pond, not a single fish surfaced for our treat. "Looks like they got eaten last winter during that midnight raid of raccoons," I recollected in disappointment.

"Probably the same ones that ate three of Grandma's banty hens," Debbie frowned. "She hadn't even named them yet."

With no fish or fairies around, Debby and I tramped through the dense underbrush, stopping when we discovered piles of empty wine bottles littering the ground outside Uncle Charlie's cabin.

To my horror, Debby took a big swig from one that still had an inch of wine left in it. She held the bottle to my lips so I could share in this pleasure. We pretended to take big slugs from the bottle and then stumbled around as if we were drunk. I accidentally swallowed some of the high-octane brew.

I spit it out immediately. "Ew—that's nasty stuff."

Nevertheless, Debbie had her own opinion and swallowed a little sip. We watched warily, waiting to see if the world would start spinning around for her, but nothing happened.

A loud snoring serenaded us through one of Unk's open cabin windows. We crept up closer, brash enough to poke our heads in to get a better view of Unk sleeping off his latest bender. Eventually Unk's snores died down so we gave up on that and headed back towards the pond. We picked several handfuls of daisies on the way and sat in a patch of sunshine to make chains to wear. Mine kept falling apart since it's next to impossible to string daisy chains with one hand.

Tired of listening to my complaints, Debbie ripped up her chain and threw it to the ground. "Let's go back and watch Unk sleeping," she insisted. "You can do that with only one hand, right? Then we can go eat some French prunes and greengages."

"Forget the prunes. Remember, Grandma told us to stay clear of the prunes because there's a lot of them that have fallen off the branches and rotted. The path's a real mess."

"Then, there's nothing left to do except watch Unk," Debbie whined. "I wish we could get inside his cabin and look through that trunk of his."

"Who knows? Maybe he'll invite us in."

The two of us trudged back up the path to the cabin and for the second time, peered in through the dirty window. Without warning, Unk bolted upright. We let out a scream and jumped back when his eyes flipped open.

"He's got a gun," I yelled to Debbie, pointing to a twenty-two rifle propped up against his bed. Unk kept blinking and scratching his bald head. "What do you damn kids want?" he barked, his speech slurred probably from having finished off the bottle of fortified wine I spotted next to his rifle.

Our overly inventive imaginations conjured up several catastrophes. We spun in our tracks and took the messy shortcut that ran right through the stand of prune trees. Over the years, I had developed a hop-skip move, using my brace to full advantage. I made good headway, almost keeping up with Debbie.

"He's coming," I said, half laughing, half crying, half hopping for my life.

Debbie whimpered. "Oh, Paula, I think he has his gun."

That threat goosed me into a faster trot, but in my rush, I fell over, landing on a pile of juicy prunes littering the path. I could feel a sticky dampness seeping through my skirt. Debbie stopped to help me up, but by then the plum dye was cast...all over my poodle skirt.

Debbie looked as horrified as me when I explored the damage done to my outfit. She picked me up, emitting a little moan. "Your poodle skirt is wrecked," she cried, knowing how much I loved it.

I looked back over my shoulder, glancing at the big red blotches of juice. Several smashed prunes still clung to my skirt.

Debbie soon ran out of her compassion and patience. "We got to hurry." She grabbed me under my arm to hasten our retreat. "Uncle Charlie looked mad enough to shoot us," she wailed. "Let's go back to Grandma's."

"But we can't. She'll see my skirt and know we broke our promise."

"We can hide in Grandma's cellar," Debbie decided, taking charge for the moment. "Maybe we can hose off your skirt while we're there."

With our shoes covered in mushy plum juice, we slushed our way to the side of Grandma's house and ducked into the cellar around the back. The earthy fragrance of potatoes and apples filled our noses as Debbie helped me off with my skirt and shot a steady stream of water at it from the garden hose.

"It's not coming out," Debbie moaned. I started to cry and she gave me a consoling hug before we collapsed onto a heap of empty gunnysacks. Feeling relatively safe and exhausted, we fell asleep, visions of Unk and his gun dancing through our heads.

I woke up with a start, nudging Debbie out of her peaceful slumber. "Listen."

Off in the distance we heard Grandma's plaintive calls. "Paula," she yelled. "Debbie. Where are you two hiding?"

"We're here in the cellar, Grandma."

When Grandma opened the cellar door, we noticed with dismay that Unk wobbled there at her side. After downing a little more wine, he somehow managed to stagger up to Grandma's and report our trespassing. The two of them searched all the places we were forbidden to go and seemed a little perturbed at finding us so close to hearth and home.

By now, my skirt had dried off, but the stain remained. Grandma pretended not to notice, just shook her head sadly and said, "Sometimes the punishment fits the crime." Which I guess was why she never told Mommy or Auntie Dot about our crimes and misdemeanors.

Grandma quickly agreed when Mommy suggested Debbie should stay overnight at our house rather than the two of us remaining with her.

"Don't know why, but I'm a little tuckered out," she wheezed.

"I hope you two didn't wear out Grandma," Mommy fretted on our drive home.

"I don't think so, Mommy. We pretty much stayed out of her way." I looked over at Debbie for confirmation.

"We didn't fight or make any messes, Auntie Lill," Debbie assured my mother. Then, in a stroke of sheer genius, she added, "I think Unk upset her cause he stayed out all night on one of his benders."

"That old drunk will be the death of Grandma," Mommy complained bitterly.

Unless, of course, *we* were.

Mommy shook her head and sighed when she saw my wrecked skirt. "Plum juice stains are forever," she told me as she prepared Debbie and my dinner of spam and eggs. It was just the three of us because Daddy had two free tickets to the Harlem Clowns, the branch of the Globe Trotters that visited puny logging towns like Eureka. He took David to see them whenever they appeared. Daddy also took David to the fights until Mommy put a stop to it when a boxer knocked out his opponent and sent him to the emergency room.

"Now you only have a blouse, a pink gingham dress and a scratchy can-can slip to wear the first day of school," Mommy remarked between bites of spam. She said this in an irritating *I told you so* way.

Debbie felt bad for me and let me wear her coonskin hat until we went to bed that night. It was nice of her, but I'd rather have had her long ringlets as my consolation prize.

25

POETRY IN MOTION

The bell rang for the fifth grade class and I shuffled my way from the playground to my desk, unlocking my brace so I could sit down. My heart gave a happy skip as I reexamined the purple mimeographed school bulletin I held in my hands. Right there in front of me, situated between next week's cafeteria menu and a PTA announcement, was my first published poem.

Mrs. Wales, my fifth grade teacher, had passed out a copy to all the kids to take home to their mothers.

"Let's hear you read the poem," the gentle southern lady coaxed me in her soft drawl. I loved Mrs. Wales, even after she scotch-taped my mouth closed when I kept talking to my neighbors.

I blushed a little, but wasted no time locking my brace and standing up to recite my ode to spring. "Hear the robin sing," I read out loud in a shaky voice, "by Paula Viale, aged ten."

Hear the robin sing,
"Tis such a pretty sound,
It is the song of Spring
That he sings round and round.

You must get up so early
If you want to hear him sing,
He is in such a hurry
To sing his song of Spring.
The dew he drinks is fresh and cool,
I always feed him bread,
He takes his bath in a little pool,
And sings to me when I'm in bed.

Now he always goes to rest
Way high up in a tree;
I think he's built a little nest
For wife and babies three.
Today instead of just one robin,
There are many more
Tiny little heads a-bobbin',
In fact, I think there's four.

I fell back into my desk, drained by my solo performance.

Mrs. Wales smiled her beautiful smile and led the class in a round of applause. That's when stupid Mark Fieg began to wave his hand in the air, seeking the teacher's attention.

"Yes, Mark?"

"I think she got the math wrong," he announced importantly. "There's a total of five tiny little heads a 'bobbin," he smirked. He thought he was so smart.

I jumped back up to defend my poem. "I didn't count the father robin, because he was there from the start," I explained, furious at Mark's criticism.

Mrs. Wales stepped in before a brawl broke out. "Paula," she informed the class, "is practicing something called poetic license. It gives her the right to bend words into appropriate rhymes and rhythms."

I had no idea what she was talking about, but a poetic license sounded good to me and put an end to Mark Fieg's snide remarks about my math abilities.

To nurture my budding talents, Mrs. Wales gave me a book called *Great American Poets*, which provided me with an introduction to Robert Frost and Emily Dickenson. She told me both of them had poetic licenses and made their living by writing. My father always emphasized the importance of me using my head and other talents so I could support myself when I grew up. Maybe writing poetry would pay the bills. Along with running our pet shop.

At my request, Mrs. Wales had re-appointed Marilyn as my monitor when I returned to Franklin. "It's good having you back in school," she told me when we sat down later in the auditorium to eat our lunches. I still carried mine in my fishing basket from first grade.

"Hey, are you going to try out for City Choir tomorrow?" she hollered, forced to yell in order to be heard over the din of students' voices that filled the auditorium.

I swallowed a bite of my tuna fish sandwich. "I didn't know they were having tryouts." I shrugged. "But, sure, I'll go. I make a good high soprano. I've sung in Sunday school and church."

"Well, you need to get a written consent form for your parents to sign. They passed them out at the end of last year while you were in the hospital. I think Miss Asslestein still has them in her office."

Although she terrorized almost everybody, even the boys from the housing project, I had a better than average relationship with our German principal. For the first few years of school, I went to her office to use her private bathroom. She also helped me pull my underpants up and down. Now that I had taught other girls how to help me, I didn't see much of Miss Asselstein.

As we ate dinner, Mommy and Daddy studied the permission slip I'd brought home. "Looks like this should be fun," Daddy remarked. He was in a good mood because Mommy had cooked him up a juicy steak, dripping with blood.

Mommy frowned. "How is she going to get there from school?" she asked. "And how will she get home?"

I ran a fork through my mashed potatoes, bubbling with excitement. "We get to ride there on a school bus. It drops us off and then our parents pick us up at four forty-five. Please sign the slip," I begged. More than anything, I wanted to ride in the school bus, something I had only done once before on a field trip to the Big Loaf Bread factory. Riding the bus was as big a deal to me as trying out for the City Choir. I'd be like a normal kid instead of one who was chauffeured to and from school by a man like Mr. Beebee.

"Well, you haven't even been to the tryouts," Mommy reminded me. "You may not make it and then you'd be disappointed."

After all the times I'd sung in church choirs, I just knew I'd be chosen. Besides, I had grown up on disappointment.

Daddy pushed away his plate and signed the permission slip. "Look, her practice ends just a few minutes after I pick up David from Little League. It'll be easy to swing by. Might as well let her try out."

So try out I did. The next day, Marilyn and I sat outside the music room, nervously waiting our turn to audition. By the end of school, we learned we'd both made the final cut.

"I'm going to have to be a tenor," Marilyn moaned to me "because not enough boys tried out."

"But just think of it, we'll get to ride on the bus," I shrieked in unmitigated joy.

Marilyn scrunched up her nose. "Who cares? I have to ride the bus every day."

Her lack of enthusiasm failed to dampen my spirits. New independence was on the horizon and I would greet it riding in a bright yellow school bus. City Choir met every Tuesday afternoon following school. I had chosen a new box-pleated skirt and a frilly blouse to wear on my first bus ride.

The handsome Italian bus driver swept me up in his hairy thick-muscled arms and took the three giant steps into the bus with ease. "I'm 'a Joe," he introduced himself with a heavy accent, "and I'm'a gonna put you right behind me so I can keep an eye on you." He winked at me. "You looka like a pretty rowdy kid to me," he teased.

I nodded. "Just throw me off the bus if I get too wild," I told him, proud that my snappy comeback made Joe smile. I wondered if bus drivers married crippled women.

Altogether there were seventy-five members of the City Choir. During our first gathering, we sat in rows of uncomfortable folding chairs as the choirmaster, Mr. Matson, ran us up and down the scales. Next, he had us stand up so he could arrange us by height. I was the shortest one there, so some other short kids and I stood on the floor. I lucked out because the risers would have been impossible for me to climb.

Mr. Matson clapped his hands. "Settle down now and act like young ladies and gentleman. I want you to walk around in a circle so I can see how well you can pace yourselves."

In spite of my limp, I managed to keep up, except when the boy behind me stepped on the heel of my oxford. "Can't you hobble any faster?" he egged me on. "You walk like an old lady."

For the most part, kids at school liked me and rarely tormented me or called me names. It caught me by surprise that such a rude remark came out of the boy's mouth. He had dirt on his face and under his fingernails, and his jeans were patched and too small.

I turned around for a face-off. "You must be from the projects 'cause kids there can't *afford* manners."

I waited for another of his wisecracks. None came; he put his hands in his pockets and skulked away, but not before I saw the hurt look on his face. I was learning to use my words as weapons, the way my peers used slapping and punching each other to fend off personal attacks. Like Daddy said: "Practice makes perfect."

David, suited out in his Little League baseball uniform, waited outside for me at the end of our first choir practice, sauntering along at my pace. He opened the door of Daddy's truck and pushed me up onto the seat.

I snuggled next to my father, telling him about the bus ride and rehearsal.

"Sounds like you two are real winners today," he congratulated us.

"We won our game by four runs and I made one of them," David spouted. What he didn't say was how much he missed Mommy and Daddy attending most of his games. Daddy continued to work Saturdays and Mommy had, as she often explained, "her hands full" taking care of me.

"When you get a car of your own, I'll ride to every game with you," I promised David, wishing my caretaking hadn't prevented Mommy from attending his games. Her hands weren't that full.

"Thanks," he said, half-heartedly. "It'll be a long time coming, me getting a car." Now that he had made it to junior high, David set up a calendar to mark off each day that brought him closer to a learner's permit. His enthusiasm for baseball died down, but we still fantasized about the prospects of outings in his future car. He planned to drive as far away from Eureka and Daddy as he could go on a tank of gas.

Mr. Beebe had continued to cart me back and forth to school. The rest of the kids from Franklin's Special Class had grown too big and aggressive for him to handle, so thankfully I was now his only passenger and could sit up in the front seat with him. I told him how excited I was about joining the choir and we were celebrating the fact when he dropped me off after school the next day.

Mommy helped me up the front door steps, a serious look on her face.

"What's wrong?" Panic seeped into my bloodstream.

"I'm afraid I have some bad news for you."

I blurted out the first thing that popped into my head. "Who died, Mommy?"

Mommy smiled sadly and sat down with me on the Chesterfield. "Nobody died, but I got a call from your choir director saying he didn't think you were up to being in the City Choir."

"Why not?"

"He's worried that you won't be able to stand up for a forty-five-minute concert and he doesn't want to ruin the symmetry of the choir by having you sit in a chair."

"The bastard!" I yelled.

Mommy never blinked an eye. "Yes, I'd say he qualifies for being a bastard."

"But if I start practicing now, I can be strong enough to stand up for forty-five minutes by the time we have our Christmas concert. You have to tell him that."

"He sounded pretty definite about it. He did say you had a lovely voice, though."

When Daddy got home and heard the news, he hit the roof. He immediately called up Miss Asselstein to register his complaint. "You tell

Mr. Matson that Paula can stand up for forty-five minutes so as not to defile the symmetry of his stupid choir. He is not kicking her out." Daddy slammed down the receiver before the principal had time to respond.

Daddy looked over at me. "Well," he asked, "why aren't you standing up? You've got your work cut out for you if you're going to stand up for forty-five minutes."

Practice began that night. I managed to stand up for fifteen minutes while watching *Rawhide* on television. I crumpled in a heap during the commercial, but both Mommy and Daddy cheered me on. "You'll be standing up through all of the *Ed Sullivan Show*, before you know it," Daddy convinced me when he tucked me into bed.

I stood up to eat cereal at the breakfast bar and spent most of every recess at school standing on the yellow line where badly behaved students were forced to remain for the entire length of playtime. I became acquainted with several kids from "low" fifth grade. Most of them lived in the cheap-rent projects. These kids' worst crimes appeared to be poverty, dirt, and grime. I came to understand how working class families were protected from such hoodlums who were fated to attend the "low" part of whatever grade they had reached while school officials channeled the most fortunate of us into the "high" grade realms of academic life. Segregation happened in lots of ways and places.

Mr. Matson resented the fact that Miss Asselstein forced him to let me remain in City Choir. By the time of our Christmas concert, I could stand for over an hour straight, so what could he say? Gradually he came to accept my presence and even assigned me a short solo to perform during our Christmas pageant. At the end of each stanzas of a Christmas carol, I sang out "dear little babe of mine" in my sweet little soprano voice. Like it or not, I was there to stay.

Mommy found me a beautiful red dress to wear for our performance. It had candy cane trim around the sleeves and bottom ruffle. Even though the dress was a hundred percent cotton and had a "made with the union label" sewed on the inside, I felt beautiful in it. Not all "union made" clothes looked ugly. Thanks to the white rabbit fur cape and matching hat Mommy had secretly put on layaway early in the summer, I could have passed for a Hollywood starlet…except for my limp and the fact that the dress lacked a pocket to hide my shriveled-up hand.

By the middle of fifth grade, my life had settled into a comfortable routine of weekly classes and for the first time, the experience of being part of a weekend gang of boys and girls who went on group outings. Marilyn and I remained best buddies, and we paired up to go places with Brad, Mark, Ricky, Susan, Laurie, and Ruth. It was the closest thing to a date I would have. Everybody's parents, including mine, ran us around town, sometimes to go shopping (and shoplifting) or spend time at the zoo or skating rink. What I most looked forward to was when they'd dropped us off at the Fresh Freeze where we wolfed down hamburgers and French fries before walking to the Eureka Theater.

The wide staircase to the loges, the plush red carpets muffling our footsteps, and the chandeliers hanging in the main lobby of the theater recalled glory days gone by, but nobody noticed the carpets now looked threadbare and three of four light bulbs had burnt out in the chandelier. We loved the bygone splendor. It offered a glittery getaway for Eureka's glamour-starved residents.

We watched very little of any movie, entertaining ourselves by throwing popcorn at each other and making trumpets out of the cardboard boxes candy came in and blowing them in unison on the count of three. Once, an usher threatened to kick us out of the theater if we didn't quiet down. That proved to be a highlight of the year, something I could brag about to my friends.

I soaked up the pleasure of being part of a crowd. None of these kids stared at me and if some stranger gawked too long, Marilyn would pipe up, "Hey, if you don't like it, shoot it."

Then the group broke out in peals of laughter while the gawker blushed or hurried away.

Though I had many a heartthrob during these pre-adolescent years, it never crossed my mind that any of the boys would develop a crush on me. I rejected their compliments except when they told me how funny I was or asked for help with homework. Daddy had prepared me so well for being an energetic self-supporting girl who would do just fine on her own, thank you, that I rarely thought of love and marriage.

Except for a serious mental block in math, I did well in all my studies. No one ever confused me with the mentally retarded kids I worked so hard to avoid. Nobody noticed if my brace squeaked or that I could only wear oxfords because of my polio foot. What I did get noticed for were the poems I continued to write and have printed in the daily school bulletins. I memorized most of the poems in the Emily Dickinson book Mrs. Wales had given me. I loved Emily who clearly understood my world of emotional pain. She must have, given she'd written "I'm nobody, who are you? Are you nobody too?"

I read that Emily lived a solitary life, never married, and devoted her time to poetry that few people even read in her lifetime. She provided another perfect role model, although I hoped the public would read my poems while I was still alive so I could get paid for them.

26

MINOR FAME

It was official. The local chapter of the March of Dimes had chosen me to be their Humboldt County poster child. I didn't like the way this organization portrayed crippled children, giving them hard luck life stories to make people feel pity for them and fork over their dimes. Like most crippled kids, the last thing I wanted was pity. I didn't mind being thought of as courageous with lots of gumption, but I hated the people who came up to Mommy and me when we went to town, patted me on the head and sighed "Poor little duffer," and stuff like that.

Daddy asked his old friend, Dave Hoppe, to come over one Saturday to photograph me and take one picture for the newspaper and one for the March of Dimes flyers, which would be stapled to phone poles and handed out to businesses. I chose my striped dress with the red pinafore, the going home outfit I had worn six months earlier when I left Shriners. I knew about the March of Dimes through my father's accounts of his futile attempts to get the organization to help cover the cost of a new leg brace. Mommy had marched with a group of neighborhood mothers, traipsing around Pigeon Point to collect dimes for the organization. She hated fundraising and soliciting for donations. I think most of the other mothers felt the same way, which is probably why the five of them only collected $5.70.

"I felt awful accepting seventy cents from the little girl at the bottom of the hill," Mommy confessed over dinner that night. "She had saved up her allowance to give to that stupid organization."

"You should have taken Paula with you," David reflected in hindsight. "I bet if she limped around in little circles once people opened their doors, you would have raised a lot more money."

I glared at my brother. He was a master at hiding little barbs in his conversation, but I said nothing, giving him the benefit of the doubt.

Just before Dave arrived, I took a last look at myself in my bedroom mirror. My hair still hadn't recovered from the Toni Home Permanent Mommy gave me every fall before I started back to school. Mommy lacked any beautician skills and even though she carefully followed the perm instructions, my hair curled up in frizzy knots like a tumbleweed on my head.

I applied *Suave* hair dressing to my kinky fuzz, but I overdid it. I hoped no one would notice.

Mommy noticed it right away. "Honestly, Paula, you'd never know we washed your hair last night. It looks so limp and dirty. I just don't get it."

I was not about to mention the glob of cream I had tried to work into my hair. It didn't help that my earlobes stuck out thanks to the time I had spent in my body cast with it pushing up under my ears. I begged Mommy to let me wear her dangling pearl earrings to hold my lobes down, but she refused.

"You're way too young to be wearing earrings," she insisted.

"Then can I tape them down?" I held up my backup plan, a roll of Scotch Brand Invisible Tape.

"Don't be silly."

I gave up arguing with her when I thought up a perfect solution. Luckily, Daddy had bought me a black Pomeranian puppy to replace old Chico when he died. During the photo shoot, I insisted on holding Cuddles by her leash while I stared down at her lovingly. The pose completely hid my ear lobes. I looked a lot cuter staring down at a dog.

By Monday morning, most of the kids in class had seen my picture in the *Standard*.

Brad Brisbon flattered me by bringing a clipping to show during sharing. Our teacher, Mrs. Killmore, who was substituting for Mrs. Wales that day, snatched it from him and shoved it into the top drawer of her desk along with all the other items she had confiscated from a rowdy bunch of students she called "hooligans."

"Let's not give Paula a big head," she cautioned Brad. "Last thing this little lady needs is another photo opportunity."

I hated Mrs. Killmore. Luckily, I had missed out on most of her class back in third grade because I'd been at Shriners. For some reason she had it in for me. I overheard her tell another teacher I was spoiled rotten because of all the attention I got. Stares and whispered remarks were hardly my idea of attention.

My photo and the news article about crippled kids got around town and the next thing I knew, our local television station, KIEM, called to invite me and Daddy to appear on *What's Happening?*, a local show that followed

Walter Cronkite and the Evening News. KIEM planned to publicize the next March of Dimes campaign so they wanted the president of the March of Dimes, Daddy, and me to be on the show.

I was well on my way to becoming a local star. "A big fish in a little pond," is how Mrs. Killmore put it after I shared the news with the kids at recess.

Daddy took time off from work and picked me up at school. "They're going to tape us at three, so we have to hurry."

"I'm kinda nervous Daddy," I confessed to him over the truck's noisy engine. "At least most of the frizz has gone out of my hair." I stroked the new red sweater Mommy had bought me for the occasion. It matched my red plaid skirt perfectly.

Daddy lifted me down from the truck, pulling out the hem of my skirt, which somehow got tucked up into my underpants. "You'll do fine, honey. Your old Dad's a bit shaky himself."

Although Daddy yelled and turned beet red when he got angry, he had a shy streak that showed up when he was in public. I would have to respond quickly if he froze during our taping.

The KIEM studio was dark compared to the bright spring afternoon. A man named Alan rushed over to us, took my father's hand, and pumped it enthusiastically.

Before I was ready for proper introductions, he grabbed my limp polio hand, and then dropped it as if it was a hot potato. "Sorry. I didn't hurt you, did I?" he stammered.

I offered Alan my good hand, but he had already turned away, suddenly intent on studying a script attached to the clipboard he carried.

We followed Alan over to some folding chairs, one occupied by Fred Watson who swayed up to greet us. "Frederick Watson," he stammered after Daddy replied "Jack Viale."

"You can call me Fred," he told us, little droplets of sweat popping out on his forehead. Fred had stuffed himself into a plaid suit bursting at the seams. He tugged at a bright yellow tie that had him in a stranglehold. "I'm president of the Humboldt County March of Dimes." He winked at me. "And this here, must be little Carla," he gushed.

"Paula," I corrected him. "I'm Paula Viale, poster girl for the March of Dimes."

By now, sweat poured over Fred's bulbous nose and down his moon-shaped face. "Ah, oh…Paula yes, yes," he stuttered, "That's what the script says so it must be true. Ha, ha."

The studio lights reflected off Fred's shiny bald dome. A lady named Rhonda bustled over and wiped Fred down, brushing some powder onto his head. "You and Paula look great," she assured Daddy and me. "Now let's get everyone seated."

We stepped onto a little stage where three folding chairs circled around an ugly coffee table. I sat between my father, who had a stunned look on his face, and Fred, who continued to frantically mop his Elmer Fudd head. Rhonda hung clunky microphones around our necks, stepped back for a final view and gave us a thumbs-up.

The host of the show, John Laponna, dressed in a three-piece suit, waltzed in breezily. His dark eyes sparkled and he looked straight into mine. He gave my good hand a hearty shake. I was sitting on my polio hand, so he wouldn't get confused.

"I like your art show," I told John, referring to his fifteen-minute program called *Let's Have Fun with Sketching.* "We buy Challenge milk because they sponsor your show," I fibbed.

"Thank you, honey. Aren't you, sweet?"

Wasn't I though?

Bright lights flashed on, beaming their heat down on us. Fred started melting even faster.

John looked into the camera and welcomed his viewers to *What's Happening?* He gave the lowdown on the March of Dimes and all the good work they did for polio victims.

Fred jumped right in, adding his bit about President Roosevelt and his fight to overcome his own bout with polio. Gosh, I'd forgotten even polio victims could be elected to run the country.

Mr. Laponna introduced Daddy next. "Tell us how March of Dimes helped your little girl, Mr. Viale?"

Daddy stared into the camera for a long time.

At some point, he came to and nodded his head, smiling at the television's home audience. The smile lasted a long time, but he finally mumbled a few words about what a fine organization the March of Dimes was.

"Didn't they help cover the cost of Paula's new brace?" John prompted.

Daddy puzzled over the question. "Well, no, actually they didn't."

John looked confused, while Fred tugged at his tie.

I knew it was up to me to save the day. "Daddy says the March of Dimes always marches right by us," I blurted out, forcing the cameraman to swivel the camera in my direction.

My voice sounded far calmer than Daddy's or Fred's.

"Paula, can you tell us how the March of Dimes helped you?" John asked, grateful for the line I threw him.

"Well, they gave us a lot of little donation jars for Mommy and our neighbor ladies to collect people's dimes in." The camera swung over to the coffee table, focusing on a sad little donation jar sitting there. I took a deep breath and continued. "And they put on the East-West Shrine Games to raise money. I have one of their posters on my wall that says, 'Strong legs run that weak ones can walk.'"

John's eyebrows shot up in surprise as he searched for an appropriate response. "Ah, you're referring to the Shriners football game," John Laponna corrected me. "Another wonderful organization."

"Shriners make really bad braces," I rambled on. "But at least they made one for me when the March of Dimes turned Daddy's request down." I was on a roll, hardly nervous at all. "My brace man, Mr. Hawkins said the bulky braces Shriners made could support a hundred and fifty-pound man." I lifted my skirt a little to show off my sleek, lightweight brace. "This one is much more comfortable to wear, but the March of Dimes wouldn't pay for it."

John Laponna glared at me, but not before I had told all my friends in TV Land that Mr. Hawkins made the best braces in Humboldt County. "When we return from this break," John interrupted, "we'll hear more from Fred Watson."

John Laponna nodded to Daddy. "You two don't have to stay for the second part of the show. I'm sure Paula's pretty tired out by all this."

"Not really," I contradicted him, but Daddy lifted me into his arms and hurried us through the front door, held open by Rhonda. "Good job, sweetie," she praised me.

"I could have said a lot more, Daddy," I shrugged in disappointment, leaning my head against the truck window.

Daddy revved up the engine and pulled away from the curb. "No doubt about that," he agreed.

"Do you think I could be a host on a TV show, Daddy?"

"I think you can do anything you put your mind to, honey."

"A radio show would be even better," I dreamed on. "Nobody would ever have to know I had polio."

I leaned back against the seat, silently reliving my moments of fame. So what if Mrs. Killmore was right? I *was* a big fish in a little pond and that felt like the perfect fit for me.

We survived the Christmas holidays without Mommy having a nervous breakdown and I was pleased with the new Bobby Brooks skirt and sweater I received. David, now a teenager, requested a buttoned-down short-sleeved shirt and a long-sleeved sweater. Jeanne, just this side of four, had Santa deliver her a bunch of troll dolls with every color of hair in the rainbow. Almost immediately, she got hold of a scissors and cut off the trolls' topknots. Pleased with the effect, she went on to cut off both of her braids and most of her bangs. Now she looked like a troll, too.

For the first time ever, my cousin Susie had come to spend New Year's Eve at my house. She had never stayed overnight with me and I felt proud that the most beautiful of all the Wahlund cousins chose to be with me. We were up until midnight helping Mommy put together the jigsaw puzzle we always did as we waited for the year to change over.

David slept over at the Barnharts and Daddy slipped off to bed at ten because he was working New Year's Day. "Half a day for twice the pay," he told me, "thanks to the union."

Daddy still never gave up the opportunity to work overtime. "Your old Dad makes as much as a college teacher," he often bragged to me, neglecting to mention that college professors got weekends, Thanksgiving, Christmas vacation, and summer off. Teachers had a life.

On New Year's morning, Susie and I sat in front of the television ready to watch the Rose Parade. I loved the floats made of nothing but flowers. "I want to be a beauty queen one day," Susie confided in me. "And you can put that in your Ponytail Girl diary."

Susie was impressed with the diary I had received for Christmas along with a matching Ponytail Girl treasure box and autograph book.

"Well, I plan to be a writer," I told her. "I can write about you winning the Miss America Contest," I joked, but Susie looked serious.

"There's a woman in Eureka who owns a modeling agency and she advertised she was looking for new students. If we can afford it, I might enroll and learn special poses and how to walk down runways."

At least learning to be a writer cost nothing "but due diligence and practice, practice, practice," my home teacher, Mrs. McCord had once told me. At ten, I'd start my career by recording daily entries in my diary, and by the time I turned twenty-one, I could be self-supporting, fulfilling one of my father's goals for me.

Later that day, after we had a big New Year's Day feast, Daddy drove Susie home while I recorded my first journal entry.

Dear Diary,

Today I begin to record my thoughts and maybe world events in my diary if we don't blow up in a Nuclear War. My diary comes with a key to lock it up, away from prying eyes. I'm hiding it in my pink jewelry box, under the lining.

My brother came to mind, so I scratched out the last line.

27

CITY LIFE

The best thing about Auntie Bert and Uncle George was their decision regarding children. They didn't want them, at least not as permanent fixtures residing in their big green house on 2225 Ward Street. Being the oldest daughter of the Wahlund tribe, Auntie Bert exhausted whatever maternal longings she might have had by being the surrogate mother to Mommy and her twin, Uncle Bill, as well as rearing Donny, the last of the line. It also fell upon Auntie Bert to wash and iron an endless bunch of white work shirts for her five oldest brothers. She escaped her indentured servitude by getting married, moving far away from home, and sharing her time with Uncle George. Just him. Uncle George's large family left him with no yearnings for little feet pitter-pattering around the house either, so they were a perfect match.

For most of my growing-up years, I delighted in being their only child. I fell into this role when Daddy got the bright idea to send me to spend my summers in Berkeley. Except for my times at Shriners, this was the only respite Mommy had from me. It kept her from going over the edge, the result of the daily grind of taking care of me. I was as eager for the break as Mommy.

Daddy and Mommy drove to Ukiah, the halfway point, to meet up with Auntie Bert and Uncle George. I usually dozed through our picnic lunch due to my father's insistence on leaving our house at four o'clock in the morning, hoping to get on the road before the highway construction crews started their endless work on President Eisenhower's ten-year project to build an interstate highway system. By eight, we were well on our way, usually wedged between giant logging trucks that drove the twisted roads even worse than Uncle George did. Truck drivers liked getting a head start too and if Daddy didn't drive fast enough, they blew on their monster air horns to honk us out of their way.

2225 Ward Street came as close to heaven as I could get. I was on my best behavior because I felt safe and happy in the upscale two-storey house. Since my aunt and uncle rented out two of the tiny upstairs apartments to professors from UC Berkeley and kept a small bedroom for visiting family, downstairs was my domain. I slept on a couch that folded down into a bed. There was a pretty wide crack where the two halves of the sofa met, but it never bothered me a bit. Pocket doors that slid open and vanished into the walls separated all of the downstairs rooms. Auntie Bert and Uncle George's bedroom had such a door, which they closed at night, along with another pocket door that shut the living room off from the dining room where I slept.

Aunty Bert and Uncle George rarely fought and as far as I can remember I never got into any real trouble with them. Uncle George loved his lawn almost as much as he loved Auntie Bert, so if a dog pooped there or kids rolled on the grass, he would chase them away with his rake. If I did something questionable, Auntie Bert might say, "You better look out, missy." And I would. At peace with the world, nightmares no longer kept me awake.

Auntie Bert radiated a good mood when I got up every morning to join her and Uncle George for breakfast.

Over spring break, Debbie and I spent two weeks there together, vying for attention but never jealous of each other because there was always enough love to go around. The change in venue sparked our imaginations, prompting us to reinvent ourselves with new stories about our lives in the big city. We abandoned our roles as poverty-stricken orphans subsisting on the prairie; when we looked into the gold-framed mirror gracing Auntie Bert's small dressing room table, a pair of confident city slickers stared back at us.

Just like my summer visits, spring break visits always included a classy lunch at San Francisco's Cliff House where, dressed up in hats and white gloves for the occasion, we spoon-fed ourselves exotic shrimp cocktails and ordered chocolate mousse for dessert. Auntie Bert did us proud, gussied up in beautiful linen suits and pointy-toed high heels purchased at Good Will or the second-hand shop on Shattuck Avenue where the wives of rich men donated their barely worn outfits. In the late fifties and early sixties San Francisco was filled with some of the classiest dressers in the world.

One of our visits stands out above the rest. With some concern about our level of maturity—or lack thereof—Auntie Bert allowed Debbie and me to sleep upstairs in the guest room. It had just been vacated by our eighteen-year-old cousin Jeff who, unbeknownst to our aunt, left behind a stash of *Playboy* Magazines in a bottom drawer of the dresser.

Although I knew only men who shopped for their wives at Fredericks of Hollywood would stoop to reading *Playboy*, Debbie and I devoured the pictures of naked women spread out across the magazine's pages. Most of the cartoons flew straight over our heads, but the flawless nude perfection of the models left us flabbergasted. We especially enjoyed reading the interviews with "Playmate of the Month." Most of these women were said to be practically geniuses along with devoting loads of time to volunteering at hospitals, old folks' homes, and after-school activities that involved poor kids and their troubled families.

"Wow, listen to this, Debbie. Miss July is the winner of six major beauty contests, attends UCLA pre-med school, and reads two or three books a week. This article quotes her as saying, 'I love this country, I love intellectual gentlemen, and I love my body, something we should never be ashamed of. I hope when readers see my words and not just my body, I can help them feel good about their sexuality and take joy in it.'"

Debbie and I roared with laughter, embarrassed by the mention of sex.

I tried to imagine taking joy in the body polio had left with me. My joy meter stopped at about two out of ten points.

One Friday night, Debbie and I excused ourselves extra early. We were in the middle of a scary story in *Playboy*, one that had nothing to do with sex. Naked ladies had begun to bore us.

"It's only seven," Auntie Bert remarked, rechecking the kitchen clock.

"All that shopping today made us pretty tired," Debby explained as we trudged upstairs. I had learned how to scoot up and down the stairs so we no longer needed Auntie Bert's help getting to our room. We shut the door and pored over the sad childhood of Miss February before getting back to a story by Stephen King.

"Do you think these women are for real?" I asked Debbie while puffing up my tiny breasts through my nightgown.

Debbie, busy attempting an erotic handstand, nodded yes.

Nights in our private guest room ended abruptly when Auntie Bert sprung a surprise visit and found us out on the roof of the front gable watching stars and scanning the skies for UFOs.

She trudged over to the window and yanked me inside. Debbie climbed in after me, jabbering about how we were searching for any signs of alien space ships stealing across the night sky. "You can see a lot better out there on the roof."

"Well, there'll be no more star gazing. You could fall off the roof and break something," Auntie Bert justified. "I don't feel I can trust you two up here anymore. I'll feel better having you move downstairs to sleep on the hideaway couch. It's for your safety and my peace of mind."

The first night we slept downstairs we suffered withdrawal from our little hoard of soft pornography, so Debby slipped away and returned with the magazines. We'd lay awake until the house settled down for the night and then sneak into the tiny bathroom, close the door and turn on the light.

Debbie was helping me compose a letter to "Playboy Forum" so I could see my name in print when Auntie Bert knocked on the bathroom door around midnight.

"What are you doing in there?" she asked.

Debbie and I froze. "We're taking a shower," I blurted out.

"At this time of night?" Auntie Bert sounded hopping mad. "Well, get back to bed," she ordered in a voice that hinted we were nearing the last straw with her.

Auntie Bert waited for us in the hallway, so we stuffed the *Playboys* behind a shelf filled with towels and washcloths.

She followed us to bed with a curt good night.

"They're gone," Debbie cried out the next morning when she reached behind the towels on the bathroom shelf and found nothing.

My stomach flipped over. "What do you mean, they're gone?"

"Gone. G-O-N-E," she spelled out.

After a thorough search, we had to accept the fact that the *Playboy* magazines had unfortunately disappeared from the bathroom. But they hadn't gone far. When we stepped into the hall outside the bathroom, they lay face down on a pile of old newspapers waiting to be burned.

Debbie and I remained so quiet at breakfast, you could actually hear the snap, crackle, pop of our Rice Krispies.

Uncle George winked at Auntie Bert before he turned to us. "Cat got your tongues?" he joked as he picked up his lunch pail and prepared to leave for work. "I want you two to find something good to read today," he called out over his shoulder.

Snap, crackle, pop...

Later we watched Auntie Bert throw the newspapers and magazines into the incinerator next to the garage. Before she lit a match, she looked at us and asked, "Anything you want to save from here?"

We broke out in nervous laughter, but shook our heads, no, there was nothing there we wanted.

Auntie Bert slammed shut the incinerator's lid. "I didn't think so." Much to our relief, she never mentioned the *Playboys* going up in smoke.

Safe on the streets of Berkeley in the late fifties, Debbie and I enjoyed long walks through the neighborhood, stopping at the corner store for our candy cigarettes.

"I'm bored," Debbie complained between puffs.

"Me too. I know, let's get into the Plymouth and pretend we're Nancy Drews."

Debbie's face lit up. "Good idea, I'll race you to the garage." I hopped along dragging my brace at a good clip.

The two-car detached garage was dark and cool when we opened one of the folding doors and stepped inside. Debbie pulled the door closed behind her and we got into the car, trading places behind the wheel every so often.

We drove through all the Nancy Drew locations we could remember. Over the moss-covered bridge, past the mysterious Lilac Inn, and up the hill of the Pine Phantom. "I'm tired," Debbie announced, "let's pull over." She climbed into the back seat while I stretched out in the front. We'd covered a lot of miles and needed a restorative nap.

I glanced at the car clock. "Yikes! Debbie, wake up!"

Her head popped up over the seat. "Four o'clock," she gasped. "We've been here for two hours."

We exited the car and skedaddled out of the garage. From far down the street, we heard Auntie Bert calling out our names. The desperate sound of her voice unnerved me. We walked down the long driveway.

At the corner, we saw Auntie Bert surrounded by neighbors trying to calm her down.

"We'll find them," her friend Oggie reassured Auntie Bert.

"I saw them at the candy store no more than three hours ago," a foot-patrol policeman added. "They'll be fine."

"Here we are!" Debbie and I yelled down the street.

Auntie Bert spun around. The rest of the group did the same.

"We were safe and sound in the garage," I said nonchalantly.

"We didn't wreck anything in the car. We were pretending to drive Nancy Drew's yellow roadster." Debbie looked over at me for confirmation.

"I was playing Bess and Debbie was playing George. You know, Nancy's best friends."

I was about to explain the role of Ned, Nancy's boyfriend, but I swallowed my voice when I saw the crowd of neighbors charging in our direction.

Auntie Bert was as close to tears as I'd ever seen her. "You were supposed to tell me when you got back from your walk," she fumed. "We've been calling you for hours."

"I'm sorry," I stammered, struggling for something else to say.

Before I could think of anything, Uncle George drove down the driveway in his work car.

"You're home early," Debbie said, grabbing him by the hand and looking sweet.

"You're damned right I'm home early," he sputtered, walking over to Auntie Bert's side. "I'm home early because your Auntie Bert called me at work to say you were lost."

For the most part, Uncle George was a gentle man, but when something stirred up his anger, his voice took on an alarming tone.

"You two get inside and help your Auntie Bert set the table," he ordered. Thankfully, Uncle George had little experience as a parent, so his frowns and glares served as our punishment. Dinner conversation never got started. Debbie and I cleaned our plates and fell over ourselves handing out compliments about how good everything tasted.

Auntie Bert sat stoic and coldly rigid. Debbie and I agreed that we'd rather have been yelled at or even spanked than have to sit through another dinner like we had that night.

Debbie took a deep breath. "Can we still go to Fairyland tomorrow, Auntie Bert?"

Our aunt remained speechless.

I swallowed the frog in my throat. "Maybe some other time," I suggested.

Debbie and I lay awake that night, recounting our past enchanting visits to Oakland's Fairyland, a tiny version of the Disneyland Walt built later. If you could fit though the entrance, which was the door of the old woman's shoe, it was free admission. Adults had to cough up $1.75.

The next morning, Auntie Bert was still cross with us for our two-hour disappearance. "I almost called your parents to confess that I had lost you two. I need to know where you go and when you plan to return. That's a responsibility you're old enough to understand and honor."

"I promise to ask your permission before I go anywhere or make plans to do something," I swore to Auntie Bert.

"Me too," Debbie agreed. "I'm sorry we worried you and awfully glad that you didn't have to call Mommy and Daddy."

Auntie Bert gave in and took us to Fairyland, but some of the old rules had changed. We were still short enough to fit through the Old Woman's shoe for free, but if either Debbie or I wanted little extras like cotton candy or an Eskimo Pie, we had to spend our own money. Auntie Bert still treated us to lunch at the Cliff House and bought us knee socks and hair clips to spruce up our wardrobes, but if we wanted an extra comic book or most anything not essential, we paid for it with our own dimes. Being little skinflints when it came to our savings, Debbie and I learned there were an awful lot of things we could do without.

Even so, we were practically broke when it came time to drive to Oakland to take advantage of *Capwells'* sale. We were determined to buy swimsuits for our camping trip when we got back to Humboldt County. We found a 75% off rack, which offered pathetic-looking swimwear. Thankfully, we each found a suit in our size. The string on mine made a deep dent in my neck and Debbie's bottom part worked its way into her crotch, but we took our comedown in swimwear like real troopers. They still looked better than anything you could buy in Eureka.

28

MISPLACED

In the fall of 1959, I started sixth grade. Times were changing. Castro invaded Cuba and the Barbie doll occupied the toy world. The news filled up with accounts of creeping Communism and the admittance of two new states, Alaska and Hawaii, which messed up the design of the American flag twice. With its statehood, it might make it easier to get to Alaska to see if I could locate my Inuit mother. I still clung to that long-ago hope of finding my place in her world.

Mr. Beebe helped me out of his beat-up car on the first day, saluting as he held the heavy front doors of Franklin Elementary open for me. I had serenaded him all the way there with my worries about sixth grade and the dire consequences of being placed in "low" sixth.

"You'll do fine," he guaranteed me, escorting me to the front row of desks. They were the modern kind that stood separated from each other, had a top that opened, and best of all, a swivel seat.

I had grown accustomed to the new brace Mr. Hawkins designed for me that year, making it so smooth and easy to bend my leg and fit it under the desk. No more kids tripping over my stiff leg when it poked out into the aisle. The ring around the top of my brace pinched my skin if I swiveled the wrong way in my new desk seat, but I was used to tiny irritants like bunions, corns, and general skin rashes and chafing.

"See you this afternoon," Mr. Beebe called back to me. "Good luck."

By 8:45 a.m., kids started trickling into the room. My heart sank as I watched one after another of those from "low" fifth hanging up their coats and sweaters in the closet. Although I recognized most of the kids from the playground, not one familiar face from "high" fifth passed by me.

I had been demoted! My pulse raced as tears gathered in the corners of my eyes. I steamed with humiliation and righteous indignation. I had received "superior" and "highly satisfactory" on last year's report card, so what was I doing in the class with kids from the rundown side of town? Maybe school officials had demoted me because I missed so much school during my stays at Shriners.

I put my head down, nestling it into my folded arms. I tried to make my feelings go dead, like I learned to do at Shriners, but my emotions remained in high gear. "Oh, no, oh no…" I whispered to calm myself. It didn't help.

Suddenly an unfamiliar voice announced, "I will now begin roll call. Please answer 'present' when you hear your name." I didn't recognize the teacher reading the list of unfamiliar names. Two boys answered "absent" when the teacher called out their names so she had to write them up and send them to the principal's office. Clearly, she had a "take no prisoners" attitude.

When the teacher arrived at W in the alphabet, my name still hadn't been called. I heard a pair of heels click over to my desk. It belonged to Miss Reed, the "low" sixth grade teacher.

"There appears to be some mistake, Paula. You're not enrolled in my class. Your class is just across the hall."

Miss Reed took my hand and led me to the "high" sixth grade class.

Thirty pair of eyes stared at me as I limped to my designated seat, my brace whining all the way. For once, it failed to bother me.

"Here you are, Paula," the "high" sixth grade teacher, Mrs. Center, informed me enthusiastically. "Looks like your driver dropped you off at the wrong class."

I remained speechless, eagerly scanning the aisles for the familiar faces of Francis Gilmore, Susan Gates, Brad Brisbon, and my old best friend Marilyn Roberts.

"Hey, you got on your new brace," Marilyn noted with gusto. I sat down, pushed the lever that unlocked the cumbersome piece of steel, bent my leg, and hauled it under the desk.

"It's the latest model," I mumbled, embarrassed to remain the focus of everybody's attention.

"But it still squeaks like your old model," Mark Fieg teased. Mrs. Center whacked him on the head with her grade book, knocking off his glasses. They hit the floor with a satisfying clatter.

Mrs. Center made sure she crammed everything she could fit into our brains right from the start. We were still trying to catch up with the Russians and fighting the commies in the Cold War. We'd survived a couple of worrisome incidents with Russia, but so far, nobody had been blasted off the face of the earth.

Times felt good if you didn't listen to the news and I mostly enjoyed myself until an official-looking letter arrived at our house. A dismal shudder passed through me as I read the return address. Shriners Hospital wanted me to come for another visit. Once again, the bottom fell out of my world.

29

THIRD TIME'S A CHARM

My third and final stay at Shriners in 1959 deprived me of most of sixth grade and all of my first year of junior high school. During the three-month hospital stretch, the doctors took one look at my x-rays and decided to perform a second surgery on my back, stiffening up my curved spine by transplanting a piece of my hip bone into it—another experimental attempt to make me whole.

After I recovered from that very painful operation and they had put me in another loathsome body cast, the doctors determined it was finally time to have a go at my good leg. "By making incisions on both sides of this leg, we'll insert a pin into Paula's knee to stop the leg's growth until her shorter leg catches up," Dr. Shultz proclaimed to the latest gaggle of interns, "thus reducing her significant limp." It never did.

The doctor paid special attention to the early muscle transplant surgeons had performed on me when I was four. "We managed to stabilize her arm at a forty-five-degree angle so rather than hanging almost backwards at her side, she is able to move the limb in useful ways."

I demonstrated how I could flex my arm a little this way and that. It did work better and definitely pointed in the right direction.

"The surgery we plan to perform on her leg has proven successful in several cases," Dr. Ramsey reported. What he didn't mention was the surgery would leave two wide parallel scars, a nasty set of red railroad tracks, running up both sides of my leg.

Doctors' Rounds put everybody in a foul mood. "The intern who stitched you up definitely flunked sewing 101, but they gotta practice on someone," Lucy Knowles remarked with a nonchalance that irked me. She never tired of ranting against Shriners experimental surgery program. "Still, it's no money out our parents' pockets," she added with a bitterness that stung.

Lucy was my one and only true friend during this stay at Shriners. I gave up on developing my social skills and I didn't have the energy to make a bunch of new friends. Besides, I hoped this would be my last time at the Shrine and I didn't want to get involved with the mean-spirited back biting practiced by most of the pre-teen and teenaged girls.

At fifteen, Lucy had all the important beauty attributes that I lacked. She looked out at the world through a pair of bright blue eyes, set off by a flawless complexion and a halo of golden curls. Not that she'd be mistaken for an angel. Her only physical curse was a misshaped left foot, which doctors would cure with some new and still unpracticed surgery. I'll admit I envied her no end, but that didn't stop me from enjoying her wisecracks that landed her in the hall cubicle more than once.

"You'll look pretty good when you get out of that turtle shell," she said good-naturedly. "Oh, and get a new hairdo."

Thanks to the body cast, the only thing nurses could do with my thick brown hair was to rubber-band it together and roll it like a doughnut on top of my head. "It makes you look like a spinster," Lucy remarked.

"That's probably what I'll turn out to be. An old spinster—but a famous writer," I added. Teachers continued to rave about my poetry and more than one of them thought I could be published someday. They didn't know I'd already been published in the Franklin School bulletin twice. Being famous would help make up for my lackluster existence and inability to attract boys.

Three months crept by and I returned home in a body and leg cast. I spent the first weeks flat on my back. Since I had to stay in bed, Mommy redecorated my room again. I now possessed a maple dresser with a matching bed and desk and an extended closet and shelves built by Daddy. He and Mommy had purchased a little black-and-white TV which sat on a wheeled cart that stayed in my room. At night, Mommy would pop corn and sit with me to watch all our favorite television programs. We especially enjoyed the *Twilight Zone* and *77 Sunset Strip* starring Ed "Kookie" Burns. Like our shared time over paper dolls and sewing a layette for my Banister Baby, I took advantage of this time and space for us to connect, even in a superficial way.

Mommy looked forward to the *Gary Moore Show* and old classic movies. She bought lots of movie magazines for us to read and she'd tell me all about Bette Davis and Joan Crawford as if they were her best friends. We talked about our mutual love of Gary Cooper and Judy Garland and once we sent away for a glossy black-and-white autographed photo of Robert Young.

Along with bringing me a bedpan umpteen times a day, Mommy had to improvise a way to shampoo my hair while keeping my body cast from getting soaked. I lay on the bed sideways and turned over on my back so my head dangled over a large cooking pot balanced on a stepstool. This served as a sink while Mommy poured water from a pitcher to rinse away the bubbles. My cast also required Mommy to give me bed baths since I could hardly soak in the tub.

My entire wardrobe now consisted of dusters—lightweight robes that buttoned up the front and could fit over my body cast. They looked like the coats doctors wore, but they came in several different colors and styles. Mommy bought me one in every design and print that she could find, but *Seventeen* Magazine didn't feature a single model in a duster...or anything resembling one.

This cast was bigger and heavier than my other one. It reached up under my chin and covered the back of my head. The cast pushed my ear lobes out and made my chin look doubled, maybe tripled. When my body went into the cast, it went straight up and down and I had no idea that breasts and pubic hair were changing the landscape of my figure.

After six weeks, I visited Shriners clinic to have my leg cast removed and for the first time I saw little black hairs sprouting up the incision on my leg, not to mention in other embarrassing locations. The depilatory sensation of the time was a gross-smelling product called *Nair*. Mommy bought me some right away to stop me moaning about unwanted body hair. By lathering my legs and armpits with the slime and waiting ten minutes, the hair died and could be wiped away. If only it worked on the bright red lines scarring up my once perfect leg.

30

PLASTER OF PARIS MUMMY

I had been shocked and brokenhearted when I found out during my three-month check-up at Shriners that I'd be spending the rest of sixth grade and several months beyond that moldering in another stinking body cast. I couldn't believe I'd be gypped out of another year of school.

I sobbed uncontrollably as the intern on duty buzz-sawed through my cast. "But what about junior high? I'll miss all of seventh grade."

Mom left the plaster room, unable to watch and hear the cast cracking open. A peppy student nurse—it was her first day at Shriners—wheeled me down to the bathroom where I luxuriated in a hot tub of water. With obvious reluctance, she grabbed a washcloth, and scrubbed off all the dirt and dead skin I had accumulated. I caught her gagging as she washed away the strips of dried skin peeling off my back. She treated me like a disgusting leper, and frankly I could have passed for one. We barely exchanged ten words, which further humiliated me and triggered my self-disgust.

Mommy waited for me back in the plaster room. She had never before witnessed the procedure. She winced as the interns balanced me on a narrow strip of canvas with my arms and legs spread out and firmly attached to what resembled a medieval torture machine. As always, the most painful part came when the doctors put a strip of canvass under my chin while attaching a sort of girdle around my hips. As they turned a large crank, my neck stretched up and my hips were pulled down. They followed this torment by preparing me for my new cast.

"I see you had a full set of crayons in your last cast." the intern laughed while slapping on strips of cold wet plaster to my body.

"Yeah, my little sister dumped a boxful of them on my head when I was watching T.V."

"That was after she locked Jeanne in the duck pen," my mother explained in my sister's defense.

"But to get back to my education," I interrupted, "couldn't I go to school in a wheelchair?"

"I don't think that's a good idea," the intern argued. "I'm sure you'll have a teacher during that time." I couldn't read the doctor's name tag because it had plaster all over it. "You'll keep up with all your studies. Right, Mother?"

Mommy nodded her head. "Oh, yes. In fact, they've already assigned a new homeschool teacher," she guaranteed the intern and me. "Paula will be able to keep up with all her schoolmates."

"But I'll be all alone in homeschool." I could barely choke out the words.

"Lighten up," the intern smiled. "Everything's been taken care of for you."

Not quite everything, I wanted to scream. Mommy and I continued the conversation while we waited for my cast to dry.

Once again, Doug Harris had volunteered to drive for the long trip back to Eureka. I continued to rant and rage against my fate until Doug turned on the radio. "Time to check out the news," he told my mother.

We listened to the latest details about the summer suicide of Diana Barrymore. The unfairness of my lot made me both angry and sad. I didn't have a single tear to spare on a brunette bombshell who threw away a perfectly good life. I imagined myself peering into Diana's coffin and asking, *"Since you don't want it anymore, can I have your body or at least some of the usable parts?"*

Mommy tried to cheer me up. "I'm sure Debbie and your cousin Janet and Sharon will visit you, especially now that you have your own television and a telephone."

"Yeah, but they'll have made new friends and done all sorts of things while I'm trapped at home. They'll have their own little world," I argued, "and they'll forget I'm even here." That fear haunted me night and day. Staying imprisoned at Shriners hospital for months at a time was isolating. I felt like I stopped existing for my friends. Sometimes I had a creepy feeling that I hardly existed to myself.

I carried on with my sob story for the whole first week at home. "You can lay here all day and feel sorry for yourself or you can learn to put up with life's little disappointments and get on with it," Mommy advised, leaving my bedroom for a cheerier climate.

I turned over on my side and cried myself to sleep. In doing so, the armhole of the cast cut into my arm. When I awoke, that limb had turned black and purple and lost all feeling. "Mommy," I yelled out, "my bad arm looks dead. And I can't feel anything when I touch it."

These sorts of dramatic announcements always brought Mommy running to my side. She winced when I showed her my lifeless black appendage. "Oh, my God, quick now, roll over on your back."

As soon as I did that, the blood rushed into that limb, causing shooting pains and biting prickles as my polio arm regained its rosy color.

"Don't do that again," she ordered.

I glared at her. "Well I don't plan on repeating the trick, fun as it was."

I had been honing my skills at making smart aleck comebacks just to get under my mother's skin. Even though some of my responses resulted in humiliating slaps across my face, it was worth it to push her buttons and watch what happened. After all, my teen years lay ahead of me and I looked forward to venting some of my anger and frustrations at my parents who, like most parents, didn't understand teenagers one bit.

Starting in September 1960, the school district assigned a home teacher to visit me three days a week. I was overjoyed when Mrs. McCord showed up at the door.

"I see you've done well at school," she noted.

"Thanks to you." It pleased me when I noticed a little blush on the teacher's face. Now that I was almost twelve, my curiosity about events shaping the world beyond Eureka intrigued me more than ever. Committed to my education, Mrs. McCord once again dedicated herself to expanding my horizons.

Part of my homework involved listening to the nightly news where Walter Cronkite signed off with "And that's the way it is." Daily exposure to current events sparked my interest in politics and social causes. Even more important, Mrs. McCord had me present a short oral report on five news articles every Friday. She listened with interest and respected my often far fetched observations and confused opinions about world events and life in the good old US of A.

She never laughed at me when I did a report on the youth in Asia. "I heard all about it on the talk show hosted by Ira Blue," I began. News radio was now my nightly companion, filling the empty spaces I tried to avoid after dark. "Ira Blue is against kids from Asia, but I bet Chinese youth are just like us, so what's the big deal?"

Without blinking an eye, Mrs. McCord explained that Blue was against *euthanasia*, the practice of allowing people who were sick and in horrible pain, to die by taking an overdose of drugs. She also explained that the minors who were not allowed to drink alcohol in bars were kids under twenty-one, not poor thirsty coal miners digging for coal.

The Cold War heated up with each passing day. "It says here," I reported gravely, "that the Soviet Union shot down one of our spy planes and took the CIA pilot, Francis Gary Powers, as a prisoner of war." I looked up at my teacher, seeing if I'd caught her interest. Clearly, I had. "I think the Russians have every right to shoot down our spy planes," I commented. "Spying should be illegal. I bet we'd shoot down Nikita Khrushchev's plane if he flew it over, say, Omaha, Nebraska." Khrushchev had such a friendly smile that I sometimes forgot his threat to bury us.

Mrs. McCord flinched. "Well, there's something to be said for spying, Paula. It's a necessary evil during these times. It's good to have a strong opinion about spying, but for now, you'd best keep that one on the back burner."

This was the golden age of television, long before news had become entertainment. The tube still aired educational and socially relevant stories. That week I had watched the first of many civil rights documentaries that both moved and outraged me. The development of my social conscience took root during the CBS documentary *Harvest of Shame,* which exposed the appalling living conditions of America's migrant workers. I took it personally when I heard on-going accounts of the Ku Klux Klan burning crosses in the front yards of Negro families. "Someone ought to set the Klan's sheets on fire," I told Mrs. McCord when she asked me what should be done about these cross burnings. I was rarely without an opinion.

I enjoyed finding news accounts of the ungodly and gruesome, partly because the macabre fascinated me and partly because I liked to watch Mrs. McCord's discomfort over some of the topics I included in my weekly reports. I took her by surprise when I opened up my news articles folder and whipped out a half-page spread, photo included, of a fat lady laying on her bed to show where an asteroid had crashed through her roof and landed on her hip, scorching her skin right through her night gown.

Mrs. McCord shuddered. "Well, that certainly is a fascinating article, Paula, but I'd like to see you focus a little more on national and world events."

My father influenced my political views although sometimes I surpassed him in my indignation over social injustices. While most members of my mother's side of the family were red-necked Republicans who bonded during hunting and fishing trips, some of the Viale clan voted for Adlai Stevenson and later John Kennedy who supported unions. Between Daddy, Uncle George, and Uncle Marsh, someone was always standing in a picket line or threatening to go on strike for higher wages.

Gradually, I began the slow, often painful process of developing a separate unique self, different from both my mother and father. "I'm going to marry a Negro or a Mexican if no white men want me as a wife," I announced as the family ventured out on one of our Sunday drives. That stirred the pot. I now identified with the poor, downtrodden and socially disadvantaged; I felt I had at least earned a place at the table with every other second-class citizen.

"*I* won't be coming to your wedding," David teased. "Maybe you could have a giant watermelon instead of a wedding cake." He smacked his lips. "That would make your husband's relatives happy."

"You're not invited," I snapped, my liberal feathers ruffled. I had an uneasy feeling that my brother had begun to develop his own ideas about politics and race relations that had little to do with mine. The solidarity uniting us in childhood could no longer be taken for granted.

31

ROAD TO FREEDOM

The summer of my second body cast proved to be bleak and never-ending. I missed Mrs. McCord when the school term ended and kept up with my recent habit of reading the evening newspaper. Things finally got interesting when Daddy's boss at work chose him to attend the convention of the Pressman's Union for the *Humboldt Standard* newspaper in New York.

Much to everyone's surprise, Mommy announced she was going with him. "It's high time for me to spread my wings." She had a gaiety in her voice I hadn't heard before.

Unfortunately, Mommy refused to fly so Daddy had to look into an alternate mode of transportation. They considered the possibility of taking the train, but when Daddy discovered the newspaper was giving him payment for his travels in a lump sum, he realized he could actually *make* money if he and Mommy drove to New York. Over the years, he had accrued more than six weeks of vacation and he could use some of that for the trip.

He drove our car to the garage for a tune-up and returned home that evening discouraged.

"Our mechanic Joe says our car will never make it across the country," he told Mommy. "In fact, he called it an accident waiting to happen."

"Just like flying," Mommy said.

That's how Uncle Ralph and Great Aunt Bertha got invited along for the ride. They owned a brand new boat-sized Dodge with power steering and cruise control. The ads on television boasted that the four-wheeled wonder could seat up to six adults...comfortably.

Uncle Ralph could share the driving with Daddy and more importantly, not only could he read maps but he could also refold them so they fit back into the glove compartment, a skill my father never mastered.

Mom would have Great Aunt Bertha for company, which would be a bit stressful since Aunt Bertha was stone deaf by then and we had to yell at her or use a pad and pencil to have a decent conversation. Because of her deafness, she couldn't hear herself when she farted and she had no qualms about farting constantly into her soundless world. "If I hear her say 'Wherever you may be, let the wind blow free' one more time, she's going to end up deaf *and* blind," Mommy swore.

The round trip would take a little over six weeks since Great Aunt Bertha wanted to visit all of hers and Mommy's Swedish relatives back east. "That's free room and board," Uncle Ralph snickered to Daddy. "That's the one thing Swedes are good for, Jack, free room and board."

"Just as long as they don't expect us to help with the haying." Daddy laughed.

The task of dividing us up while Mommy and Daddy were away wasn't a problem. Jeanne, just four at the time, would stay with Auntie Bess. My aunt refused to host David, whom she believed exhibited all the signs of juvenile delinquency. My brother had to stay with some people where Daddy worked. They were new in town and knew nothing about boys who had reached the dangerous age of fifteen and a half.

David had just passed his driving test, earning him a learner's permit. Shortly before leaving for New York, he talked my father into taking him on a practice spin around Pigeon Point. My brother beamed with enthusiasm as he slid behind the wheel of our black and white Ford. "Hey, Paula, when Mom and Dad get back from New York, I'll be old enough to take you anywhere you want to go," he yelled through the car window, his hair sparkling with the Butch Wax he used to keep his long side wings plastered flat against his head.

Daddy sat down in the front seat and slammed the door shut. "That's putting the car before the horse," Daddy joked with me.

David started up the Ford and Mommy, Jeanne, and I watched it jerk down the hill, Daddy's head bobbing around like a puppet. The moody silence at dinner that night hinted that the test drive had not gone well. "I don't know how much it's going to cost to repair the stripped gears," Daddy complained to my mother later.

Naturally, Auntie Bert and Uncle George agreed to take me on for the six or seven weeks my parents would be gone. School started a week after I arrived at their house, still trapped in my body cast. Berkeley City Schools sent out a home teacher so my studies would not be interrupted.

Mrs. Benson and I got along immediately. She helped me improve my writing skills and introduced me to a new level of classic American novels. I devoured Jack London, Edna Ferber, and a stash of trashy paperbacks Auntie Bert inherited from a forward thinker named Cousin Elsie. Not bothering to examine the books closely, Auntie Bert shelved them in the dining room bookcase. *Peyton Place, God's Little Acre,* and *Lady Chatterley's*

Lover, banned in America for years, advanced my interest in and knowledge of the human body and the sexual act—although I remained hazy about the latter subject.

Things looked up for me as soon as I settled in with my aunt and uncle. Knowing how self-conscious I felt in my plaster jacket, Auntie Bert came up with the idea of tying scarves around my neck to camouflage my body cast. She also bought me two new dusters that looked more like dresses than robes.

"I wish my cast didn't come halfway up the back of my head," I moaned, catching my reflection in Auntie Bert's dressing room mirror.

"But look," my aunt beamed, proud of her success with my makeover, "not one piece of plaster shows anywhere."

"I know. I just wish I didn't look so lumpy."

A ring from the telephone interrupted me. Auntie Bert ran to catch it. "It's for you, Paula. It's David."

A wave of homesickness for my brother rippled through my chest. Long stretches at Shriners had gradually accustomed me to life without parents so I learned not to miss them, but there were times when I'd cried myself to sleep thinking about the long distance separating me from David and Jeanne.

I sat down at the breakfast table so I could hold the phone by myself. "Guess what, Paula?" The excitement in David's voice shot through the telephone lines.

"Just tell me," I demanded, anxious to hear his latest news.

"I just got out of the hospital *and* we're buying a new car," he announced jovially.

"Are you okay?" I asked, fearing he had lost a leg or split his head open. I started to cry.

"Don't worry, I'm just fine. Isn't it exciting that we're getting a new car?" he persisted.

"Yeah, I guess so. I never knew Daddy planned to replace our Ford. I thought the mechanic told Daddy it was in good enough shape to drive around town."

"Not since I totaled it."

Stunned by this catastrophe, I dropped the phone and started shaking.

Auntie Bert rushed into the kitchen and wrapped her arm around me. "What's the matter, Missy," she asked, troubled by my hiccupping sobs.

"Daddy's going to kill David," I sputtered, with visions of my father punching my brother into the next state. When angered at David's poor sense of responsibility or his smart aleck attitude, Daddy still beat up on him although David had learned some defensive moves and even threw a punch or two at my father.

Auntie Bert picked up the phone and listened as David filled her in on the details. I could hear him from where I stood. "Ran off a fifteen-foot embankment," he reported, "rolled the car over three times, and escaped with minor injuries. Got a ticket for joyriding and driving with a learner's permit, but without being accompanied by an adult twenty-one years or older."

Auntie Bert hung up the phone after saying she was just thankful nobody got hurt.

"Well, he's going to have major injuries when Daddy gets back from New York, I can promise you that, Auntie Bert."

It turned out that Daddy *was* furious, but he ended his lecture with an arm around David saying "I'm just thankful you're alright." It was the closest Daddy ever came to expressing his ambivalent love for his son.

As my twelfth birthday approached, I checked the mail daily for cards and packages. I always wrote letters as a way to practice my writing skills, so I both sent and received a steady stream of correspondence while I stayed in Berkeley. Now a stack of parcels accumulated on the table in the front hall. Most were marked with "DO NOT OPEN UNTIL BIRTHDAY" or words to that effect. The tower of loot enticed me every time I walked by.

Auntie Bert took me shopping a day early, purchasing a frilly duster that made me feel as pretty as you can feel in a body cast. Thinking ahead, she invited my Uncle George's niece, Rosalie, just my age, to share in my upcoming birthday festivities.

Whenever I stayed in Berkeley, Rosalie served as my friend away from home. Rosalie had dark twinkling eyes, coils of jet-black hair she pulled back into a swinging ponytail and a perfect tan because like Uncle George, Portuguese blood ran in her veins. Best of all, she shared my love of paper dolls. Uncle George called her his "Rosie Posey, full of vinegar" to tease her, but we became soul mates right away.

Earlier that summer, Rosalie had persuaded me to buy a newly minted Barbie doll in spite of my advanced age. With Auntie Bert's help, we made our dolls a fully furnished apartment, complete with cut-away milk cartons that we covered with material. We constructed dressers out of glued-together matchboxes, side tables from empty spools of thread, and beds from Popsicle sticks and vivid imaginations. Auntie Bert knitted us throw rugs and bedding to add that cozy touch.

"So, do your friends know you play with dolls?" I asked as we prepared our Barbies for a relaxing day at home. Certainly mine didn't.

"Who cares," Rosalie responded, hands on hips. She went to a school on the wrong side of Oakland and had learned early on to stand up for herself. "Besides, Barbies are fashion figures, not dolls."

"And we're fashion designers," I added, overjoyed that we weren't too old for that fantasy.

We celebrated my birthday on Saturday so Rosalie and Uncle George could attend the party.

Auntie Bert set a beautiful store-bought cake in front of us after lunch. Chocolate shavings and vanilla frosting covered the double-decker delicacy. "Happy Birthday, Missy," the message proclaimed in iced writing. This was no little kid's cake. I got the piece with the beautiful pink roses on it. Just eating it made me feel grownup and mature.

After her third slice, Rosalie stood up with a warrior's cry and bellowed "Time for the presents!" She gave me the airline stewardess outfit for my Barbie doll. "Sorry, but Mattel hasn't made a writer's uniform yet," she joked.

"Never mind," I told her. "Poets and writers live for years and years in poverty, so I can dress her in rags." Even Uncle George laughed at that one.

My presents from Mommy and Daddy came from New York City's finest souvenir shops. First I opened an everlasting desk calendar with the Empire State building planted in the middle of the base, its pointy tower serving as a paper spindle just like the one Lorraine used at the newspaper. That was from just Daddy. My just-from-Mommy surprise came from Macy's—a genuine black leather purse with a poodle key chain and a secret pocket for hiding away your cash. I found a five-dollar bill concealed there. They both chipped in on a gold-plated Statue of Liberty figurine for my desk back home.

Finally, Mommy filled up all the empty spaces in my birthday box with bars of miniature soaps she saved from every hotel they'd stopped at from San Francisco to Coney Island. Those scented my underwear drawers for years.

After we oohed and aahed over the birthday loot I had collected, Rosalie and I sat out on the front porch and began the process of catching up with each other's lives. I expressed my fears to her about starting eighth grade having missed seventh.

"Is your junior high an all-white school?" she asked.

Her questioned puzzled me. "What do you mean?"

For the next hour, I learned about a junior high that existed worlds away from mine. Rosalie went to an integrated school attended by Negroes, Mexicans, and Asian students.

"I wish I could get to know people from all over the world," I noted wistfully.

"They're not from all over the world, at least not many of them. They were born right here in the good old USA," she explained, giving a military salute, "just like me and you."

"Our world history book said we were the melting pot of the world so I guess that's why. Everybody here used to live somewhere else." A funny thought crossed my mind. "I wonder why kids at your school aren't beige-colored by now?"

Rosalie snickered. "We live next door to a black and white family, you know. Mr. and Mrs. Jepson are really nice."

The revelation fascinated me. "What do you mean—black and white?" From the little I learned from Walter Cronkite on the evening news, kids in the South, wherever that was, went to separate schools; one for whites and one for Negroes. In fact, I did a report for Mrs. McCord about segregation, but talking with Rosalie now made the story come to life.

"Well, the husband is black and the wife is white. They have three kids; one beige, one who looks white and I guess you could call Mariah chocolate. Mariah is one of my best friends."

Memories of Erma White looking at me across the ward at Shriners flashed in my mind. "I had a Negro friend, too," I recollected. "She wasn't my best friend, but she came pretty close."

"Does Mariah stand out because she's black?" *Like I stand out because I'm crippled.*

Rosalie laughed, shrugging her shoulders. "Where I go to school more than half the kids are black."

Her words amazed me. "I get tired of white, white, white in Eureka. I'd blend in better in your school," I added. "I could have lots of Negro friends."

"Not everybody thinks like that," Rosalie informed me. "Before they bought their house, Mariah told me a bunch of white men presented them with a petition that said 'You are not welcome in this neighborhood.' It had a lot of signatures. And some neighbors even threw rocks at Mariah's house. When they asked Dad to sign the petition, he tore it up and they had to start one all over again."

"They must have been mad."

Rosalie shrugged. "Judging by the number of rocks they threw at *our* house, you could say that."

Rosalie's exotic life enthralled me. I imagined Mr. and Mrs. Jepson inviting me over to have dinner with Mariah. They'd take to me right away because, like them, I had something different, something wrong about me.

Auntie Bert stepped into the dining room. "Time to get your stuff together, Rosalie."

We said our goodbyes, but not until we agreed to write to each other in code. We exchanged letters for the next two or three years, all written out substituting the Greek alphabet for our own ABCs. The effort proved to be so labor intensive, we finally abandoned it.

When Uncle George returned from driving Rosalie home, we sat down to a boring dinner of meat and potatoes. "Did you have fun with Rosalie?" Uncle George asked.

I nodded enthusiastically. "Did you know she goes to school with kids who are black?"

Auntie Bert shuddered in disgust. "That's because she lives in East Oakland; that's nigger town."

My mouth went dry. "You mean 'Negro' town," I corrected her.

A look I'd never seen on Auntie Bert's face shocked me into silence.

"I know what I mean," she snapped, giving Uncle George another helping of potatoes.

Uncle George broke in quickly. "Almost time for Lawrence Welk," he announced, glancing down at his wristwatch. By the time the television host who played the accordion finished "The Midnight Polka," the tension died down and Auntie Bert made Uncle George and me our cinnamon toast, just like it was any regular Saturday night.

Auntie Bert tucked me into the sleeper couch and kissed me. "Sweet dreams," she smiled, looking like the old Auntie Bert, but I lay awake for hours, mystified that an aunt I loved so much, an aunt who I knew loved me back, could say 'nigger' with all that hate. Maybe she'd had a rotten day or misplaced her glasses and that made her slip into a bad mood. Those excuses sounded phony. Hearing the word 'nigger' made me cringe the way I did when people called me lame or crippled. That night a little of the glitter from Auntie Bert's crown fell off forever.

32

HOLDING ON

As soon as Mom and Dad had returned from New York, I'd learned that my body cast was about to become history. Doctors would saw it off and I could take a million bubble baths and wear the latest dress styles instead of the dusters I'd come to hate. I was too excited to sleep, and woke up with a dopey smile on my face, recognizing the familiar wallpaper in Auntie Bert's upstairs guest room.

Mommy snored peacefully in the bed next to me—we were pooped after the long trip from Eureka to Berkeley. Daddy had driven us as far as Ukiah where Auntie Bert and Uncle George waited for us in the park. After Daddy's cautious driving, it took a few minutes to adjust to Uncle George's who according to Mommy, "drove like a bat out of hell." The last leg of our journey whizzed by with Uncle George honking at slow drivers and passing on blind curves. I hoped I'd survive long enough to have my turtle shell removed.

I drifted off and had a nightmare about stepping into Shriners large waiting area. I looked at the rows of kids, some getting casts put on, others having them cut off. Over in one corner, I spotted a girl getting her body stretched out in preparation for a body cast.

"No," I cried aloud. Mommy stirred in her sleep, but never woke up. I imagined her snuggling in bed with me as we made plans for my re-entry into the real world. I let go of these reassuring fantasies and I turned to my backup support in times of stress. I pulled up the bedspread with my teeth and started to fuzz away my fears.

For the first time ever, I looked forward to Shriners; I would leave my body cast behind. Just thinking about it made me want to break out in a song, but I couldn't recall a single Broadway hit that had the right lyrics.

Nobody knew it then, but this was to be my last trip to Shriners. When we entered through the double doors the next morning, all eyes in the waiting room were on me, turtle girl. My brace squeaked as I made my way to an empty chair outside the plaster room. My shell, the second one in three years, was coming off. I knocked on my plaster chest, thinking that soon I would be knocking on my own skin.

I talked with Auntie Bert and Mommy, listing all the things I planned to do with my time once they removed my plaster anchor. "There'll be no stopping me," I exclaimed.

Mommy sighed and patted my hand. "I don't doubt it."

A student nurse called out my name and escorted me to a narrow aluminum table in the plaster room. Before lifting me up, she took off my duster, but at my insistence left on my underpants. I spotted the awful contraption used to stretch me out when they mummified me in plaster of Paris. *No more of that,* I thought in relief.

"Hello, Paula," a burly resident said, winking at me. He had wild, curly red hair and a badly trimmed beard. His clownish attitude irked me when he brought one hand out from behind his back and produced the dreaded buzz saw. Like all doctors, he turned on the saw and cut across the palm of his hand. "See, can't hurt you." I knew better. I had my share of bloody nicks, I guess because tender young skin was different from a man's calloused hand.

"You may have trouble sawing through the middle of my cast," I warned him." I used a peacock feather to scratch those hard to reach places and it got stuck there."

"Not to worry," the doctor grinned.

I took a deep breath as the saw cut the plaster around my neck, working its way down to where the cast ended at my hips. The doctor broke it open with his bare hands. Taking a large pair of scissors, he cut off my body stocking, removing the only piece of clothing I had on. Two teenaged boys waiting to get new leg casts gawked with mounting interest. Self-conscious, I folded my arms across my breasts as the doctor lifted me out of my plaster carcass. The nurse finished peeling off a few stuck-on pieces of the stocking and helped me sit up.

For the first time in my life, I had the opportunity to study my budding breasts. The boys across from me were studying them too so I immediately folded my arms back over my chest to protect my modesty.

I felt dizzy and a bit unreal, but mostly, I felt light as a fairy.

"Can you take a few steps for me?" the doctor asked, lifting me off the table and helping me stand up.

As soon as my feet touched the cold tile, I swayed back and forth a few times, and then nodded yes. *Kazam!* I was back in Grandma Ida's kitchen, my feet planted on her floor. Like then, I used the square tiles to guide me out of the plaster room.

I managed to walk down to an empty examination room. We sat in one of the wavy glass cubicles and I wondered what came next. Another intern poked his head in, smiling. "I'll be back in a minute so you just wait."

"Wait? Wait for what?" I cast a nervous glance in Mommy's direction. I resented the cold hardness of the aluminum chairs seeping through my underwear.

"And then I can go home?" I called out to the vanishing doctor.

"We'll see about that," the intern shouted over his shoulder as he left for another kid's room.

The shock of his words "we'll see" turned my heart into a lump of ice. It was time to shut myself down before I fell apart. I let the faraway detachment I had perfected over the years sweep over me, slowing down my racing heart, and replacing the panic with numb emptiness.

I remained in this dead calm while an x-ray technician lifted my body onto the narrow table and positioned a large apparatus above me, aiming its long nose cone at the middle of my chest. I began shivering, still naked except for my underpants. I heard a voice command me to "take a breath and hold it, don't move." The massive machine hovered over me, shooting my body with death rays of radiation.

I thought about the atom bomb and all the warnings I had read about radiation in those pamphlets mailed to our house from the Civil Defense Department. "Are these the same rays that come when an atom bomb explodes?"

"Oh, goodness no," the tech laughed. "These x-rays are perfectly safe. You know those machines in shoe stores that let you look at the bones in your feet?"

I thought of David using that very machine when we went shopping for shoes. "Hey, Paula, I've got skeleton feet," he had cried in wonder. My mother had to yank him off the contraption because of the long line of kids clamoring to see their own bony toes.

"This machine is just as safe as the shoe store model. Scout's honor."

I wondered why she stepped behind a screen every time she pressed a button that caused the machine to emit a soft purring noise. I wished I could duck and cover just to be on the safe side.

When they finished x-raying every part of my body, a nurse stepped in holding a white hospital gown. It was Miss Brite from the ward upstairs.

"You must be freezing," she fussed gently, sitting me up to tie the back of my gown.

"It's good to see you," I said, some of the numbness draining out of my body.

"You too. What have you been up to since I last saw you?

"Well, I'm getting ready to start the eighth grade," I boasted, proud of my maturity. "And I got two poems published and was on television and in the newspaper."

Miss Brite smiled. "My, you have been a busy little girl."

"I'm almost a teenager, you know."

She assisted me into a wheelchair and rolled me down the hall. "How would this almost teenager like a nice warm bath?"

"I'd love one," I cried out, close to tears, grateful that I was in Miss Brite's capable hands.

Miss Brite glanced at the watch pinned to her uniform. "Gotta go, kiddo," she sighed. "I'm so glad to see you and catch up a little." She kissed my forehead and rushed from the room.

I sat in the tub in the same bathroom I had used since I was four. Same frog waterspout and same Hexol poured into the tub to kill the cooties on me.

Mommy poked her head into the bathroom. "We'll give you a nice bubble bath when we get back to Auntie Bert's."

Even after the hospital bath, I had a lot of dead skin hanging on me. Like always, I would be shedding for days.

Mommy wrapped me in a towel, and we half-walked, half-stumbled into one of the examining rooms where Mommy had stashed my newest duster and underwear. She eyed the two small bumps that stuck out from my undershirt. "When you get back to Auntie Bert's we're going to need to take you shopping for some new underclothes."

Mommy was buttoning my duster when a husky doctor strutted into the room. It was Dr. Ramsey, my favorite Nazi.

"Is she ready to go?" Mommy asked, a little frown wrinkling her forehead.

"Let's not get ahead of ourselves," he cautioned, holding up the before and after x-rays for Mommy to see.

Mommy looked from one x-ray to the other," her eyes misting up. "They look the same to me," Mommy snapped at the doctor, pushing the folder away.

"Exactly," the doctor agreed. "There's no noticeable change in the curvature of her spine which is why she'll probably need at least one more operation and another year in a body cast."

Out of nowhere, I heard somebody scream a violent *'Noooo!'*

That was my scream. The feelings I had turned off an hour ago refused to be stifled any longer.

"Feel better?" the doctor joked.

It was no laughing matter. Tears streamed down my face and my voice choked up with anger. "No way am I going to wear another body cast, Mommy," I yelled at her. "It's my body."

"Hey, Paula, that's no way to think. There are many more surgeries we could do to help you move around normally." A self-satisfied smile lit up the doctor's face.

Mommy looked at me in dismay, unknotting the handkerchief in her hands and wiping first her eyes and then mine.

"Don't cry, Mommy. Maybe I could come back here in a couple of years, but right now I need a rest."

Dr. Ramsey raised his eyebrows. "Now's not the time to take a rest."

Mommy threw back her shoulders and put up her chin. "Dr. Ramsey, Paula's father and I have agreed to let her decide if and when she wants more surgery. She's been through a lot, with not much to show for it."

It felt wonderful to have Mommy on my side.

Dr. Ramsey shook his head in bewilderment. "Mrs. Viale, you can't let a twelve-year old make a decision that will affect the rest of her life." He took the x-rays and said, "I'll be right back."

"This is your decision to make, honey. All Daddy and I want you to do is realize you might regret it later in life and blame us. You have to accept responsibility for your decision. Can you do that?"

I nodded yes. "I promise."

A sense of freedom and responsibility came alive in me, overpowering the old numbness I had retreated to earlier that morning. My body was in my hands and the first choice I made was to never take it back to Shriners.

Mommy had finished buckling up my brace when Dr. Ramsey returned to the exam room with two more doctors in tow. The three of them tried to convince Mommy to change her mind. "We'd like to speak to your husband and make sure he wants to stop Paula's treatment."

"Get up, Paula," Mommy prompted, putting her hand under my arm. "Can you walk to Auntie Bert's car?"

"I could fly there, Mommy."

"Then let's go. I'm taking her home." Mommy brushed away the three medicine men like they were bugs caught in a cobweb blocking her way.

When we reached the car, Mommy turned to me as she opened the back door. "Remember, this was your decision; if you regret it later, you aren't to blame Daddy and me."

Like all kids, I blamed my parents for many things down the road, but granting me some control over my wimpy little body was one of the best gifts they ever gave me.

Auntie Bert started up the car. "Where to, Sis?"

"Home to your house." The word never sounded better.

That night I sat at Auntie Bert's dressing table smiling into the mirror. My new flannel nightgown felt soft against my skin. I ran a brush through my hair, freeing it from the stupid donut on top of my head. My brown tresses fell below my shoulders in soft waves. For the first time in my life, I felt pretty. I ignored the rash of pimples breaking out on my forehead—after all that's what Cover Girl was for. I'd be normal, hiding blemishes just like all the other ordinary adolescent girls.

33

BACK IN THE SADDLE

The summer day brought blue skies and warm temperatures to our normally overcast weather, turning Eureka into a place anybody might want to live. That is if you liked fog and lumberjacks and only two television stations. I was finally free of my plaster jacket and could get started on a tan. Earlier that morning, Debbie and I had smeared ourselves with baby oil, lay down on a blanket in Grandma Ida's backyard, and let our fish belly white arms and legs sizzle in the heat.

Debbie sat up and leaned over me. "I think your body is done on this side."

"Thanks," I yawned, turning onto my stomach and studying a picture of Clint Eastwood on the cover of the *Movie Screen* magazine I had purchased the day before. "Wow, Clint Eastwood is starring in a new movie called *Yellowstone Kelly*. Plus, Ed Kookie Burns is in it, too. Want to go see it with me?

"Maybe." She shrugged.

I looked at the bright pink blush that covered her back and shoulders. "I think you're getting a bit overdone in the sun too," I warned, already planning to go to the movie with Claudia Ann, a cousin I had played with since I could remember. Two years my senior, I knew she would be more enthusiastic about Ed Kookie Burns than Debbie.

We crossed the field to Debbie's house where two large pieces of cardboard leaned against the porch. Debbie grabbed both and dragged them over to the top of the hill that slanted down to the road below. We positioned our cardboard sleds next to each other, looking out over the sea of tall, dry grass swaying back and forth in the breeze.

Debbie helped me sit down and gave me a hard push. I sailed over the slippery grass, working hard to remain upright for the whole ride. A fence post I hadn't noticed brought me to an abrupt stop. Before I caught my breath, Debbie smashed into me and we rolled over, laughing all the way.

The climb up the hill took a lot of energy, but we each had three more rides before I said, "That's enough for me."

"Me, too," Debbie echoed, rubbing her sunburnt shoulders as we headed for her house.

Auntie Dot met us at the doorway, helping me step up into the kitchen. Her round face and dark curly hair set off a warm smile. She had introduced us to the sled game, at first sitting behind me as we glided over the grass, but eventually letting me slide on my own.

She studied us for a minute and whistled. "You look like a couple of overcooked lobsters. Go get washed up and I'll make you some lunch."

When Debbie pulled down my underwear so I could take a pee, we noticed a rusty red patch on the crotch. "Where'd that come from?" I asked her.

"I don't know. Maybe it's stains from the cardboard."

I felt a cramping in my stomach, but wanted to get out of the embarrassing situation, so I said nothing.

Hours later I was screaming at my mother who had just finished explaining menstruation to me and how it would visit me once a month for years and years.

"That will never happen to me," I vowed. "It's almost as bad as having polio."

"Well, it's already happened to you," she pointed out. Mommy wasn't good at explaining bodily functions, but the next time I was at Debbie's, Auntie Dot filled us in on some gory details.

Shocked by what she told us, Debbie and I both said we had no questions to ask.

A few months later, Auntie Dot continued her facts of life lectures filled with references to the man's "thing" and foggy images of a woman's nest of eggs just waiting to be released. At least it was less embarrassing than hearing about sex and babies from my mother, who happily relinquished that chore to Auntie Dot.

The threat of an atom bomb demolishing our world overshadowed the drama of my reluctant entrance into womanhood. John Kennedy looked as if he might be our next president, keeping the world free for democracy…or from it, if Communism spread to our shores.

As I grappled with the possibility of being annihilated, I almost wished I still had the protection of my body cast, which might have kept my body in one piece. The age of anxiety had arrived. In an attempt to replace fuzzing with a more mature way to relax, I ordered and paid for my first product from the *Sears* catalog.

The pink and white clock radio arrived with all kinds of modern features making it well worth the $19.99 price tag. I could set either the alarm or radio station to wake me up in the morning and set it again to shut off after I fell asleep.

The habit of listening to late night talk radio brought world and local crises to my attention and took my focus off the growing dread I'd developed about returning to school. I listened to many of John F. Kennedy's speeches and hitched my wagon to his star. The world would be made free for democracy and triumph over Communism unless the atom bomb reduced our cities to rubble. Our military might be kept in check by the Soviet Union's military might. We kept them from bombing us by our threat to bomb them. President Kennedy called the new foreign policy "mutual assured destruction."

Our family's politics continued to support working class men and women. Daddy refused to buy table grapes in a show of support for Caesar Chavez and his boycott. We only wore union-made clothing and both Mom and Dad were disgusted by the South's treatment of Negroes. Piece by piece, the fabric of my social conscience stitched itself together and I planned to fight for human rights for everyone. Eventually I'd include myself, but right now, the threat of my imminent entrance into Junior High was what kept me awake at night.

34

MAINSTREAMING IN A LEAKY BOAT

If I had learned one thing from my home teacher Mrs. McCord, it was how much she feared I would do poorly once I returned to regular school and had to compete with my thirteen–year-old peers. I counted a slew of other disadvantages she hadn't even considered. For instance, by being homebound during seventh grade, I missed a week of orientation where you learned all the rules, regulations, and pitfalls of entering junior high. Sharon Barnhart said I also missed the sex education movies—one for girls, the other for boys.

"The teenager in our sex movie was a dead ringer for Snow White," Sharon revealed. "She gets her period and has cramps and they show these little bunches of eggs in her ovaries. When an egg drops down and a boy's sperm doesn't fertilize it, you bleed it out during your period."

"I already know the facts," I interrupted, anxious to avoid this subject.

There was no stopping her. "What they didn't show was Snow White getting pregnant and kicked out of school."

"What happens to the boy who gets her pregnant?" I asked.

"I don't know. I guess they cover that in their movie."

"Geez, Sharon, I'll never catch up with the other eighth graders. I wish I was going to your junior high so I'd know someone."

However, that was not to be. My already flattened spirits and battered self-confidence were crushed when I learned I would not be attending the same school as my friends from Franklin Elementary. School officials had determined that I would go to the newly constructed George C. Jacob's Junior High because, unlike Eureka Junior High, it had no stairs. I would be among total strangers who had already experienced a school day divided into several periods and knew the ins and outs of locker assignments and dress codes, and the location of the cafeteria, bathrooms, and library.

For an entire week, I fretted over all the possible things that could befall me once I started back to school. My new clothes lacked style and my perm made me look like Shirley Temple with the added attraction of a bunch of teen pimples spotting my face. Worst of all, my brace man, Mr. Hawkins, still had me wearing clunky white oxfords from the fifties. Except for the girls that went to St Bernard's, nobody wore them. I wondered if I'd be better off attending a Catholic school where everybody had to wear the same drab uniforms.

I spent hours gazing at myself in my bedroom mirror trying to determine which was my best side before I realized I had none.

"You're just going through the gawky stage," Mommy teased me.

"Easy for you to say because you started off as a blonde-headed, blue-eyed cutie pie who never had a gawky day in her life." I turned away from my reflection. "How long does the gawky stage last?"

"Beauty comes and beauty goes," she told me, completely ignoring my question.

Under the watchful eye of my seven-year-old sister, Jeanne, I practiced putting on lipstick and applying a too-dark shade of Cover Girl that left a ring under my chin where the makeup stopped and my white neck began.

Jeanne no longer held me in the high esteem of her toddler years when she thought I resembled a fairy princess. "You look like a clown," she howled, running out of my bedroom laughing. "Mommy! Paula looks like a clown."

I slammed my door shut and pored over a pile of *Seventeen* magazines. The models they featured applied their makeup perfectly and the letters readers wrote to "Ask Ellen" had simple problems like attracting a boy, breaking up with a boy, and recovering their spirit if the boy dumped them.

Not once did I read letters featuring a handicapped thirteen-year-old with bad skin, a squeaky brace, and scrawny arms and legs that barely worked. I could just imagine "Ask Ellen" writing back *"Good luck with that, Paula."*

When I complained to Daddy that I couldn't imagine how I'd carry textbooks, my lunch, and my purse with only my good left hand, he considered the situation. "Your old Dad will think about it, just give me time." He ransacked the attic and located the creepy flesh-colored leather satchel he'd received for attending the big union meetings back in New York. The case was the size of an extra-large mailing envelope. Instead of closing in the back though, the flap flipped over to the front and fastened shut with a clasp.

"This won't work," I whined to him. "It will be too heavy for me to carry even with my good arm and hand."

Before I had time to generate another fountain of tears, my father waved the case in my face and said, "Stop. I'm not finished."

I had a lot of faith in the many modifications Daddy had made for me and I really had no other options, so I put my waterworks on hold.

A few days later, my father tracked down a shoemaker and had him sew a loop onto the back of the leather case. By slipping my good left arm through it, I could carry all my textbooks, my lunch, and other supplies in one satchel. I purchased a purse with a chain handle I could hang on my right shoulder, like normal girls did. This balanced out my walk and even though I felt like a pack mule, one worry had fallen off my list thanks to good old Dad.

Over the summer, school officials arranged for me to be driven to and from school by Art Henshaw, an insurance salesman. Mr. Henshaw's 1959 Cadillac looked and smelled brand new. Gone were the gum wrappers and peanut shells that littered the floor of Mr. Beebe's jalopy. I was proud to be seen sitting in the front seat next to a man who resembled a balding Dick Van Dyke. On the down side, since I wouldn't be riding on the school bus, I missed out on an opportunity to get acquainted with my classmates and share the thrill of badgering the bus driver by throwing spitballs and acting rowdy.

Mom (I wanted to stop calling her Mommy), with her new drivers' license, offered to drive me to my first day of classes. "It's for moral support," she explained.

"Didn't Daddy say he talked to the school and they have everything set up for me?"

Mom nodded. "Absolutely. Everything is ready for your first day."

"Then I'll just ride with Mr. Henshaw."

Mom sighed with relief. She dreaded facing school bureaucracy or having to get all dressed up so she would be "fit to be seen in public."

I observed that she had tied one of Jeanne's old diapers around her head like Aunt Jemima's red turban. Most of the mothers in the neighborhood followed this fashion because they had lots of babies whose worn-out diapers were very absorbent. Their newly shampooed hair, done up in pin curls or curlers dried faster using this method. Still, what if Mom had insisted on wearing a diaper turban?

"I can handle it."

I repeated those words when I checked in at the front office and discovered Miss Freedman, a busty school secretary in her mid-thirties, had no record of my enrollment.

She knew nothing about me or the assistance I'd need throughout the day.

"Maybe I misplaced your paperwork, honey." She looked like the type of blonde bombshell who could do that. "So sorry."

"Does this mean I don't have a monitor?" I asked, my voice small and quivering.

The secretary blinked her mascara-clumped eyelashes and gazed across the desk at me. "A monitor?" she echoed, blowing on her cherry red nails.

Evidently, I had interrupted Miss Freedman's manicure. "What's a monitor?"

Anger and fear flooded through me. The bombshell remained mute.

My stomach turned over. I slipped into the detached state I'd perfected at Shriners and heard my foreign voice take over the rest of the story. "A monitor is a person assigned to walk with me from class to class, carry my book bag and help me with my locker, my lunch. Stuff like that." By now I realized there would be no one to assist me in the bathroom, so I didn't bother to mention that detail. Already I could feel my bladder filling up.

"I'm sorry, Paula, but I'm lost," Miss Freedman repeated, taking off her reading glasses and letting them dangle from a chain around her neck. "We simply aren't prepared for you. But don't worry, we'll get things straightened out." She gave her little blonde ponytail a toss and swayed back and forth on a pair of stiletto heels. "Just let me find out what to do next."

I watched her totter into an office marked 'Principal Wade.' She shut the door, but I could hear a man's voice declare, "I know nothing about a Paula Viale."

I sat there stranded, a beached whale with no ocean in sight.

Several minutes later, the principal's door opened and a man in a wrinkled brown suit accompanied Miss Freedman into her outer office. Principal Wade stood about five-feet two on his tiptoes, and he chugged over to me like a tired out steam engine. He took a few fingers of my good hand and attempted a nervous damp handshake. His tongue darted from one corner of his mouth to the other like a snake ready to strike.

"I think we have matters straightened out, Paula." I heard a faint whine in his voice.

"Evidently your father spoke with the superintendent of schools and Mr. Sachs failed to pass along the information about your, ah, special needs. I'll phone him right now. Miss Freedman will accompany you to your homeroom; the teacher there will assign you a locker. Meanwhile, I'll fill in the paperwork while you're gone."

Shazam! Once again, I was on my own.

Miss Freedman shrugged her bony shoulders. "Just follow me, Paula. Can I give you a hand with your, er...briefcase?" From the way she shied away from my beige-colored book bag, Miss Freedman must have thought it was made from human skin.

"I think I've got it." My brace squeaked loudly as we walked down the hall.

I passed a red-haired girl and we exchanged smiles. She wore a geeky hairdo and had an overbite. I didn't see her as friend material. She waved as Miss Freedman ushered me into a crowded classroom. A tall, slender teacher with her black hair done up in a glamorous French roll turned away from the blackboard. She gave Miss Freedman a perplexed glance and then flashed me a candy-pink-lipped smile. It was love at first sight. I wanted to be her.

"Miss Carlson, this is Paula Viale. She's new to Jacobs and we've put her in your homeroom," Miss Freedman explained.

"Excellent." The teacher spoke in a firm yet silky voice. "Paula, why don't you take a seat here in the front row and we'll get you settled in."

I squeaked over to the empty desk and unlocking my brace, sat down. Miss Freedman handed Miss Carlson a large card and gave me a wink before clicking her high heeled shoes out of the room.

Miss Carlson returned to the blackboard. "As I was saying, class— lockers are assigned alphabetically and please remember to record your combination someplace where you won't forget it." For the next twenty minutes, she wrote out her homeroom rules, stressing that if you applied yourself appropriately, you could get much of your homework done in that hour. A paper airplane whizzed by her head and she caught it midair. "Bobby, please pretend that you're a big boy now and save your flying stunts for your future career in aviation."

I appreciated her sarcasm. The class tittered, then settled down for the remainder of that period. Everybody rushed through the door when the bell rang.

I sat still, studying the various initials carved in my desktop. My heartbeats built up speed, thumping in my ears. I closed my eyes and tried to relax. I wanted to open them and find myself at home, shopping with Auntie Bert on Telegraph Avenue, or even back at Franklin with the retarded kids.

What I did see was Miss Carlson's beautiful bright eyes and sweet smile. I could tell she liked me. I wanted to sing. I wanted to slow down my runaway heart and call it back home again.

"Paula, why don't you come up here and we can go over your class schedule during lunch," she suggested.

"Fine by me," I chirped enthusiastically, limping forward and dragging my leg so my brace wouldn't squeak. I leaned over Miss Carlson's desk so I could see the print out. I read it aloud. "First period math, second period history, third period homeroom..."

The teacher picked up where I dropped off. "I see you have English with me after lunch, then science followed by choir and journalism. That's quite a load you have there."

"My home teacher said I'll probably have trouble competing with the other kids," I told her. "On account of me missing so much school while I was in the hospital."

"Well, let's not get ahead of ourselves. I'll be happy to help you any way I can during homeroom." She looked at my satchel. "Got your lunch in there?"

I pulled out my brown bag. I refused to use my old fishing basket, even though it would have been easier.

"Yep. I think I'll eat it outside." I put my good arm through the leather case's loop and wedged the paper bag up under my polio arm. Miss Carlson opened the door for me and I made my way down the hall and outside to a courtyard. Kids lounged around the edges of two big planters, but I opted for the nearest bench. I had almost reached it when my lunch bag dropped out from under my arm and fell to the ground. I tried to pick it up, but my book bag kept slipping down my arm and getting in the way.

Several kids watched as I kicked the bag the rest of the way to the bench. A couple of boys pointed at me, and one whistled. "Nice shoes she's got there," he joked with his friend.

"I guess they're kicking shoes," the friend replied. "Good for kicking paper sacks."

My face burned red, but I managed to get out my tuna fish sandwich and choke down a bite, all the time pretending that I hadn't heard them. I hated my oxfords, my book bag, and the creeps laughing at me. I wanted to dissolve into oblivion.

I couldn't dwell on that idea for long because a new challenge occupied my mind. I needed to find a bathroom. Thanks to Shriners inflexible rules, I'd pretty much trained myself to hold my pee for seven or eight hours, but my bladder was on another schedule that day.

I crossed the courtyard to the girl's bathroom and leaned against the heavy red door to push it open. Someone pulled it open from the other side and I lost my balance, careening over to a sink, which broke my fall.

"Are you okay?"

I turned around. It was the geeky girl I'd encountered earlier. Her red hair was long and frizzy and her bangs covered her eyebrows. A pair of tortoiseshell glasses kept them out of her eyes, which she had focused on me.

"I'm fine," I said. *But my bladder's not.* It was now or never. I took a deep breath and blurted out "I could use some help in the bathroom, though." The girlish chatter in the room died down. A dozen pairs of eyes concentrated on me

I pushed open one of the stall doors and motioned for the redhead to squeeze in with me. She looked confused, but not rattled. "What can I do?"

I took a deep breath. "You can pull my pants down and after I'm finished, pull them back up."

She nodded and acted as if pulling down a stranger's underwear was all in a day's work. "My name's Paula," I said midstream. Relief at last...

The girl grinned at me, then handed me some toilet paper to wipe myself. "I'm Daphne. Daphne D. King." She pulled up my pants as if she'd been doing it all her life. Then Daphne helped me get a hold on my book bag and we walked out of the stall, past a line of gape-mouthed girls, who probably thought we were weird. Frankly, I was so grateful to Daphne that I couldn't have cared less.

It turned out that Daphne was in the eighth grade like me and we had choir and science together. She became my first friend, loyal to a fault. I learned something important about myself that day. I was a poor judge of character. All the popular girls moved around in a tight little pack and I could see there was no room for me. So, I cast my lot with Daphne D. King and later Katie Hamilton and Mary Sue Ellis. None of us were very popular, but when I stopped worrying about that, my life as an eighth grader improved. All of us were smart and funny and before long, I looked forward to my days at George C. Jacobs Junior High.

Except for the first weeks of school when I cheated off other kids' tests, having no confidence in my answers, I adapted to teenaged life like any thirteen-year-old. One day, Miss Carlson kept me after class. "You know, Paula," she confronted me, "most of the answers you copy are wrong. The ones you come up with yourself are usually correct."

Tears stung my eyes. "I'm sorry, I cheated," I mumbled to her. From then on, I stopped copying other kid's test answers and my grades shot up from mostly Cs to straight As.

However, I did almost flunk out of algebra until my teacher suggested I stop asking my father to help me and instead, come early to her class for assistance. That was some of the best advice I ever had. It broke a no-win pattern.

From the fifth grade on, I had always asked Daddy for help with math. He grew very impatient if I didn't understand one of his lengthy explanations and when I refused to do my division problems the way they did it back in his day, he'd get frustrated. I'd make a sarcastic reply, which he responded to by slapping my face. Later, he'd slink back to say sorry, but his smacks humiliated me and no way would I accept his apology. I had perfected a withering look that cut him to the core. Then he'd slap me again.

The days of being Daddy's girl were gradually ending. We disagreed on more and more things, even little ones. Like so many fathers of the 1950s and 1960s, Dad failed to understand my teenaged individuation. He missed my childish adulation and the early days when I had agreed with everything he believed to be true. I now enjoyed developing my own ideas and this could get him so riled up that I stopped sharing much with him.

While I established meaningful friendships and performed well academically, home life was another matter. I realized lots of girls fought with their parents, but the mother-daughter relationship between Mom and me seemed riddled with misunderstandings, a tinge of jealousy, and remarks designed to cut off any meaningful discussions.

Anxiety and depression plagued me, removing gumption from the equation. To fight the lows, I tried drinking coffee to pep me up a bit. It did lift my spirits, but I hated the taste. Like many good Swedes, Mom drank up to thirty cups a day, partly to counteract the drowsiness that was the side effect of her nerve pills.

Working long hours of overtime, Daddy used NoDoz caffeine tablets to keep him alert and he shared them with me anytime I wanted a pick-me-up. Caffeine increased my anxiety, but it did fend off feelings of despair over my situation in life. Once I arrived home after school, I transformed from a cheery little cripple into a malcontent who skulked around the house doing my best to project my disdain for Dad's Pollyanna attitude and vying with my mother for the role of drama queen.

In an effort to escape interactions with my parents, I perfected a morose attitude and a sulky stare that gradually erected a wall between us. Growing up, my reputation as a hysterical child who treated my parents with disrespect grew along with me. I hinted that I entertained suicidal thoughts, like following in the footsteps of a great uncle who blew himself up with dynamite or taking the less dramatic path of an older cousin by shooting myself.

"If you don't snap out of it, I'll get you the gun." Words to live by. My mother interpreted my painful, often futile struggles to gain a foothold in the world as more gripes from Moaning Mary. It wouldn't hurt her to listen. Then again, maybe it would.

My parents and relatives dismissed my fluctuating emotions as immature behavior and theorized I suffered from self-pity and hormones mixed with a bad attitude. My mother's cold dismissal of my depression increasingly enraged me. From the time I could remember, she had called me evil when I upset her. That four-lettered word damaged my self-image much more than polio.

Once I accepted the monthly curse of menstruation and the depression it could cause, I initiated a ritual that included lying down on my bed, slipping a plastic bag over my head, and waiting until a buzzing sensation filled my body. This lightened the weight of gloom and doom on my chest. One morning, Mom burst into my room without knocking. She took one look at me before yanking the bag off.

I lay there unresponsive, my beet-red face slowly returning to normal as I took in deep breaths.

Mom began one of her lengthy interrogations, searching for answers in the deflated plastic bag she held out before her. "What in the hell are you trying to do?" she grilled me, a look of concern and frustration creased her forehead. "What were you thinking?"

"I was thinking how nice it would be if you could knock on my door before you storm into my room." I relayed this desire in my newly developed ho-hum response to parental interrogations.

"I want a straight answer, not another of your sarcastic remarks."

"If you really want to know, I'm practicing for choir. We're learning breath control this week."

Relief filled Mom's face. "Oh," she sighed, "well I think your music teacher should give you less dangerous homework. Do you want your father to call him?"

"No, please don't do that," I begged. Every child's nightmare—a mother's or father's call to a teacher, ostensibly on your behalf though it usually resulted in making things worse.

"I originally came in here to ask what you want for dinner, Chef Boyardee spaghetti or tuna over toast?"

I looked at my mother, astonished at how easily she accepted my lie about the plastic bag. "Tuna, and could you put Velveeta cheese on it." This was a new food sensation, sweeping across the country and turning up along with green olives on toothpicks at cocktail parties.

Mom nodded. "Sure thing." Soon after her departure, I heard the familiar sounds of pots and pans banging together in the kitchen and a few "oh, shits."

I worked at reducing my suicidal thoughts, pushing them far back into the recesses of my mind whenever they cropped up. I talked to nobody about my emotional pain, choosing to contain my anger and hopelessness over having been permanently maimed by polio in the pages of my diary.

I found real comfort in the writings of Henry David Thoreau and Ralph Waldo Emerson. Ralph's belief in the importance of self-reliance and the ability to compensate for things you didn't have by developing the abilities you *did* have rang true to me. I couldn't run so I would write. I couldn't get dates on the weekend so I would devote more time to developing my voice and singing on the radio every Sunday.

I spent hours reading my favorite sections in the Gideon Bible, my surgery gift from Shriners. The Psalms were especially soothing, and at the bottom of every page of my diary I scribbled *"Faith as big as a mustard seed"* as a way of consoling myself. Maybe someday I could work up that much faith. The phrase motivated me to be a good student, a decent human being and to hang on until I turned seventeen and a half and could escape my parents and Eureka.

35

MISSILE AND OTHER CRISES

Just as sixth grade had been a dry run for junior high, ninth grade was a dress rehearsal for high school. Ninth grade taught me the dos and don'ts of the adolescent soap opera of lost loves, failures to make the cheerleading squad, and the numerous groundings suffered by those rebels who broke their curfew, flunked a test, or shoplifted items worth more than $5.

By balancing between being a smart ass and a serious student, I earned a name for myself as a class comic and decent scholar. Years of singing in the Baptist Vacation School Choir and taking serious singing lessons resulted in a well-trained voice that landed me quite a few solos in the school choir. I also developed a journalism style that elevated me to editor-in-chief of *The Trojan Scroll*. That was my winning entry for the "name the school newspaper" contest.

I hung out with Katie Hamilton and Mary Sue Ellis during lunch and after school. We remained outsiders for the most part, but by joining choir and CLOC Club, short for Christians Living on Campus, I tried to mingle with some of the more popular kids. Boys in particular.

Mom let me dress however I wanted. Naturally, she couldn't help but make comments about the length of my skirts (too short) or my sweaters (too bulky). I continued to gain strength and stamina, but still needed help dressing and getting my brace on, even though I could walk now without it. I begged my parents to let me leave it off when I went to school, but that was a lost cause.

Just in time, Mr. Hawkins designed a new brace for me, one that I could wear with any shoe. Suddenly I sported Hush Puppies and tennis shoes and pointy patent leather styles my Mom had to struggle to wedge my polio foot into. The pain was worth it and I never complained about the big blisters on my heel and toes.

I enjoyed the envy of girls with perfectly formed feet. Even better, in an effort to save himself from listening to the weekend fights Mom and I continued to have over her hairstyling failures, Daddy paid for me to go every Saturday to the beauty shop where Sandy, a middle-aged marvel, shaped my locks into perfect "flips" and "bubbles" straight out of *Modern Hair Styles*. Many of my school outfits came with Bobby Brooks labels featured in *Seventeen*. My life improved.

So too, for my brother. David had "straightened out" so he managed to avoid Juvenile Hall. He played big man on campus in his senior year of high school. His upbeat attitude and striking good looks made him popular with both teachers and naturally, the cute girls who trailed him around like puppies. I got to know some of them, enlarging my circle of upper crust friends.

With admirable determination, David had conquered his thumb-sucking habit, but not before it left his teeth protruding a bit. He seemed to have a brighter outlook on life and now, instead of sucking his thumb, he used his hand to push in on his teeth every chance he got. His method worked—a good thing since Daddy couldn't afford orthodontia.

"I have to tell you, Paula, reading *The Amazing Power of Positive Thinking* has changed my life," he told me one afternoon as we sat reminiscing about our troubled childhood. "You can make things happen just by believing they will happen."

Not if you've had polio.

"Really. Just by thinking positive thoughts, I managed to buy a car and some cool clothes. I'm learning how to make people feel good about themselves which makes most anybody like me, even my boss Harry." My brother was now working at a dry cleaners where he eventually earned enough money to buy a '57 Chevy.

I looked at Norman Vincent Peale's bestseller, but I had given up on positive thinking when I learned to shut down at Shriners. "I think your car was what really changed your life," I told him. "You can get out of here anytime you want."

"Yep, I can clear out of here on weekends before Dad hits me up with a list of what needs doing. I'd rather do twenty-four hours of yard work for that old battle-axe Mrs. Turner than spend time on one of Dad's shitty lists of chores." From the day he turned thirteen, my brother had taken on all kinds of jobs just to avoid time at home.

I smiled at David, happy that he had survived our father's beatings and our mother's indifference. Now he looked forward to attending Humboldt State University where he planned to join the best fraternity on campus and continue his escape from Pigeon Point.

One of the best days of my life was when Mr. Henshaw caught the flu and David had to drop me off at Jacobs in his spiffy 1957 Chevy. Several girls flocked over to the car, surprised that this handsome dude was my brother.

"I just love your shoes," a cheerleader named Bobby Jo gushed at me. I smiled, duly flattered.

"You look great today," David told me when helping me out of the car. "I've got one cute sister," he added, loud enough for all the girls to hear. Love and gratitude swelled inside my chest as David hung my briefcase over my shoulder. "See you tonight," he called out before driving away. Two of the girls actually walked with me to class and I shone in the afterglow of my brother's presence. To be handicapped and popular had never seemed an option until now—thanks to David and his power of positive thinking.

In eighth and ninth grades, I suffered the heartache of every other girl not asked out on a date. Thankfully, outsider girls formed a large group and helped each other deal with the rejection of every boy on campus. We invited each other for sleepovers, attended every Doris Day and Rock Hudson movie en masse, and prayed our intelligence would bring us male attention somewhere down the line.

I had been an anxious child from the get-go, but now a dull ache came to life in my chest. Mom continued to call me moody and her 'little Moaning Mary' when I slouched around, desperate for the weekend to be over. Debbie often slept at my house or I slept at hers, but she blossomed into a svelte young woman pursued by a bunch of junior high boys.

We still had our fun though. Once, when we were over at Grandma Ida's, we stood together along the roadside, pointing at the tires of people's cars as they passed and waving our hands wildly. Sometimes a car pulled over and the driver got out to look for a flat. We hid in a nearby dahlia patch when that happened, but one man caught up with us and read us the riot act.

"You girls should be ashamed of yourself," he shouted, driving off in a huff.

I looked at Debbie. "I'm not, are you?"

Debbie shook her head and we laughed so hard I fell on my butt. It took forever for the hilarity to die down and for me to get up. Each time Debbie started to lift me under my arms, peals of laughter swept over us and I'd slip out of Debbie's grasp once again.

The other game that kept me from despairing over a dateless existence was making prank telephone calls.

"It's your turn, now," Debbie said once we had recovered from her calling up a man and saying "I'm pregnant," then hanging up.

I took the phone and dialed a random number. A man answered. "Daddy, the movie's over and a weird man is stalking us in front of the theater. Please hurry, because this is my last dime."

I slammed down the receiver and we burst into laughter, the snorting kind that shoots snot from your nose.

Later that night when we lay down next to each other in the dark, Debbie turned over to face me. "I can't go to sleep," she confessed.

"Me either. I keep thinking about the man we called to come pick us up," I admitted, feeling a twinge of guilt.

"Do you think he's still out there driving around in the dark looking for us?"

I broke the silence that followed. "Let's not think about it," I recommended.

Besides, we had more important issues to occupy our juvenile minds—like WWIII.

October marked the start of the rainy season in Eureka and I had to choose between wearing a stiff raincoat that imprisoned me like a straitjacket or fighting off the damp and cold with a bulky wool ski sweater that smelled doggy the minute it got wet. Most of the time, the sweater won out. I couldn't fit a boot over my brace so the shoes I wore remained moist and my feet chilly until May, when the rains stopped. I hated living in a logging town where curtains of precipitation made life so miserable.

World politics played havoc with the halcyon days of our youth. After we tried to invade Cuba in the Bay of Pigs and blow Castro up with an exploding cigar, I wasn't surprised that Russia tried to come to the aid of their tiny satellite. If that made me a Communist, well, I hardly posed a threat to National Security.

My attitude changed when an American U-2 spy plane snapped pictures of scores of Russian-built missile launch sites pointing in our direction. After all, Cuba was just a stone's throw away from Florida. Now the Communists had sent off a boatload of missiles to arm their sites. President Kennedy declared a boycott on any Russian goods headed for Cuba and US boats sailed off to blockade the Russian ships.

On a Friday afternoon in October, Mr. Lawson, my favorite junior high English teacher, brought his radio to class so we could listen to and sweat out the Cuban Missile Crisis with the rest of the world.

My cousin Debbie and I had given up hope for building bomb shelters in our backyards and now that Russia had exploded a hydrogen bomb, the largest bomb in human history, there was nowhere safe to hide anyway. As President Kennedy put it later, we were on the "abyss of destruction."

Thanks to Mister Lawson's fancy transistor radio, my attention turned once more to thoughts of personal and global annihilation as two ships prepared for a head-on encounter.

The radio reporter's voice tightened as he gave a minute-by-minute account. No one spoke. We gripped onto our desks and mentally rehearsed duck and cover strategies while waiting for World War III to be announced momentarily.

To distract myself I studied the cool, calm demeanor of Mr. Lawson. The teacher, a short balding man who wore elegant suits, had an air of sophistication about him that made his colleagues look like refugees from the flood that had swamped Eureka on Columbus Day. He jolted my conscience awake by assigning us sad, at times demoralizing, novels and short stories about the futility of war. Mom had gone to high school with Mr. Lawson, and heard that he had returned from WWII a broken man and dedicated alcoholic, which explained his frequent consumption of breath mints.

Mr. Lawson had good reason to take to the bottle. He told us that near the end of the war, he had piloted a plane that accidently bombed a German hospital. He had already released the bomb when he made out a large red cross on the building's roof. You could tell that this disaster haunted him and he set out to make pacifists of us all by assigning books like the *Red Badge of Courage, Catch 22, Farewell to Arms, 1984* and *Hiroshima*, John Hersey's account of the lives of Japanese survivors of the A-Bomb. As tiny sparks ignited the first fires of the peace movement, I planned to walk straight into the fire, fanning the flames.

Suddenly Walter Cronkite's voice replaced the other news announcer's coverage. It cracked with an unusual tension that broke my reverie. "At this time, navy officials have stopped a Soviet Chartered freighter at the quarantine line set up by President Kennedy. They have been permitted to board the Russian vessel to perform an inspection." We held our breaths as CBS news announced US inspectors had found no contraband military supplies. We were returned to our regular programming schedule.

Nobody in the classroom returned to their regular schedule.

The crisis continued, coming to a head when a freighter known to carry missiles stopped at the "do not cross zone" and just waited. By the weekend, the crisis had been resolved. Khrushchev ordered the missiles back home and Kennedy lifted the embargo on all things from the USSR. Once again, WWIII stalled on the frontlines.

Still convinced that a thermonuclear blast could wipe out everyone's future plans including my old dream of Paula's Pet Parade, I took every opportunity to keep our impending extinction uppermost in my classmates' minds, hoping they might relay some of the gloomy possibilities to their parents. I did a report in my history class on the nuclear winter that would follow even if a medium-sized blast wiped out most of the people on earth. Survivors would die off from starvation if radiation sickness didn't kill them first, according to my favorite scientist, Carl Sagan.

"Don't you get depressed writing about this stuff?" Katie asked after I had laid out the probable scenario facing my ninth grade comrades who had the misfortune of surviving the mushroom cloud and radiation poisoning.

"How can I think of anything else? You know about the Doomsday clock a bunch of scientists created last year?"

Katie glanced at her watch. "Vaguely."

"Well, they just set it at three minutes 'til midnight. Meanwhile we're supposed to continue life as usual. You know, just stick our heads in the sand, or better yet, duck under our desks at school."

Katie agreed it proved nearly impossible to forget our imminent destruction when public service announcements flooded the radio and TV airwaves stipulating where local fallout shelters were being built in case anyone survived the thermonuclear blast. As good Americans, we were expected to whistle while we worked and waited.

Death could be just around the corner. I had recurring dreams of lying on a gurney in the hallways of Shriners Hospital, alone until being wheeled into the surgery where a mask was placed over my nose and mouth. I struggled against the ether, and then when I could hold my breath no longer, I inhaled the poison and waited for oblivion. Other nights I dreamt I was sitting in a large stadium filled with hundreds of people looking up at the sky as a radioactive mushroom cloud exploded overhead and a fiery flash burned its way through my eyelids. *This is the A-bomb exploding. This is the end of everything. This is the end of me.*

It would be years before those nightmares receded into the archives of my personal history. Until then, my Sears clock radio filled the airways with lullaby talk of a doomsday clock counting down the hours, then minutes until we blew ourselves up.

36

STAIRWAY TO HEAVEN

Entering tenth grade brought me up against a new obstacle. Stairs. Two flights graced the entrance to Eureka High, plus the building was two-storied. I had an instinctive fear of stairs, having fallen down a few in my lifetime. Once, I knocked myself out and forgot where my next class was. I had to spend an hour in the nurse's office until my head cleared.

I remembered my success years ago in managing to make the citywide elementary chorus when I practiced standing for hours to strengthen my legs enough to sing through an entire performance. I had only been ten at the time. Surely at almost fifteen, I could learn to tackle stairs.

School authorities thought my confidence was misplaced. In a curt letter they sent to my father, they decided Eureka High was not the place for me what with the possibilities of falls and lawsuits. They were considering the option of sending me to the local St. Bernard's Catholic High School where it could be arranged for me to have all my classes on the first floor. However, I had already been forced to attend a different junior high from my grammar school classmates and I wasn't about to be separated from the friends I'd made at George C. Jacobs Junior High.

Dad came to bat for me. He tore up the letter and insisted on meeting with the superintendent. It was a relief knowing he had taken things into his hands.

The relief didn't last, however. Dad came home looking a bit frazzled. "I argued with the board of education for two hours, Paula. I'm sorry, honey, but you'll have to go to St. Bernard's or have a home teacher again."

I burst into sobs. "No way, no way," I yelled at him and the world in general.

Dad hugged me and even Mom tried to soothe away my hysteria.

"The school superintendent says the stairs at Eureka High will be too big an obstacle."

"But Daddy, I *can* go up and down the stairs if someone holds my arm to steady me."

"I pointed that out, but Mr. Bartholomew said that would place too much of a burden on other kids."

"What if I could go up and down stairs by myself?"

"I don't know. First off, you can't do stairs by yourself. Secondly, what if you fell?"

"You could really get hurt," Mom added.

"But I fall down all the time," I argued, forgetting that my parents had no idea just how often. Refusing to give up, I searched for a way to be with my friends.

My regular trip to Berkeley offered me the perfect opportunity to face down this latest obstacle to my life. Once again, Auntie Bert and Uncle George had invited me for the summer. I loved Berkeley where I could walk the four blocks up to Telegraph Avenue to mingle with the aging socialists, beatniks, and kids like me, soon to blossom into flower children.

Every other summer I had used the time to buy my fall wardrobe which set me a good six months ahead of the styles Eureka girls were limited to. Although I still intended to purchase my radical outfits for my first year of high school, I set my main goal while in Berkeley to building up my leg strength and balance so I could bound up the stairs of Eureka High. No way was I going to St. Bernard's.

Luckily, my aunt and uncle's house had steps at both the front and back and since the back stairs were steeper, I figured if I could conquer them, I'd definitely have no problem with the less steep ones at Eureka High.

On my first morning in Berkeley, I was up in time to eat breakfast with Uncle George before he left for work. Auntie Bert helped me dress and buckled up my leg brace. "Now where are you off to?" she asked when I headed out the back door.

"I'm going to do my stair exercises," I told her, swallowing the last of my English muffin. We stood side by side at the top of the stairs.

"I don't know about this," Auntie Bert fretted.

"Just take my arm and hold on to me while I practice going down."

Auntie Bert stifled her fear of me plunging headfirst down the steps. By supporting me under one arm, I was able to go down the stairs, slowly but surely. To my surprise, climbing up proved much easier. By leaning my shoulder against the railing, I could take each step without any help.

"Ta-da!" I laughed, giddy at my accomplishment. "Let's go down again, only this time just stand in front of me in case I lose my balance."

Reluctantly, Auntie Bert let go of my arm and spotted me while I took a deep breath and went down the first step. To my prideful satisfaction, I maintained my balance and took the rest of the steps weaving only slightly, but the feat took its toll. When we returned to the kitchen, I slid into the nearest chair, exhausted and a bit discouraged.

"That's enough for now," my aunt told me. "Let's get in the car and go slumming on Shattuck Avenue."

I always loved "slumming" with Auntie Bert. We'd hit every charity shop and second-hand store up and down the street. Auntie Bert had class and style. She could hunt through racks of used clothing and come out dressed like the wife of a rich doctor or lawyer. "That's because these *are* the barely worn clothes of the wives of rich doctors and lawyers," Auntie Bert revealed. While I stood in the back of the store where they kept the used books, Auntie Bert disappeared into a dressing room and danced out in a beautiful blue silk dress with matching shoes and purse. "Look, the dress still has the price on it." She pointed to a tag that read $44.

"Wow, that's a lot of money," I ventured. And it was in 1960.

Auntie Bert beamed. "Yes, that's quite expensive, but this whole outfit, dress, shoes and purse totaled just $6.99. And all that money goes to charities."

My aunt's bargains always impressed me, but I preferred to buy my clothes new. However, I was more than happy to get used books for ten and fifteen cents each. For less than $2, I came home with a stack of novels by all of my favorite authors: Alcott, Dickens, Shirley Jackson, Margaret Mitchell, Steinbeck, and Jack London plus a collection of Irving Stone's historical fiction about Lincoln, Gauguin, and Van Gogh.

I was especially pleased when I found the biography of Marie Curie, written by her daughter Eve. Marie had discovered x-rays, the same rays Shriners shot through my body every chance they had. It only cost five cents because it was missing its book jacket. Here was a bona fide woman scientist. The winds of the sixties were triggering the tiny sparks of rebellion within me, waking me up to a world of unexplored possibilities.

By the time I returned home to Eureka, I was able to show school officials that I could easily manage stairs. They agreed to admit me in September. My triumph over the stairs at Eureka High brought me a sense of pride and revived my "can do" attitude. If I kept up my grade point average, I knew I had a ticket out of town following my graduation. My spirited participation in every club I joined increased my popularity and ensured that my picture showed up frequently in our yearbook.

For my own safety, I left class five minutes early to stay ahead of the chaotic rush of students between classes. The school district continued to pay someone to chauffeur me to and from school. That's how Mr. Goetz came into my world.

Almost seven feet tall, Mr. Goetz drove a pick-up truck so large he had to have one of his woodshop students build a two-step stool for me to climb just so I could reach the seat. Like many shop teachers, Mr. Goetz had a military air about him and shied away from the towers of academia. The mass of short black curls framing his face softened its features and the deep brown of his eyes, enlarged a bit by his black-framed glasses, caught your attention.

He introduced himself as a no-nonsense disciplinarian, but with me at least, he was all bark and no bite. "So that's what you're going to wear the first day of school?" he asked as he helped me climb the two steps into the cab of his truck. "I wouldn't cross my legs or bend over too far in that skirt."

"You sound just like my mother," I shot back, a flush of embarrassment spreading over my face. I had found my voice and I used it, no longer afraid of losing my "good girl" status.

"I see. Well, I'll take that as a compliment." He studied me carefully as we made our way to school.

"You drive just like my Uncle George," I accused him.

His face broke out in a wide smile. "Feisty little thing, aren't you?" He laughed.

"I know how to hold my own," I replied with teenage flippancy.

"So they say, so they say. I also heard you beat out polio at six weeks and lived to tell about it."

I hadn't spoken that phrase for years so his remark undid me. "Who told you that?" I spat my angry words at him.

"School records have interesting comments in them. You've got yourself quite a reputation. The words 'willful, stubborn, and spunky' came up once or twice. And I see you maintained a three-point-five average throughout junior high."

"What are you, a Communist?" I blurted out. "You just go around snooping into other people's lives?"

"Only the people that interest me."

I searched for the perfect comeback. "Why? Because I'm a crippled A student and not some mental retard?" I regretted the words as soon as they left my mouth.

"Can we move on to a more stimulating conversation," Mr. Goetz replied. "For instance, what classes are you taking this year?"

I was so relieved to change the subject, I rattled off my list without taking a breath: "History, English, Biology, French II, and Introduction to Speech. Oh, and I take choir as my elective."

"Matter of fact, I'm told you're a music lover from way back and have a good voice."

That response made me hopping mad. "According to my school record?"

"No, according to your voice teacher, Mrs. Hopkins. We're neighbors."

I sighed. "Just my luck." For the last three years, Hoppy-Toad had been giving my sister Jeanne piano lessons to build her self-esteem and offered to give me voice coaching at a 50% discount. Mr. Goetz's knowledge of my private life both infuriated and flattered me. Maybe I had become an interesting person without even knowing it.

We drove the last few miles to school without talking, something that didn't bother Mr. Goetz at all.

"See you this afternoon, Paula." The giant shop teacher helped me out of his truck and hung my brief case over my arm as if he'd been doing it for years.

"Guess so." I shrugged.

I spent all of lunch telling Katie and Mary Sue what a creep Mr. Goetz was.

Mary Sue threw her lunch bag in the trash. "You two looked kinda funny walking side by side."

Katie stood and pulled up her baggy knee socks. "Yeah, you barely come up to his waist," she snickered.

"Ha, hah, very funny," I responded, glad that fourth period started in five minutes. I set off for class without even saying goodbye. I looked forward to English class, which was taught by Fred Wilson. He had a big belly and chest, but he liked my compositions and gave me A's on every one. He covered my pages in bold red writing that said things like "good point" and "well-stated."

When I turned in a scathing review of *The Old Curiosity Shop* dismissing it and its main character, Little Nell, as "soppy sentimental tripe" his comment at the bottom of the page was "I hope you give Dickens another try!"

Fortunately for me, I did and fell in love.

This was not the case with geometry. Not only did the math confuse me, but I also had to steady the compass with my chin in order to draw circles. The big red dimple imprint lasted for two or three hours. Mrs. Armstrong, my teacher, grimaced every time she caught me battling with the compass. "I just hate to see you hurt yourself," she remarked more than once.

Actually, she thought my struggles showed determination and fortitude. Without them, I never would have passed her class with a B-. Pity came in handy.

37

TRAGEDY IN CAMELOT

"They've shot President Kennedy," Don Dean yelled out to me as I left choir class late in November 1963. Don's reputation as a class clown made him a favorite among students, but this time he'd gone too far.

"That's not funny."

"Paula, I'm not kidding," he said, grabbing my arm and turning me to face him. "Someone shot him while he was riding in a parade in Dallas."

We stood outside our history class, watching the teachers and students milling around in a daze. They piped in constant updates of the attempted assassination through the intercom system so we stayed in class, listening to Walter Cronkite relay the grisly details.

"You are living through one of the most important times in the twentieth century," Mr. Kantan, our history teacher stressed. As if the constant threat of nuclear war didn't even count. As if it wasn't historical enough to hear the air raid warning drills that repeatedly sent us into "duck-and-cover" mode crouching under our desks. By the time I could get down there, both the world at large and I would be blown to smithereens.

School let out early that afternoon since half the kids had wandered off campus to return to the relative security of their homes. Later that day, I watched the rerun of Cronkite's dismal announcement, stunned when he removed his glasses and swiped at a tear. "President Kennedy is dead," his voice croaked. I viewed that part of the tape over and over again, trying to imagine the world as it had been just hours earlier. The assassination brought an end to our country's wild love affair with Camelot and the king who lived there.

"I never think of you as being handicapped," Katie assured me one sunny afternoon not long after President Johnson had settled into President Kennedy's oval office. Out of habit, she pulled up her perpetually baggy knee socks for emphasis.

We sat on the lawn behind the school eating our lunches and planning a trip to the movies on Friday since neither one of us had dates, which was par for the course.

"Not even when you help me in the bathroom or carry my books?"

She shrugged "I mean, at first, I noticed you had a brace and couldn't use your hands very well, but I liked you because you were smart and funny." She stuffed her sandwich wrappings into her lunch bag and jumped up. "Come on, or we're going to be late for fourth period."

"I'm going to be extra late if you don't help me up," I told her.

Katie laughed her wonderful infectious laugh and ran back. She expertly slipped her hands under my arms and lifted me up. "See, I forgot I needed to give you a boost. It's no big thing, just a background detail."

I thanked my lucky stars for friends like Katie, Mary Sue, and yes, even Jerry Wilcox.

As far as I was concerned, Jerry Wilcox lived just this side of Camelot. His scrawny physique and a voice that had yet to overcome the up and down slide of puberty, made him a poor match for Sir Lancelot. I knew Jerry liked me when he started carrying my books from class to class. I must admit that when we talked on the telephone almost every night after I'd done my homework, I could conjure up the picture of a tall, blonde beach boy while I fantasized myself as a bright, funny, not too bad-looking girl.

Politically speaking, we disagreed about everything.

"If Barry Goldwater wins, we'll be out of Viet Nam in no time," Jerry proclaimed with absolute confidence. Viet Nam posed no threat to his future since his horrible eyesight qualified him as a 4-F.

"If Barry Goldwater wins, *we* will be out of this world in no time," I noted sarcastically, thinking about Barry's plans to bomb Hanoi as soon as he became president.

"So, you would actually prefer creeping Communism to living in a democracy where free enterprise is allowed?"

"I'll still have polio no matter who wins the elections."

Jerry laughed. He appreciated my off-handed comments about my disability. We felt comfortable with each other. "Are you really going to sign up to debate me in civics class?"

"I already have. The debate is about whether or not we should bomb Hanoi, Jerry. Personally, I'd prefer to avoid World War Three if at all possible. I don't think my nerves can take another Cuban Missile Crisis."

"Aha, better red than dead," Jerry taunted.

"I look good in red," I joked.

"Actually, you do." Conservative or not, Jerry caused my heart to skip a few beats.

Still, there was no getting around the fact that I was a girl who had polio and a body to prove it. Throughout my high school years, I channeled my energy into academic and creative pursuits while enjoying the good will and banter of teachers I had crushes on. Mr. Ritz, my handsome biology teacher, enjoyed my sarcastic remarks and my endless supply of cheerfulness and determination. Except for being male, he had nothing in common with Jerry Wilcox, but by combining Jerry's cynicism and intelligence with the repartee I shared with Mr. Ritz, I made peace with being dateless every weekend.

By now, I had relinquished any hope of abandoning my whining uncomfortable leg brace. I could walk fairly well without it, but I required the brace's support to keep my leg from buckling. Thankfully, I had at least a dozen pairs of stylish shoes to help me forget the one firmly attached to a leg-iron.

I attended all the football games on Friday nights and rode to out-of-town games in hopes of striking up a school bus romance. I was part of a quartet that sang on the radio every Sunday morning, but even among Christians, it was lean pickings for a person with a gimpy hand and leg. My playful, sometimes risqué, humor gained me popularity with both boys and girls. In truth, I maintained several meaningful and satisfying relationships with many guys on the road to higher education or hoping for a football scholarship to get them there. I loved team projects for class because it was yet another way a boy could get to know me better. Even popular handsome guys chose me as a partner since they knew I would do the grunt work necessary to get an A on team projects. It never crossed my mind that some of these boys might be attracted to me beyond a Platonic interest.

I desperately searched for recommendations about how to live and love in the world if you had a handicap. I spent hours at the Humboldt County Library looking for anything I could find on disabled people. The options were scant and discouraging. I didn't want to check out any of the three books on disability the library offered. First off, I didn't want anyone to know I read stuff like this. Secondly, not one of them talked about *being* a disabled person, just *raising* one—like I was a chicken.

One book, *Not My Child*, dealt with the disappointment and despair of being the parents of a less-than-perfect baby, which led to "the disruption of parent-child bonding." It forecasted that such a disruption resulted in mothers and fathers who could not effectively connect with their disabled child.

Everything spiraled downward from there. According to the experts, "Emotional distancing, shame, and guilt" were just a few of the problems parents faced. I did find some of the research interesting. I immediately diagnosed my mother as having a disturbance in her bonding with me and guilt and shame had certainly cast a shadow over Dad's and my relationship. After all, he'd told me more than once that God had punished him by giving me polio. I knew he was proud of me, but he definitely wasn't comfortable.

So Your Child is Disabled, a thick volume with a cheery bright red jacket, listed important developmental stages your child might or might not reach and how to cope with any anger or disappointment this could bring up for the already overwhelmed mom and dad. It provided several options to raising your child at home, pointing out that the stress of coping with a severely disabled child often brought on the couple's divorce and created resentment among their other children. It casually reported that disabled kids were twice as likely to be abused as normal children, leaving the impression that institutionalizing your son or daughter might be in the child's best interest.

The most disturbing aspect of this book was a section devoted to the negative effects a handicapped child could have on his or her siblings. For the first time in my warm little narcissistic shell, I seriously considered what effects my polio had on David and Jeanne. David's failure to thrive, his neglected teeth, and Dad's physical abuse—did my disability cause these things? Certainly, it contributed.

By the time Jeanne came along, Mom had improved her bonding skills, although my sister suffered from obsessive-compulsive disorder, which manifested early in her ritual hand washing. Thumb sucking, fuzzing, and hand washing…our youthful attempts to make peace with the hostile atmosphere we lived in. I was glad Mom rocked and cooed over Jeanne while I watched and absorbed any leftover affection. In my own way, I had tried to be the perfect big sister, patting Jeanne to sleep at naptime, reading her books I wished had been read to me, and playing silly pretend games with her. I hoped this would prevent too much suffering in her life and protect her from the minefields of our dysfunctions.

Coping with a Disabled Teen upset me as well, suggesting ways you could redirect your child's physical energies towards socializing with others, reading, painting…but nothing about redirecting sexual drives. Did handicapped people ever have sex? Would I? The hormones flooding through me certainly made me want to. Especially after reading the stash of pornographic paperbacks my brother stored under his bed.

No mention was made of dating, marriage, or parenthood as possible options that a disabled teen might anticipate sometime in the future. The book pointed out the fact that many handicapped men and women maintained jobs and led rich and productive lives, but except for President Roosevelt's triumph over polio and Helen Keller's blind victories, I had no role models to guide me through the perils of being a handicapped teenager.

Not one of the six hundred students in my graduating class suffered from a physical disability. In fact, I remained the only handicapped student throughout junior and senior high. Truthfully, I didn't want to associate with my kind, even when I could. I aimed to pass as a normal person and not be mistaken for the retarded children I had happily abandoned back at Franklin Elementary School. Being in a crowd of handicapped people, accepting that I was a part of that crowd, had to be avoided at all costs. My own prejudice placed me outside of both the disabled and 'normal' worlds. Left on my own, I struggled to create a self-image I could present to the rest of humankind.

Dad constantly reminded me that my brains would save me from a life of dependency and low-paying jobs. "You could become a tutor," he recommended, "or maybe work with children. Visit people in old folk's homes and sing to them. Remember you have a good voice as well as an above average mind. You could go places," he concluded resolutely.

"The first place I want to go is out of Eureka," I sassed. "Besides, have you ever seen a handicapped teacher or lawyer? Not a lot of crippled singers either." I didn't mention my literary companions. Daddy had absolutely no trust in writing as a means of earning a living and besides, I could hardly compare myself to famous authors. To compensate for my lack of role models, I determined that I would be *one* of a kind. I found lots of examples of lonely, but brilliant women who were writers and poets. I set out to join that illustrious legion of creative females. Emily Dickinson, Elizabeth Barrett Browning, and Katherine Mansfield became my role models.

Isolated geniuses were a dime a dozen if you did the research. I felt closest to Katherine and Elizabeth because like me, they fought both depression *and* serious physical illnesses. Unlike me, they weren't born physically deformed and their beauty attracted many male admirers. In some ways, I had most in common with Emily because although she had no deformities, shyness and despair crippled her and she missed out on love and marriage.

I spent most weekends lost in these women's biographies as well as their art. I devoured their letters and diaries as if they were written to me personally. My journal entries evolved into an imaginary correspondence with them. I modeled myself on their lifestyles, learning how to use poetry as a means of recording and assuaging the loneliness and depression that I suffered throughout my childhood and adolescence. My fantasy friendships with these authors rivaled those with my closest flesh-and-blood companions. Their uplifting words spoke to me in ways that the psalms and the sermons of Jesus failed to do.

38

CHURCH-HOPPING

My friendships with both the living and the dead poets brought me companionship and consolation, but I still searched for something more, something that was missing from my life the way my mother's love was missing. Ever since Daddy's Sunday sermons at home, religion had sparked my curiosity regarding spiritual matters. I never gave up completely on becoming a born-again Christian in hopes of receiving a miracle cure for my polio-damaged body or, at the very least a cure for my depression.

Lured by the exciting projects and awards I won for memorizing Bible verses, I became a church hopper at the tender age of five, starting with the Southern Baptist summer Bible school. Usually I rode along with the Barnharts, but sometimes my mother accompanied me to make sure kids didn't knock me down and step on me. The Bible School teacher told us stories about man-eating whales and tigers, burning bushes that cropped up in the desert and Jesus performing miracles with fish and loaves of bread. She was no competition for Daddy's meanderings about the mysteries of God's universe, but she offered another perspective.

I especially liked the stories where Jesus made the lame to walk. I imagined myself sitting in a desert, sweating as I watched Him rummaging through his bag of miracles until he found the one for "making the lame to walk." I visualized the special techniques He might employ to perform the miracle—perhaps He'd touch my forehead and I would spring up and sing a round of halleluiahs while I kicked sand into the faces of the non-believers and some of the meaner people in my life. I prayed hard and made Jesus all sorts of promises if He'd heal me from polio, but He turned a deaf ear.

By the time I reached eleven, I based my church attendance on the quality of its choir, devoting myself to congregations where I got to sing solos. I understood the ministers sometimes chose me because my pitiful condition compelled parishioners to cough up bigger donations, but I also realized it was another way of drawing people's attention to the fact that I had a good voice and not just polio.

I waited patiently to be born again; after all, some of the kids I knew had been reborn three or four times, but I never heard the call encouraging me to be washed clean of my sins. The pressure to give my heart to Jesus increased as I entered junior high and high school. It came to a head when the Baptist Sunday School teacher said if I wasn't "born again" before Easter, I would be booted out of the choir.

I came home that afternoon, threw myself on the bed, and experienced my first dark night of the soul. I took out my Jesse Jesus doll from my jewelry box and held the paper talisman close to my heart. She/he had always been there, not as the Child of God, but as a quiet cardboard companion to my loneliness, the secret witness to the grief that sometimes swallowed me up. Jesse Jesus had been there with me when I longed for a loving mother, a courageous father, or for a body that could run and jump and fly out over Grandma Ida's deep green gulch, my hands wrapped firmly around the braided robe hanging from the ancient weeping willow tree.

Jesus words were written in red on the pages of the small white Bible Daddy had given me one Easter, the one inscribed with my name in gold print on the front cover. Most of His words made good sense. Jesus felt quite real to me and I experienced a genuine desire to live the life He recommended, but I never believed Jesus was the Son of any God; I envisioned Him as an older wiser brother who would have thought highly of me, imperfect body and all. It was His personhood and not the surgeries at Shriners that made me feel almost whole.

A peace settled over me one Sunday as I sat alone in a front row pew at the Swedish Covenant Church (having left the Baptists). My Christian friends knew the pressure was on as I watched them, one by one, walk to the front of the church to accept Jesus as their lord and savior, their one-way ticket to paradise.

When Mary Sue Ellis returned to sit beside me, she leaned over, a sorrowful look on her face. "I guess you still haven't heard the calling, huh?"

"Not even a whisper."

Once I gave up on listening for the voice of Jesus my Lord and Savior, imploring me to let Him into my heart, my relationship with Him improved—it felt warm and comfortable, like a kid leather glove slipped over my polio hand. I figured this was my own way. What a relief. Now I could join the best choir in town, Baptist, Presbyterian, or Swedish Covenant and remain true to myself, free from all the confusing dogma that suffocated the Holy Spirit. I wasn't born again like so many of my friends, but I felt my life shifting to a higher plane of being. I no longer capitalized all the he's and him's spellings when referring to Jesus in my diary.

I finally joined the Covenant church, even though I disagreed with most of the teachings of this strict Swedish offshoot of Lutheranism. I hoped that by hanging out with an uptight congregation and increasing my practice of prayer, some unsuspecting Christian boy would be blinded by the Holy Spirit and overlook my disqualifications for the Miss America Pageant.

39

WE ALL FALL DOWN

The dress immediately caught my eye as Katie and I hurried past the display window at Dalys. I turned in my tracks and scrutinized the light gray flannel dress worn by a headless manikin. A large white square collar draped down in the front and back and reached across the shoulders of the garment. "I wish I could buy the whole display, Katie. I'd just screw my head on the dummy and voila, I'd be a new woman, *sans* polio."

Struggling through my second year of French, I practiced the language whenever I could. "Do you think it would make me look like a pilgrim with the white bibbed collar and all?"

Katie and I dressed as if we came from separate planets. At the moment she wore stylish white go-go boots and a dress with a wild geometric pattern. She stepped back, squinting her eyes while I stood beside her, drooling over apparel appropriate for sailing on the Mayflower. Her answer pleased me. "I think you'd look very Audrey Hepburnish." We had recently seen *Breakfast at Tiffany's*.

Secretly, I identified with Hester Prynne, the heroine of the *Scarlet Letter,* which we had read in English class. Conceiving a child with the village vicar certainly put Hester in my circle of hell, though she gave birth eventually. Just as I had to face my disability every day when I decided to get out of bed, Hester's daughter Pearl haunted her with a constant reminder of the burden she carried. I could wear that dress as a sign of solidarity with fallen women around the world.

Katie poked my shoulder. "Hey, you! Come back from wherever you went. I do like the line of the dress," she confessed. "So, what do you think?"

"I think it's graceful, though it's a bit prim. Anyway, will you help me try it on?"

She rolled her eyes. "Lead the way," she ordered, backing open the department store's heavy glass door.

Minutes later I turned my reflection in the mirror this way and that, smiling at the somber, yet sophisticated dress. "So Audrey Hepburn, you think?"

"Except Audrey wouldn't be wearing a girl's size twelve—how sophisticated is that?"

"So what? I buy half my clothes in the girl's department. Skirts and sweaters look pretty much the same no matter what size they are and a girl's size twelve or fourteen costs half as much as it would in the teen department."

"Well, as your friend, I have to tell you I was relieved when you had your Mom remove the Tinkerbelle patch from that last sweater you bought."

"And that simple removal saved me $3.95. Anyway, I'm going to buy this dress so *fermez la bouche*. Oh my gosh—look! It even has pockets," I crowed.

Katie automatically slipped my polio hand through the hidden pocket on the side. How well she knew me. Out of sight...and out of mind.

I couldn't wait to get home and model my latest purchase after dinner.

At eight years old, my brainy sister Jeanne still held me in high esteem most of the time. "You look very historical," she nodded approvingly.

David threw down his dinner napkin and gave me a wolf whistle. "You look like the Flying Nun."

"A lot you know. The girls you date dress like Barbie dolls and I don't mean that as a compliment." I pushed my stool away from the bar and went into my room, slamming the door behind me. I was slamming a lot of doors lately, prompting my mother to note that I must be premenstrual.

Except for a day of cramps relieved by Midol, my period didn't even rate a day home from school. Maybe my hormones did stir up my emotions. Some mornings when a large pimple appeared on my nose (made bigger and redder by my attempting to squeeze it away) or my hair refused to bubble or flip, I carried on like a maniac, throwing my brush at the mirror, stamping around the house and giving in to a torrent of screams and tears.

Oddly enough, my parents endured my tirades. They had given up on day-to-day parenting. As long as I remained dateless and sulked in my room for hours reading biographies of women writers, there was no need to restrict my curfews or take away phone privileges.

Jeanne, however, would shy away from me after such hysterical episodes. "You're scary when you act like that."

"Like what?"

"Like Mommy." She came over and wrapped her arms around my waist. I had given little thought to the effect my behavior might have on others. Certainly, I never acted like this at school.

"I'm sorry, sweetie. Don't worry, I'll never turn into Mom." I said this to convince myself as much as my little sister.

I waited for the start of a new week to wear my Quaker-style dress. Sun streamed in when I opened up my bedroom shades and the cherry blossoms outside my window smelled sweet and full of promise.

Mom finished buckling up my brace and stood back so I could get up. Dad had oiled the squeak the night before and now her fingers were sticky with the black stuff. She wiped them on her jeans. "Mr. Goetz is out in his truck waiting, so get your stuff together."

I pointed to my trusty leather briefcase, now covered with autographs from my friends. "I'm packed," I told her, galumphing to the front door and allowing Mom to take my arm as we descended the stairs. She would never trust me alone with stairs even though they were now a permanent feature of my life at high school.

I was in no mood to hear Mr. Goetz's opinion about my dress, so I glared at him when I got in the truck. "Don't say anything."

Noting I was under some sort of duress, the shop teacher turned on the truck radio and we listened to the news of Albert Einstein's death and the public's mixed reactions to sending our troops to Viet Nam. Neither of those stories lifted my spirits.

By the time we reached school, I had recovered my questionable stability and Jerry Wilcox brightened things considerably. "I like your dress," he complimented me when I walked into French class.

"Thanks." I sat down at my desk and lifted my skirt up over my knee to reveal a lacy black garter that had a YES! button attached to it. Mom had reluctantly helped me put it on.

Jerry blushed and raised his eyebrows.

"I'm no pilgrim," I laughed, using my Mae West voice.

Nerd that he was, Jerry stumbled to his seat at the back of the class, chagrined by my risqué behavior.

Monsieur Pepper called on me first to read a section from our French book. By the dumbfounded looks on everyone's faces, I knew I had slaughtered the passage.

Monsieur Pepper gasped out his horror. "It seems Mademoiselle Viale has not yet swum the English Channel over to France."

Maybe I'd just sink and drown.

Five minutes before the bell rang, I turned around to Katie and motioned to the clock. I still left classes five minutes early to avoid the mad rush of students. Katie stood up and walked to my desk, grabbing my briefcase and following me out the door.

"I must say, you look good in that dress; it suits you."

I was just about to ask her what she meant by that when the lock on my brace gave way, causing my leg to buckle under me. I fell to the floor and hit my head so hard I actually saw stars.

A warm liquid puddled around my neck and shoulders. Memories of all my falls, broken arms, bruised chins, and skinned knees flickered through my head like a home movie. The kind you didn't want anyone to see.

Katie bent over me, a look of dismay reshaping the features on her face. "Let me sit you up," she whispered, backing away a little to keep from stepping in the blood. We stared at the YES!" garter now wrapped around my ankle. Without asking, Katie whisked it off and stuffed it in her handbag.

All the commotion brought Monsieur Pepper to the door. "Mon Dieu!" he cried. "Quickly, Mademoiselle Hamilton, take Mademoiselle Viale to the nurse's office."

By then Katie had me up on my feet, which caused blood to gush down my neck and over my pristine white collar. She searched for a wadded-up tissue from her purse, holding it to my head to stem the flow.

"Oh, this isn't working," she cried. We both stared down at the red stain I had left on the floor. I was humiliated when the bell rang and kids started filling the hallway, stealing glances at me.

"Make room for her," Katie yelled in a shaky voice. She pushed us through the gawkers and down the stairs to the nurse's office. Katie smiled nervously at the nurse as she led me over to a cot and helped me lay down.

The clear-headed, no-nonsense Mrs. Twine sat me up again and cleaned my wound with peroxide. It fizzed loudly.

"Sorry, sweetie, but I think you're going to need stitches for this one." Mrs. Twine had tended to my first aid needs after some of my less dramatic falls.

She finally stood up and noticed Katie. "Are you okay, sweetie? Do you want to have a glass of water?"

Having witnessed both the fall and medical intervention, Katie looked worse than I did. "No thanks. I'll go to my next class—if that's okay with you, Paula?"

I nodded yes, and then burst into tears when she left the office.

Mrs. Twine sat down beside me on the cot. "I don't think it's too serious. Head wounds always bleed a lot," she added, taping some gauze to my injury.

I stared down at my red-soaked dress. What a joke. *Now I'm wearing a scarlet letter*, I thought bitterly. *Be careful what you ask for*, I heard my mother say. This was one fall I wouldn't be able to hide from her.

Mrs. Twine flipped through the Rolodex on her desk. "Should I call your father first?" she asked, knowing my present condition could bring on my mother's hysteria.

I nodded while she searched through the lost-and-found box, eventually finding a sweater for me to cover the top of my dress. "There, now, nothing shows."

This included my hands, which disappeared in the sleeves of the too-big sweater.

Neither Dad nor Mom could be reached, so Mrs. Twine called the third person listed on the "In case of emergency" list. It was Debbie's dad, my Uncle Bill, who picked me up at school.

"Quite a spill you took there, Pumpkin," he mused sympathetically on our ride over to Dr. Ely's. Just hearing him call me 'Pumpkin' reduced my panic and seething anger at God. Something my mother's reactions would have failed to do.

"Not you, again," Dr. Ely joked when he waddled into the examination room where I waited sitting on a long table. Uncle Bill excused himself and the doctor came over to me, parting my hair to better expose the split in my scalp. "Yep, you're going to need six or seven stitches for this one." He called in his nurse and told her to wash and shave the area around the wound.

I flashed back to Shriners where I had experienced my first head shave. *Would there never be an end to my pain and humiliation?* I wondered, already composing a diary entry to write out once I got home.

"You didn't black out, did you?" Dr. Ely asked as he shot my scalp full of Novocain and stitched me up.

"I don't think so," I blubbered. My sobbing came not from that pain, but from the prospect of having a six-inch bald spot in the middle of my head.

Uncle Bill and I didn't talk much as he drove me home, which I appreciated. He said he had called my mother and carefully broken the news to her.

She waited for me on the front porch, shaking her head wearily as she helped me up the steps.

"Were you hurrying too fast?" she asked, looking for a place to fix the blame.

"No," I yelled at her. "My brace came unlocked. It was a mechanical failure, not mine, so put that in your pipe and smoke it." Once we reached my bedroom I threw myself face down on the bed crying, "I just want to be dead!"

"Shall I go out to the barn and get your Dad's shotgun?" Mom's attempt to make me laugh myself out of the doldrums ignited a smoldering anger in me.

After damning God, any god, every god, I settled down and rolled over.

"Do you think you could hug me?" I flinched when I heard the words slip out.

My direct request startled Mom, and seemed to confuse her. "I don't think so." She said this in an off-handed way as if I had asked her for a stick of Juicy Fruit gum and she had none.

As she backed out of my bedroom, she promised to see if she could get the bloodstains out of my dress. "I'll come back in a while and help you into your nightgown."

In the early sixties we had no Biz or Shout to remove Scarlet Letter stains so I had little hope of rescuing my one-of-a-kind outfit. At least Hester Prynne didn't have to face a return to high school.

The next morning, I heard Mom calling Mr. Goetz to tell him I would be absent for the next few days.

I got up and slid onto a bar stool where Mom had my favorite breakfast, soft-boiled eggs on toast, waiting for me. "I hope you don't think my hair's going to grow back in the next few days," I snarled.

"You may be surprised. Go get a scarf and I'll make it into a turban," she offered. "Then we're going for a little ride."

"I'm not going anywhere," I shouted.

"Come on. You'll be glad you did."

We got in the car where I hunched down in the front seat, sighing loudly and trying to look pathetic. We headed downtown, pulling up in front of a store called "Justine's Wigs and Hairpieces."

It took some pleading on her part, but I eventually gave in and followed Mom into the shop.

Justine couldn't have been happier to see us. "You must be Mrs. Viale," she said, shaking my mother's hand. "We talked on the phone this morning," she explained to me. "And this little lady is Paula, right?"

I glared at Justine.

"We're here to buy a wig," Mom told Justine. "A human hair wig."

Justine scowled. "Ma'am, *all* our wigs are made from human hair."

Mom spent hours with me, trying on long and shorthaired wigs in dozens of styles. She put on a red one, which made us both laugh. "I look like Lucille Ball," Mom kidded with Justine.

We decided I looked best in a medium-length style that matched the color of my hair. Justine opened up a large fashionable wig carrier, placing the dead human hair on the Styrofoam head inside. "With the carrier that comes to $55.00."

I stood by in stunned surprise as Mom laid down six ten-dollar bills like she was Mrs. Rockefeller. She smiled at me. "I guess you're worth it."

This came as close to a hug or an "I love you" as Mom could get and I willingly accepted the gesture.

A SOLO IN THE WILDERNESS

However much I fantasized about becoming a writer, it was my voice that brought me a modicum of recognition during high school. I sang first soprano and was able to reach impressive high notes without screeching. In choir, I hit it off with pixyish second soprano Brenda Phillips and chubby-cute alto Gail Davis, and we met together at lunchtime to form the Noon Trio. We convinced senior Bonnie Foster to serve as our accompanist. A year older than us, Bonnie added a touch of elegance and grace seriously lacking in our group.

After rehearsing a series of old and new songs, we took our show on the road. Our debut at an early morning student assembly meeting brought on a few hoots, but mostly the audience applauded our fledgling group. "You gotta get a better name than the Noon Trio," someone yelled from the stands. "And better outfits," another high-pitched voice jeered.

Like our name, our outfits were understated, but matching. I wore pale yellow, which made me look jaundiced, but by the time my mother got around to buying the fabric, the pretty blue, pink and lavender bolts of gingham cloth were already taken.

The four of us agreed that better names and costumes could come later. "A record company might help us with a snazzy name and outfits," Gail reflected, then noticing our raised eyebrows added, "Well, it never hurts to reach for the stars."

Most of our friends and quite a few upperclassmen crowded around us, impressed with our planned foray into show business.

"How much money are you going to charge for each show?" Katie asked, dollar signs registering in her eyes.

"We haven't set a rate yet," I explained. "Maybe twenty-five dollars a performance."

"Oh, at least that," Brenda countered. "But we think it will be better if we let the adults come up with the amount since they may be more generous than we think. We don't want to shortchange ourselves."

"I should hope not," Bonnie interrupted, "especially after we bought the gingham for these matching outfits. "My dad wasn't too thrilled having to lay out eight dollars for this," she noted, picking up the hem of her dress. "I thought handmade clothes were supposed to be cheap," she said in a grouchy voice, mimicking her father.

"I hope you told him that included a McCall's pattern," I muttered.

Ever the optimistic entrepreneur, Daddy guaranteed us we would earn back the cost of our outfits after one or two performances. Despite the fact that he knew nothing about the current music scene and couldn't carry a tune in a bucket, he saw potential careers for all of us, so he wasn't surprised when The Daughters of the American Revolution booked us for our first off-campus performance.

"Gee, I'm dying to know how much a famous organization like the DAR will pay us," our tiny second soprano Brenda speculated as we geared up for our noon performance.

Gail, the group's alto, had hopes as high as her ratted blonde beehive. "My mom says the DAR has lots of rich old ladies in it, you know, whose ancestors came over on the Mayflower."

It had been my idea to pepper our usual repertoire with "America, the Beautiful" and "This Is My Country" to ingratiate ourselves to the revolutionary daughters. "As long as we act patriotic and polite, I think we should make a pretty big haul."

We arrived at the dismal gray DAR Hall decked out in our new attire, having added white gloves for dignity and glamour. From the age of the audience, it looked as if we'd be entertaining the *great-grandmothers* of the Daughters of the American Revolution.

A shrimp-sized woman bordering on a hundred years old introduced us to the group of aging matrons. "Ladies, you're in for a real treat," she cooed, just this side of audible. We took our places beside Bonnie as she checked to make sure the piano was in tune. She had perfect pitch.

Before we started, the shrimp lady waved her hand wildly. "Ladies, will you please stand for the Pledge of Allegiance." This request provided many of the daughters with their most demanding physical exercise of the week. Some of the older ladies needed to be helped to their feet, but those in wheelchairs remained seated.

We were about to take our places on stage when we were again interrupted. "Madam Chair, Madam Chair!" an agitated voice cried out from the back of the hall. "Don't forget the minutes from last week and old and new business must be discussed."

A top-heavy woman with her hair coiled up on the crown of her head and sprouting an impressive dark mustache stood up and rambled through the notes of their last meeting. "First item," she began, "our letter to President Truman demanding he stop the Red Menace from invading our shores was approved and sent."

A voice from the back cried out, "It's Johnson, Millie. President Johnson. You know, LBJ. I recommend that we make appropriate corrections to that letter and possibly send our request to the current sitting president."

This did little to deter Millie from continuing to read the minutes. "Second item, our building has been approved as an official bomb shelter and the Red Cross will be here next week to distribute medical kits for anyone who takes a hit from flying debris or radiation poisoning. Furthermore, an inspector from the Office of Civil Defense calculates that our basement will be able to shelter and feed twenty-three to thirty people for at least a full week. There is no new business." She sat down with a dull thud.

I turned to Gail and whispered "Bombs away!" which got us all laughing and brought some hostile stares from the ladies who had turned up their hearing aids.

Finally, our turn came. We were still laughing about my "bombs away" comment and messed up on "This Is My Country," but we sang "America the Beautiful" without a hitch. Then, the daughters insisted we perform an encore so we did that old Kate Smith favorite, "God Bless America."

We seated ourselves at a rickety card table to share tea and cookies with the president and treasurer. They both wore fur stoles, one with two minks hooked together, the other a flattened-out fox head chewing on its tail. After our snack, the two women excused themselves for a minute and then returned carrying four small boxes which they presented to each of us along with four envelopes. We were running late for our afternoon classes, so we thanked the women, took our bows, and excused ourselves.

We straggled back to school and sat on a bench by the fountain to examine our spoils.

"There's probably money in the envelope," Gail speculated. "It's awfully thick." When she ripped it open, a thank you card with a DAR pin attached to it fell into her lap. Brenda, Bonnie, and I stared at the tacky pin in disbelief.

Brenda shook her box, listening for the sounds of fine riches. She opened the lid and removed a miniature cherry pie. "Is this a joke or what?"

Clearly, we weren't yet on our way to fame and fortune. We all tossed our pins in the trashcan like live hand grenades. "No wonder the Communists are taking over the world," Brenda griped. We decided to eat the cherry pies to keep our spirits and sugar levels elevated.

"You know," Dad told me over dinner that night, "Eleanor Roosevelt resigned from the DAR because they wouldn't let a famous black singer perform at their hall. Then Eleanor invited that same lady, Marion Anderson, to perform on the steps of the Lincoln Memorial and she drew a huge crowd."

"But how can such rich old DAR biddies be such a bunch of skinflints?" I asked with heart-felt indignation.

"Well," Daddy explained, "they're a bunch of rich Republicans, so what do you expect?"

I'm going to write Mrs. Roosevelt and tell her nothing's changed with the DAR, I noted in my diary that night. *And I'm never ever going to vote for a Republican,* I added, feeling the first stirrings of my identification with Democrats like Eleanor. When I looked her up in our World Book Encyclopedia and saw her homely picture, I realized that if Eleanor could be famous with her big nose and buckteeth, maybe the Democratic Party had a place for handicapped people like me.

41

MY OWN KIND OF MUSIC

Early in my fifteenth year, I brought my father's dreams and future plans for our pet store crashing down on his head. The tragedy opened on a Saturday afternoon when Dad agreed to take me to Maxon's Music where I intended to spend the $15 I had saved up from my allowance and babysitting money.

At this point in my life, I had developed my own taste in music. I'd collected several albums of Broadway musicals, always performed by some second rate company because their records were cheaper. I still loved the twangy sounds of Hank Williams, Pete Seeger, Gene Autry, and the yodeling laments of Little Jimmy Dickens. What he lamented the most was being only 4'11," my exact height. As a little girl, I cherished their songs and because my mother had signed me up for a Country and Western record club for my third birthday, I assumed cowboy ballads appealed to her as well. Occasionally she would come into my bedroom and listen to them with me.

Even now, sitting there on the bed next to her that morning, I continued to imagine we both shared a brokenhearted sorrow over cowpokes who "drifted along with the tumbling tumbleweeds" or "dotted each 'i' with a teardrop." I thoroughly appreciated the sense of connection we formed through music. Besides, the lyrics were usually about losing love or being cheated out of it and I could easily identify with the misery. Maybe Mom could too.

Then again, maybe not. That afternoon I asked her why she enrolled me in a Country-Western record club in the first place. "Was it because you liked sad songs and handsome cowboys like I do?"

Mom shook her head and laughed. "It's not because I liked country music," she explained, brushing my bangs out of my eyes. "I accidentally checked off Country Classics instead of Children's Classics when I signed you up for the club."

Her answer left me speechless. All this time I'd been feeling connected to Mom because we shared a love of the same music, but it had been a mistake. This realization replaced my sense of connectedness with a painful emptiness.

Mom jumped up and went out to the kitchen, returning with the latest record catalogue that had arrived in the mail. "Looks like it's time to pick out a different category for you." She riffled through the catalog while I looked on. "See anything you'd like besides *Back in the Saddle Again?*"

Irritated by her levity, I turned to the magazine and grabbing a pencil, checked the box for "Broadway Show Tunes." I ordered *Camelot* and *The Damn Yankees.*

"That it?"

I nodded, watching her fold up the order form and stuff it in the return envelope.

"I'll put this out in the mail box for you. Then I'm going to make you and your Dad's favorite dinner, chicken and dumplings."

"Thanks, Mom," I nodded in an off-handed manner.

When she was gone, I rummaged in my desk drawer until I found my diary.

Dear Diary,

I'm beginning to enjoy the lyrics of Broadway musicals. They're not all that different from country-western music, except for being more sophisticated. I can relate to songs about loss and the lyrics that urge poor lonely people to climb every mountain and dream impossible dreams. Like country ballads, Broadway songs cover some pretty down-in-the-dumps stories, but somebody usually comes out okay with a lot of hard work and singing and dancing.

The next day I went with Dad to donate my cowboy records to the Salvation Army Thrift Store. We sat in the cab of our pink and white pick-up while he revved the engine; I'd become accustomed to riding around in the former ice-cream truck, so when we arrived in downtown Eureka, I no longer scanned the streets, worried that one of my high school friends might see me disembarking from the cartoon vehicle. Having disposed of my collection of country-western records, I now had my eye on a four-record set of Tchaikovsky's *Nutcracker Suite* on sale for $9.99 plus tax.

We swung through the doors of Maxon's Music and I walked up to the counter to ask for the slickly produced L.P. I joined my father in the audio booth where he sat waiting for me. We shut the glass door and motioned for Mr. Maxon to turn on the music. The sounds of the orchestra filled the booth and I closed my eyes in pure rapture.

"Yep, this is the set I want, Daddy."

A bemused look crossed his face. "You really want to buy this long-haired music? Do people really like this stuff, Paula? Or do they pretend to like it because they want to impress people? Can you say you like this sound?"

I ignored him. Mr. Maxon winked at me when I handed him a ten-dollar bill and pocketed the penny. At least *he* understood and appreciated classical music.

Dad helped me back into the pick-up and shoved the album in my lap. "Guess you've outgrown the music we commoners enjoy." He slammed the door harder than necessary.

I resented his mocking tone, holding back my response until he had pulled into the street. "I love *The Nutcracker Suite* and I plan to see the ballet as soon as I get out of this stupid red-necked cowpoke town. Goodbye fog, rain, and lumberjacks," I smirked.

I couldn't help notice Dad's body sag a little. "What about the pet store we are going to open when you graduate? I suppose we could play this classical stuff over the speakers."

My heart cringed. It had been ages since we'd discussed the future of Paula's Pet Parade. I had no idea Dad still clung to what had become a silly childhood fantasy that no longer held the slightest appeal to me.

A twinge of guilt reminded me that I'd never gotten around to telling Dad I had no intention of following through with that enterprise. I swallowed hard and dropped my bombshell on him. "I don't want to own a pet shop with you, Dad," I confessed once I finally found my voice.

I glanced at him out of the corner of my eye, praying that he wouldn't start crying. I had provoked him to tears more often now in my role of rebellious teenager. "I want to go away, far away and attend college after graduation, Daddy. I'm sorry, but that's what I want to do. My English teacher thinks I'm a pretty good writer and could do well as an English major." I delivered my newest intentions to my lap.

"And just how do you plan to pay for that?"

My hackles shot up. "I'll get a job," I proposed, though I still wondered if that was even possible for a handicapped girl.

All the way home we remained wrapped in our own separate space, beginning to construct a wall of hurt between us, a wall of misunderstanding that thickened and hardened and seemed to grow twelve feet higher with every passing day.

Daddy never fully recovered from this breach in our relationship and the pain proved mutual, but a few weeks later, he got me a job as a proofreader down at the newspaper. I wasn't old enough get a work permit for another six months, but the *Humboldt Standard* hired me anyway at $1.50 an hour. Daddy launched me into the workforce even though it meant I had abandoned both him and our pet shop dream.

42

DINNER AT EIGHT

The fact that I was the first in my class to have a professional weekend job enhanced my reputation among my friends and classmates. Not only did I maintain my grades, but I could also afford to buy some of my school clothes as well as save for college. Little by little I was learning how to overcome, or at least sidestep the obstacles that polio had placed before me—my brace and funky arm—I began to accept them as part of the gear of my life.

I loved working as a proofreader at the *Humboldt Standard* Newspaper. At fifteen, I shared and performed the work with women in their thirties and forties, thanks to my facility for spelling and the English language. My father took great pleasure in my employment at his personal stomping grounds. My presence there softened the blow of my rejection of our pet shop dream.

I sailed through my junior year, continuing to write articles and poems published in both the school newspaper and various campus poetry collections. My literary voice slowly matured as I turned from recording childish meanderings in my tacky Pony-Tail Girl diary to exploring deeper issues within the gilded pages of a leather bound journal. I struggled with and finally concluded that my contracting polio was the results of bad luck and timing, not God's way of punishing my father for his faltering faith. With a few pen strokes, I let both God and my father off the hook. I concluded that how I handled my fate was up to me and I optimistically assumed I would be up to the task of making a life for myself.

I joined the Young Democrats Party on campus and signed up for the debating club while continuing to sing my heart out in choir and the Noon Trio.

I packed my senior year of high school full of pleasures, choosing classes that challenged my attitudes and sparked my creativity. Speech, French and Spanish, and creative writing electives expanded my knowledge of the world beyond redwood trees and saw mills. As part of a journalism class, my assignments included covering special events and activities which I never would have been invited to on my own. I did my best to be one-of-a-kind.

Adults' constant request for my babysitting services took the sting out of dateless nights and other missed social opportunities. I did well to hide my longings for a soul mate, a Mr. Rochester to play the wounded lover of my Jane Eyre. I kept a stiff upper lip, but suffered silently when both Katie and Mary Sue snagged themselves invitations to the proms.

Sometime after Easter, Mr. Goetz and his wife Cathy invited me over for dinner. They had something they wanted to discuss. I couldn't imagine what they had in mind.

I rode home from school with Mr. Goetz, anxious to see the new house they had just completed. Cathy opened the front door and I entered an enchanted world beyond my dreams. Each of the rooms featured a different decorating style or theme. Each room took my breath away— clearly, I had landed in Oz.

The kitchen offered a bar with stools lined up under it: a working replica soda fountain stood next to the refrigerator and colorful hand-painted tiles covered the floor. The sink and drain boards reached my shoulders to accommodate the pair's height—they towered over me.

Mr. Goetz claimed the den as his own private get-away. A large black recliner took up one entire corner and I envisioned Mr. Goetz snoozing there.

The library clearly belonged to Mrs. Goetz. Endless shelves of books, and pottery purchased as souvenirs from around the world jam-packed the chamber, complete with a stained-glass window casting a paint box full of colors onto the hardwood floor.

"Oh, I love that picture," I raved. "And that one too."

I stood next to Mrs. Goetz as we studied a magical impression of a French study. "We have similar taste, Paula. Those are prints of Raoul Dufy's work. He's a favorite of mine."

Charles, a college boy who I found reasonably handsome, joined us for dinner. Mr. and Mrs. Goetz had more or less adopted him after his parents kicked him out of his home at the tender age of fourteen. Charles had recently turned nineteen, the perfect age for a mature senior such as myself.

Italian stoneware graced the ten-foot oak table in a large dining room. Moose, deer, and elk heads stared down at us as I sampled my first taste of beef stroganoff. I pitied the polar bear, domesticated into a rug stretched out in front of the fireplace, but kept my opinions to myself. Mom and Dad encouraged me to practice self-censorship on a more regular basis, especially when out in public.

This issue had surfaced after I called Great Uncle Ralph a liar during our Thanksgiving dinner. "Well," I argued with Dad, "he said unions are infiltrated by Communists and that *is* a lie." Mom thwarted any kind of disagreement between people while dining. "Even so, you can't go around calling your elders liars during a holiday."

Mom's ban on political or controversial topics during meals made meaningful discussions impossible. The Goetzes posted no such restrictions against arguments as long as they remained respectful. Mr. Goetz embraced the Republican's perspective on national and world events while I entertained a decidedly Democratic one. By the arrival of chocolate mousse, a favorite of mine, we had agreed to disagree on short dresses, the Viet Nam War, and plans for a space race.

Mrs. Goetz nudged her husband as she refilled his water glass. "Why don't you tell Paula what we'd like to give her for graduation?"

"We've discussed this with your parents and they've okayed our proposal," he announced, and then sat in total silence until I lost all patience.

"What proposal?" I demanded.

Mr. Goetz executed a comical jump in his chair as if I had scared him. "Why, I thought you'd never ask." He teased me with one of his sly smiles. "Cathy and I want to take you to San Francisco next weekend. We can visit some art museums, I'll show you my seaplane parked in Sausalito, and on Saturday night we have four tickets to a Broadway show. It's *Brigadoon* starring the Irish singer Dennis Day."

I sat there stunned by this opportunity of my lifetime. "Wow, our choir's performing all the songs from *Brigadoon*. I love the lyrics and know them by heart. And I've never been to a genuine art museum."

Mr. Goetz proceeded to present the plan for our upcoming adventure. "You can bring a packed suitcase to school next Friday. Cathy will pick us up and we'll drive as far as Willits. We'll spend the night there. Then, we'll get on the road early Saturday and start our tour of San Francisco." Happiness filled me up until I floated, a helium balloon, bobbing in midair. I longed to get up and throw my arms around Mr. Goetz, exasperated that polio crippled my hugging arms, putting them permanently out-of-order. "Thank you, Mr. and Mrs. Goetz. This is one of the best presents I've received in my whole entire lifetime."

I toned things down a bit when I saw Charles grinning at my display of childish enthusiasm. He probably thought I acted like some little hick from the Ozarks. It turned out Charles was coming too, so the four of us sat around the table studying a map of San Francisco and circling landmarks we wanted to visit. Mr. Goetz drove me home at ten o'clock.

Mom stayed up to help me get undressed and remove my brace. "I hope Mrs. Goetz won't mind it when I ask her for help. What if she can't get my brace on or isn't prepared to help me in the bathroom? Maybe I should stay home and not have to feel anxious over everything," I tentatively proposed.

"Maybe. It's up to you."

Later I wrote myself a note in my diary: *Don't back out of things just because they make you anxious. If you do, you'll never get off to college.*

Or out of Eureka, I realized. A very scary thought.

Early Friday afternoon, Mr. and Mrs. Goetz sat in the front seat of their Dodge station wagon while I shared the back with Charles—another giant like the rest of them. Charles fell asleep, his head lolling back and forth as we took on the curves of Old Redwood Highway. He dressed just like David, in a striped shirt with an Ivy League buttoned-down collar under a sports jacket. He sported a bad case of acne and his eyes sat too close together. His thick brown hair, a little too long for Mr. Goetz's liking, softened a long pointed nose, and emphasized china blue eyes.

Who knew? Maybe a short holiday romance?

A dribble of spit ran out of the corner of Charles's gaping mouth. Then again…forget the romance.

I considered all the drives our family had made to San Francisco with Daddy at the wheel. Butterflies had always fluttered in my chest. Those trips had been packed full of tensions: fears of getting lost; fears of missing the last ferry to Berkeley; fears of our car's transmission pooping out, leaving us stranded on the empty stretch of highway between Ukiah and Hopland; fears of *what*, life?

Motoring along with the Goetzes, it dawned on me that life could be different, *was* different from the constant turmoil and chaos atop Pigeon Point Hill.

I leaned back against the seat of Mr. Goetz's completely reliable car, soaking up this new realization. *Hope.* I felt hopeful that if only I could get through until graduation, I had a chance of moving far away, entering a world of my own making.

We ate a late dinner at Francine's café where the waitress knew the Goetzes from their regular stops there.

I stared at the menu. "Go ahead," Mr. Goetz urged me, "the sky's the limit."

Luckily, the sky only reached as high as the $7.99 steak dinner, but I ordered the modestly priced hamburger with cheese.

"Do you want that or the patty melt?" the waitress asked.

Hmm, a choice. I summoned up my courage. "I'll have the patty melt," I decided with conviction, having no idea what a patty melt tasted like.

Soon I savored what turned out to be a hamburger on rye bread, covered with cheese and onions. Not bad.

"So, tell me again, what colleges have you applied to?" Mr. Goetz took a bite of his blood-red steak. It looked delicious.

"Well, Dad forced me to apply to Humboldt State University in case I get turned down everywhere else. Then there's Sonoma State, but it's even smaller than Humboldt. I'm hoping that Fullerton State accepts me."

"That's a long way from home," Mrs. Goetz remarked.

"Exactly." I folded my napkin up and tossed it on my plate, like everybody else did. "I want to be where there's sunny mornings and warm nights." I didn't mention Fullerton was a stone's throw from the razzle-dazzle of Hollywood. That just sounded phony.

We said our goodnights, and Cathy and I went to our room at Willit's Skunk Motel, a pretty pink and white place that smelled quite good actually. Mr. Goetz and Charles retired to the room next to us.

"Sweet dreams," Mrs. Goetz called out in the dark.

"Thanks for helping me get undressed, Mrs. Goetz."

"No problem, Paula. Do you really sleep in your brace most nights?" she asked. That had been my first white lie on our trip. Fearing that Mrs. Goetz wouldn't know how to put on my brace, I had decided to sleep in it and save her the bother. "I don't always sleep in it," I reassured her. "Just when I'm on the road and want to get an early start before dawn."

"Well, we won't be leaving before six thirty, so there's no worry."

Her words echoed through my head before I fell asleep. "No problem, Paula," and "there's no worry" struck me as phrases from a foreign language. Nobody in the car that day noticed my crippled hand or leg. I didn't feel like I was ruining their adventure by tagging along. They *wanted* me there—brace or no brace. I tingled all over, but I didn't shut down. I reveled in the giddy sensation of experiencing and enjoying my feelings and looking forward to Saturday.

43

UP, UP, AND AWAY

"Hold on to me tight," I yelled at Mr. Goetz as he picked me up and jumped across the little stretch of water lapping between the pier and the seaplane. He strapped me into the seat of the tiny aircraft while I struggled to straighten out my clothing. I couldn't worry about my skirt bunching up over my brace or that my sweater had twisted sideways. Mrs. Goetz and Charles shrank to domino-sized figures on the tarmac below as the plane sputtered, then lifted into the sapphire skies of Sausalito.

Mr. Goetz banked the plane steeply, watching to see my reaction. I wasn't scared—I was thrilled! "Let's do a flyby of the Golden Gate," he suggested, starting to circle the famous landmark.

"Everything looks so different up here." I pressed my nose against the window.

I watched a group of sailboats fanning out in every direction and I longed to be on all of them.

"It's a whole new perspective, isn't it?" Mr. Goetz hollered over the roar of the plane's engines.

"And how!" I yelled back. I winced at my mundane reply. If I was going to be a writer, I had to work on expanding my vocabulary.

For the next forty-five minutes, we soared over the city where Tony Bennett left his heart. At my request, Mr. Goetz flew us over Auntie Bert's house in Berkeley. It was too small to see very well, but I waved at the people inching along on Ward Street.

"That's where all the beatniks live," I noted, secretly hoping they would wait for me to graduate and join them down there on Telegraph Avenue.

"I'd rather see than be one," Mr. Goetz joked. "How about you?"

"I wish I could be a beat poet," I admitted. Unlike my Mother who responded to everything I liked with a *no you don't,* Mr. Goetz permitted my fantasy to unfold. "I plan on taking creative writing when I get to college. Dad said it's a poor man's trade, but I don't care."

The engine whined as we began our descent. "I see you had two poems published in the school paper. Looks like you're on your way." He gave me a thumbs-up as we glided back to Sausalito.

Mrs. Goetz and Charles had spent their time scouting out the little boutiques sprouting out along the streets of Sausalito. I wasn't a bit sorry I'd missed that. Nothing could compare to flying high in the skies of San Francisco.

We ate lunch at Fisherman's Wharf where I ordered an abalone sandwich. I was ready for anything; the rubbery meal tasted delicious. I couldn't wait to tell my Mother I had eaten food she declared was "as tasteless as old tires," even though I don't think she'd ever tried it.

I noticed things about me that were different from my parents' timid and resistant approach to something new, whether it involved flying or eating an abalone sandwich.

"I want to try lots of new things," I told Charles and the Goetzes as Mr. Goetz paid for the meal.

"See that you do," Mr. Goetz advised me. "By the way, you mentioned you hadn't bought your sweater for senior pictures. How about we check out Macy's while we're here?"

I'd been so lost in my dreams that I hadn't noticed the store's iconic sign at the corner.

"Good idea," Cathy agreed. "I want to look for some new shoes."

"I'm going to check out the bookstore," Charles declared.

Once again, I was torn between wanting to do two things. But there was no Macy's in Eureka while I could always get used books there.

It felt funny poking through sweaters in the teen department with Mr. Goetz standing beside me. I was relieved when he left to see about a necklace he'd ordered for Mrs. Goetz. I wondered if that was what some husbands did for their wives. Dad gave Mom the latest Hoover vacuum model for her last birthday, but I couldn't see him ordering her jewelry. Dad never shopped for himself or anybody else. He left that to Mom. He went alone once to buy some shoes, but he returned with the wrong size.

My eyes fell upon a gorgeous pink angora sweater in my size. I stroked the softness. *Hah, perfect for fuzzing.* The tag read $12.99. Holy cow! Luckily Dad had supplemented my allowance and given me a twenty-dollar bill for the trip.

I returned home with much more than a fuzzy pink sweater. The Goetzes provided me with a birds' eye view of life beyond the limits of a redwood curtain and I liked what I saw. There was no going back and I felt heady just thinking about an exciting future awaiting me.

44

REALITY 101

I suffered from an emotional crash landing following my high-flying weekend with Mr. and Mrs. Goetz. Once home again, I fought to maintain my ebullient spirits given life back here on earth. Even though I never expected to be asked to the Senior Prom, it hurt when I wasn't. The closest I came to that event was singing with the Noon Trio during intermission. I remained dateless throughout my high school years. Fortunately, for the first time in my experience, days rocketed rather than dragged by, leaving me little time to brood.

My senior yearbook picture turned out better than I could have ever imagined. Dressed in my pink angora sweater with my smooth bubble-do resembling a space-age helmet, I put on a Mona Lisa smile, knowing all my teenaged acne would be airbrushed away by the photographer.

My luck didn't hold when Dave Hoppe photographed me in my cap and gown. The stupid square pasteboard hat flattened my hair, making it stick out in wild directions while my body disappeared in the folds of an oversized gown. I scowled at my reflection in the living room window.

"Shit, I look like the Nutty Professor, Mom."

"You'll be sorry if you don't have a memento of your graduation outfit," she fussed.

"I couldn't agree more," Dave nodded, positioning me on the bench in front of our piano. "Jesus, Jack, can you believe our little cowgirl will be leaving the paddock?"

Dad shrugged. "What I can't believe is how much I'm paying for our little cowgirl's books and tuition," he joked.

"I'm paying for some of it," I protested.

"That's true, but she can thank her old dad for steering her to the hidden treasure. Tell Dave about the book I found for you," he prompted.

I rolled my eyes in disgust. Dad ignored me. He picked up a thin paperback laying on the coffee table, reading the title out loud. "*Little Known College Scholarships That Go Begging*. It lists small scholarships that nobody applies for. I had Paula apply for two and she got both of them, didn't you honey?"

I flashed back to our school awards assembly in May when the scholarship presentations had been made. The Italian Son's of Italy sent a Mafia-type emissary to award me $300. Blood money, no doubt. Then a patriotically-dressed matron from the DAR thrust another $200 check in my hand, giving me a salute.

"Yep, that book was worth its weight in gold," Dad reiterated.

A bright light struck me in the eyes as Dave began his last photo shoot of me.

The number of gifts I received during the weeks leading up to my graduation surprised and delighted me, especially since Mom had refused to let me send out announcements. "That's like asking for a present. Or bragging."

"It's to let people know I made it, Mom. How's that bragging?"

She never answered.

Auntie Bess and Auntie Bert pooled their books of green stamps and bought me a matching three-piece luggage set in what they called "a grasshopper plaid." Cousin Debbie gave me a nifty pen and pencil set to support my nascent writing career. I received enough items to decorate two dorm rooms: colorful bedding, a throw rug, a travel alarm clock and from Mom and Dad, an exquisite wristwatch dainty enough to fit my scrawny arm. Mr. and Mrs. Goetz presented me with a red leather thesaurus inscribed, *May you never be at a loss for words. Love, Bill and Cathy.*

It came as a shock when David announced his intention to marry his steady girlfriend Joyce. How had I not seen it coming? Lately he had spent most of his time hanging out on campus or at the fraternity house where his good looks and upbeat attitude made him a popular pledge. I missed our late night talks when he filled me in on campus life and I shared my dreams about becoming a writer. Now he would be sharing his world with Joyce, not me.

My hopes for a graduation party and send-off to college evaporated as the newly-engaged couple upstaged me with plans for their wedding. I liked Joyce, but I hardly knew her. David was preoccupied with becoming a husband and fulfilling his lifelong goal of moving out of our house. Well, *almost* out. He would be renting one of the two new houses Dad had built as his first venture into real estate. It took his mind off our failed dream of running a pet shop with me.

Katie and I were thrilled to receive acceptance letters from Fullerton State College. Katie had planned on attending Humboldt State for financial reasons, but to provide me with a familiar companion as I entered the foreign world of academia, Dad persuaded the Department of Rehabilitation to pay Katie a stipend to be my *monitor* roommate at Fullerton. Now she could afford to join me.

My rehab counselor argued that there were no state funds set aside for "monitors," but Dad convinced him to put Katie under the category of "miscellaneous equipment" which had a substantial budget. I doubt if Katie would have appreciated being lumped together with wheel chairs and crutches.

In lieu of World War III, the Pentagon introduced us to The Viet Nam War featuring napalm and Agent Orange. David excelled in college and as a husband and student teacher, he earned a temporary deferment from military service. I couldn't bear the thought of him following in my uncles' footsteps, never to return home from the swampy jungles of Southeast Asia. The undeclared war had already taken the lives of two of his closest friends. The *Noon Trio* suffered its own loss when Gail's brother Gary, was killed in action. I delivered an impassioned anti-war speech in my civics class, winning a debate over my nemesis, Jerry Wilcox. I broke down in tears several times reading off the names of three fallen classmates while students squirmed uneasily in their seats.

"You did great," Katie comforted me as we stood in the girls' bathroom, gazing in the mirror while she ratted my hair into a perfectly round bubble.

"Two of my uncles died in WWII," I reminded her.

"I know. I saw the memorial plaque the zoo put up in your Uncle Robert's memory. He won the Congressional Medal of Honor, right?"

"He didn't win anything except a final resting place in the city zoo."

Katie squeezed my shoulder. "Still, it's something, isn't it?"

"I guess. They never found the body of my Uncle Raymond though, which is worse."

"Lost at sea...lost at sea." Katie repeated. She turned to me with a woeful expression that wrinkled her forehead. "Just like us," she reflected. "Just like you and me."

Was she getting cold feet about accompanying me to Fullerton?

Buoyed up by *The Amazing Power of Positive Thinking,* David managed to survive all the wedding preparations in good spirits. Our last conversations fell flat though, each of us willing for the present to skirt heavy emotions left over from our childhood. Time for that later. "You'll have to come visit Joyce and me on your winter break," David said, but I sensed he and Joyce would be celebrating their first Christmas focused on each other. For the time being, my brother was walking out of my life without leaving a forwarding address.

David's and Joyce's wedding went off without a hitch. Mom created beautiful floral arrangements that graced the sanctuary and hinted at the maternal love she left unspoken. A crystal blue sky greeted all the family and friends attending the celebration.

I sat in a back row pew next to Jeanne, feeling that old and oh-so familiar urge to activate the emotional cutoff I had mastered during my days at Shriners. I fought to remain present, fully alive.

Jeanne had crawled into bed with me the night before, begging me not to abandon her to our parents. My heart still ached from the guilt she inspired. Abandonment was the last thing I wanted her to endure, but escape to Fullerton offered me my only chance for a life of my own.

I promised I would bring her to live with me in Fullerton after she graduated.

"But even with my skipping a grade, that won't be for six years."

"You can always visit me in the summer."

She looked doubtful.

I listened solemnly as David and Joyce repeated their final wedding vows. From some dark and unexplored depth, I felt a sob rise up in me. A bark really, not even sounding human. I broke down in wails of grief, causing some in the audience to turn around and stare at me.

The minister brought things back to the event at hand, asking everyone to stand and sing "All Things Bright and Beautiful." A peaceful calm returned to the sanctuary as people rose to take their leave, making their way through the receiving line and offering their best wishes to the newlyweds. I said a brief hello and rushed away, too ashamed to apologize for my hysterics.

"What in the world happened to you back there?" my mother asked as she settled in the car with my father, Jeanne, and me.

I took Jeanne's hand, giving it a gentle squeeze. "Life happened to me," I whispered in her ear. "And I promise I'll help it happen for you."

The next week I graduated with honors and very little fanfare.

45

THE LAUNCH

The time had arrived. I stood in the midst of suitcases and packing boxes, preparing for my long-anticipated departure from Eureka. Katie and I compared notes during frequent frantic calls both day and night. Together, we agonized over what the 1966 co-ed should be wearing to the fortress of higher learning. I decided on a professionally collegiate look, purchasing a red and white houndstooth suit with a slightly feminine blouse. I'd seen a similar outfit in the "College Bound" issue of *Seventeen*. I noticed my subscription had just expired.

Katie decided on a complete personal makeover. She'd lightened her dishwater-blonde tresses and learned to accessorize. She looked smashing in a short pink and black polka dot sheath with a cowl collar. For footwear, she selected a pair of white go-go boots that she planned to wear over black fishnet stockings. Together we presented a study in contrasts, me galumphing along in my Wall Street business ensemble and she ready to flash-dance her way down the hallowed halls of ivy.

The phone rang. "Are you taking your hairdryer?" Katie asked for the third or fourth time that day.

"Yes, along with my electric razor, two dozen sanitary napkins, and a year's worth of NoDoz."

We left no potentially useful item behind.

"You're going to have wrinkles in your beautiful new suits," Mom fretted as she sat on one of my suitcases to zip it shut. "I can't believe how much you crammed into your luggage."

I patted her arm. "Katie's bringing her iron, Mom." I gently pushed her out of my room and locked the door.

I filled one last box with my favorite books and record albums of Broadway hits. At the last minute, I decided to bring along my wallet-sized senior pictures to pass out to any cute boys I might meet at college. Or maybe I'd write to a guy slugging through the mud in Viet Nam. I wouldn't have to tell him I was handicapped. Plus, if the war dragged on, there would be loads of disabled Veterans who might want to date me...if they made it home.

Convinced that the early autumn traffic would be awful, Dad hounded us into leaving Eureka's city limits a little after 4 a.m. on a Monday. Jeanne and I had a tearful, sleepy-eyed farewell before Mom, Dad and I squeezed into our overburdened car. Dad had to tie the trunk closed with rope and strap my typewriter table to the roof. I said my goodbyes to my brother and Joyce before they left on a three-day honeymoon at a resort just outside of Garberville.

Mom frowned at our car. "We look like a clan of Okies from the Ozarks," she despaired, displaying her geographic ignorance of anything past San Francisco.

News talk radio filled in for our lack of any meaningful conversation. The trip took fifteen hours, including two hours of backtracking when we passed our freeway exit. Twice. *Motel 6* stood out like an oasis in the desert when we checked in on the outskirts of Los Angeles.

"I feel like I'm in a dream," Mom said that night as she helped me off with my clothes and brace for what might be the last time. Her eyes glazed over in the way I remembered them from childhood. In a maternal gesture, she tucked me in before crossing to the bed she shared with my father. I shut my eyes, smiling at the snores buzzing from their corner of the room.

A call from Katie served as our alarm clock the next morning. She had ridden the Greyhound bus from Eureka and just wanted us to know she had made it to LA. "The depot stinks," she said disgustedly. "The bus to Fullerton is getting ready to leave so I gotta go. I'll meet you around eleven, in front of the dorms." Her voice cracked. "That is if I don't get kidnapped by the creepy little man that's been sitting next to me since San Francisco."

"I'm sorry we couldn't fit you into our car," I attempted to apologize, but Katie had already hung up. Our lack of coordinated plans unnerved me, especially since Dad figured we could afford to miss the orientation and early registration Fullerton State offered in-coming students. "There's no need to pay for an extra night at a motel," he reasoned.

I pictured myself back on my first day at Jacobs Junior High School where they neither expected nor planned for my attendance. Showing up for "Late Registration Day" seemed like a poor way to begin my academic career. Was I destined to miss orientation days for the rest of my life?

"You don't mind if I stay here at the motel, do you, honey?" Mom asked. "I think it would just be too nerve-wracking for me."

"No, I don't mind," I assured her.

Dad rushed around, carrying my suitcases and boxes out to the lobby where we would wait for the taxi he had ordered.

I kissed Mom and promised to write and let her know how I was doing. She took my hand and rubbed it, her way of saying goodbye. "If I started to cry I would never stop."

I smiled, remembering the few times I had seen tears in her eyes. For her, tears posed a danger to be avoided at all costs. Dad and I turned back to wave to her before heading for the lobby.

46

SUN CITY

I sat next to my father on a torn plastic couch, making small talk until a down-at-the-wheels cab pulled up in front of *Motel 6*. We stepped outside; Dad dragged two of my suitcases while I draped my book bag over my good arm, hung my gargantuan purse over my bony polio shoulder and carried my cosmetic case in my teeth.

The Negro cabbie jumped out and introduced himself as "Larry-at-your-service," running his words together like a first name. He squinted at my father. "*All* those boxes in there yours?"

Daddy pointed at me. "No. Hers."

Larry removed his hat to scratch his head. "It's gonna be a mighty tight squeeze," he calculated, "but I think we'll make it."

Daddy scurried around helping load my suitcases and boxes into the purple and white taxi. He had never learned the art of just standing around watching somebody else wait on him.

"I think she has her rock collection in this one," Dad laughed nervously, pitching a heavy box into the trunk of the taxi.

Larry nodded and helped me and then my father settle into the backseat. He arranged us on opposite sides of a stack of boxes towering to the ceiling of the cab.

"These won't bother you, will they, sir?" Larry inquired. "Just couldn't fit them into the trunk. And there's no more room up here in the front seat where we piled her shoes."

Although I couldn't see Dad over the boxes, I felt his irritation. "We'll manage," he replied. "And please call me Jack," he requested in a friendlier tone.

Jackass seemed more appropriate.

"You're going to Fullerton, that right?"

"Yeah, to Cal State Fullerton," I directed Larry.

The cabby turned to give me a quick wink. "You want to take the scenic or the historic route?"

"I want to take the historic route," I interjected before Dad could state his preference.

We cruised along the jammed freeway for ten miles, swerving around cars and constantly changing lanes, serenaded by frequent blasts from Larry's horn. After successfully missing two stalled cars and dodging one on fire, a daily occurrence according to Larry, we exited the freeway onto a street lined with yawning door-less refrigerators, beat up couches, and abandoned cars. "Welcome to Watts," Larry announced, creeping through the streets of the fire-blistered town.

I flashed back to the summer of 1965, the summer of the Watts Riot, when two white policemen had a scuffle with a black motorist suspected of drunk driving. A crowd of unemployed Negro-Americans, tired of what they saw as another racially motivated incident of police abuse, had seen enough. The riots that erupted raged on for six days and resulted in thirty-four deaths and millions of dollars' worth of property damage. The thirty-four victims were forgotten by now, but the damage and hurt remained, evident in the rows of vacated apartments and ravaged businesses we passed.

I peered around the boxes between us and saw my father tapping his knees nervously.

"Are you sure we're going in the right direction?" he asked Larry.

Larry nodded.

I knew we were. I was entering a place where History with a capital H surrounded me.

And I wanted to be a part of it. Change it. Maybe limp along on a march with Martin Luther King. It thrilled me to think I might have to put my life on the line for my beliefs. It would certainly liven up my journal entries.

The sight of refurbished homes and businesses indicated we were leaving the most hopeless parts of town. I spotted a small corner grocery store with an "open for business" sign.

"I want to stop here, Dad, just for a minute."

Dad looked around anxiously at the piles of garbage and shadowy skeletons of buildings. "Stop here? But where? Where is here?"

"It's plenty safe this time of day," Larry said in a soothing voice meant to calm my Dad's frazzled nerves.

Larry pulled the taxi to the curb, leaving the engine running as he helped me out of the cab. "You want to take pictures, miss?"

I shook my head. "No. I just have a hankering for something cold and sweet. Maybe an *Eskimo Pie*."

He ran ahead to open the door of the grocery store and I stepped in. The sudden darkness startled me although my eyes soon adjusted to the neon lights flickering overhead. A young black guy wearing a do-rag looked up at me. "Can I help you?"

I drew in my breath, sucking up as much courage as I could. "Do you have Eskimo Pies or Fifty-Fifty bars?"

"Nope. Don't carry anything needs to be frozen," he explained. "Still don't have our freezers up and running. They're coming as soon as we get our damn insurance money from the fires last year."

I considered the candy bars in the rack beside the cash register. "I'll have a *Butterfinger* then." I pulled a quarter out of my skirt pocket. When he reached over for the money, I spontaneously touched the storekeeper's hand, then hastily withdrew mine.

"I'm sorry about your store," I stammered, the empty words of a stupid white girl.

The clerk grinned at me. "Don't believe you were here to do the damage," he laughed. We exchanged looks for half a minute before I picked up the candy bar and moved towards the door, still held open by Larry.

"Be sure to come again," the clerk winked at me. We both knew that was unlikely.

Larry assisted me back into the taxi, watching with interest as I unlocked my brace and twisted my leg to fit it in the cab. "See you got your moves down," he cajoled me as I reached around the boxes and handed Dad the candy bar. "Our favorite," I said, taking the half he handed back to me.

We drove in a comfortable, almost reverent stillness for the next forty-five minutes. I thought back to all the rides Dad and I had shared in his pick-ups—rides to school, to hospitals, to the library, to record and bookstores. Some of those trips had grown contentious as I spouted off my anti-war, pro-civil rights rhetoric - mostly my young adult attempts to draw the line of distinction between his life and mine, between parent and child.

"Now, right here at this corner we're about midpoint between Watts and Disneyland." Larry pointed out Cal State Fullerton on a map he carried.

How appropriate it was for me to spend the next four years of my life in a place equidistant from the ghetto and fairyland.

Dad peered around the boxes, steadying them before he asked, "You okay? Got what you need?" His face radiated both hope and sorrow.

"I'm fine, Dad," I told him, annoyed by his anxiety.

I felt guilty about my excitement over the things to come. Here I was, my heart beating like a drum marching in a protest parade as I prepared to desert Dad and the vestiges of his dreams for a business partnership in Paula's Pet Parade. So many marches and boycotts to attend, so little time. I knew I had enough gumption to see me through the rest of the sixties. Just not in Eureka.

Fullerton State was a small university in a big grove of orange trees, but given its proximity to Los Angeles and Hollywood, I knew I was right where I belonged.

Shortly after entering the city limits, Larry stopped the cab in front of an uninspiring building marked "Fullerton State College, Women's Dormitory." The gray brick edifice resembled the new humane prisons that were being built in the mid-sixties.

My heart sank, but then gave a little leap of joy. "Look, Katie's here," I cried, eyeing a lost-looking soul sitting on the edge of a bed of oleander, her feet stretched out on her father's old army footlocker. Even after a sixteen-hour bus ride that left her as discombobulated as I felt, the teal green suit Katie wore captured the essence of a polished collegiate woman. I had severe misgivings about the boxy plaid suit Mom convinced me to buy.

Despite our brave greetings, we collapsed into each other, Katie catching me by the arm before I could fall. The grab had become instinctual with her.

"For some reason I thought you wouldn't come," I confessed, leaning up against her shoulder.

Blinking back tears, Katie gave my arm a squeeze. "I thought you wouldn't be here either," she admitted.

"This is it," the cabbie announced, eager to remove himself from the spectacle of two young women on the verge of hysteria. "Need a hand?" he asked Dad after depositing my gear on the sidewalk.

Dad handed Larry a wad of bills for our fare. "Thanks, but we can manage from here, Larry."

Katie and I babbled on at the curb with no sign of stopping. Dad picked up some of my suitcases, helped Katie get a stranglehold on the handle of her locker, and shepherded us inside the dormitory's lobby.

An arctic blast of air conditioning left us shivering.

Katie and I signed in at the registration desk while a thirty-something dorm mom named Sandra looked over our paperwork and presented us with two keys to room 106.

It took forever, but Dad finally had all my stuff hauled into the room Katie and I would share for the next six months. "It's kind of stark in here," I observed, claiming the bed and desk on the right side of the room. I picked up a jockey strap wadded up on my mattress.

Dad and Katie watched silently as I threw the apparatus into the wastepaper basket. Later I learned that the LA Rams used the dorm as their summer residence while they practiced on one of the nearby athletic fields.

Our Spartan accommodations discouraged me. "Thank God for graduation presents. We'll have this place looking like the ones featured in *Seventeen* Magazine," I said, trying to sound upbeat. Or maybe the less exclusive *Woman's Day* that offered tips on how to make a nifty desk out of an old door and a pair of sawhorses.

"I've got a new Joan Baez poster for my wall," Katie chirped in an effort to erase the disturbing image of the jock strap. Katie was so with-it in some ways. I doubted if I'd ever hang up my poster of Robert Goulet in a tuxedo. What had I been thinking?

"I'm going down to get our sheets and towels," Katie said, bounding out of the room. "See you at the registration building. It's the one with a thousand people waiting in line," she hollered, slamming the door behind her.

"Do you want me to stay to help you register?" Dad offered.

"No, now that Katie's here, I'll be fine. You go back to your motel and tell Mom I arrived at my destination all in one piece."

We both laughed. I walked my father to the front lobby where I kissed him goodbye.

"I guess this is it, Sweetie...I guess this is so long for now." He inspected me carefully. "You're sure you have everything you need?" he asked one more time.

I looked deep into his teary eyes and smiled so he'd know my answer was sincere.

"Yes, Daddy. I have everything I need."

AFTERWORD

Memories can't be counted on, but I have, to the best of my ability, told the story of my childhood as it unfolded. Some names have been altered for confidentiality purposes. Writing from the vantage point of a sixty-eight-year-old lady, I know I must have a few details mixed up and muddled. I ask for the reader's understanding and forgiveness in advance.

In July of 2016, I attended my 50th High School Reunion in, yes, that soggy little town that I escaped from back in 1966. Many of my friends were there—Katie, Don, and Gail from the Noon Trio. Mark Fieg died in a plane crash before he graduated. Several others have also passed on. I've lost touch with Jerry Wilcox.

My father died many years ago, but the family recently celebrated my mother's ninety-fourth birthday. In 1984, I married my husband Rusty Jorgensen and helped raise his two children, Sara and Sven.

David and I remain in close contact. He lives with his second wife Linda in New Mexico. His son Dave and daughter-in-law Tiffany have four daughters: my grand nieces Julianna, Jessica, Isabella and Sofia. David's daughter Dana Warrior is the proud mother of two daughters, my grand nieces, Indiana and Mattigan. Dana's husband, known in the wrestling world as the Ultimate Warrior, died in 2014 and left us all broken-hearted.

Jeanne and her husband Chris Chapin remain on the hillside overlooking the family homestead on Pigeon Point while Cousin Debbie and her husband Bob Argo live in the house Auntie Bert and Uncle George built after they retired and returned to Eureka.

Now that the redwoods have vanished along with most of the salmon, Eureka has revamped itself into a pretty little tourist town; still, I never regretted leaving and moving first to Fullerton, on to Laguna Beach and finally settling here in Santa Rosa, California. I've enjoyed giving poetry readings in dark bars around town and over the radio. I remain a political activist. My wanderlust was satisfied by trips to Mexico, Canada, much of Europe, and Australia. I never did make it to Alaska.

I spent the early part of my career working in the media, doing public relations and freelance writing when opportunities fell my way. I later opened a practice as a Marriage, Family, and Child Therapist and have now retired. Complications from polio forced me to buy a bright purple wheelchair in which I whiz around the neighborhood, walking my dog Pumpkin. I continue to write using the old "stick-in-mouth typing method" I perfected in my youth. My gumption and joy are renewed weekly at Kids Street Learning Center where I volunteer as a reading tutor to six-year-olds. Thanks to wonderful teachers like Mrs. Hopkins, Mrs. Wales and Miss Carlson, I remain a life-long birder and avid reader. Life has been good to me.

Made in the USA
San Bernardino, CA
26 November 2016